The Enigma of Globalization

Globalization, that most controversial and widely recognized term, is theorized in this excellent book as an emerging new stage of capitalism. Robert Went takes us on a journey from the historical roots of globalization through to its relevance in the modern day world.

The Enigma of Globalization is a well-written and timely addition to an important debate and covers such themes as:

- International trade,
- Free trade and international movement of capital, and
- The future of the global economy.

This accessible and intriguing book is a must not only for students and academics working in the field, but will also prove an interesting read for all those with a general interest in the modern global political economy.

Robert Went is at the University of Amsterdam, The Netherlands.

Routledge Frontiers of Political Economy

The Enigma of Globalization

A journey to a new stage of capitalism

Robert Went

London and New York

First published 2002
by Routledge
11 New Fetter Lane, London EC4P 4EE

Simultaneously published in the USA and Canada
by Routledge
29 West 35th Street, New York, NY 10001

Routledge is an imprint of the Taylor & Francis Group

© 2002 Robert Went

Typeset in Times by
Integra Software Services Pvt. Ltd, Pondicherry, India
Printed and bound in Great Britain by
TJ International Ltd, Padstow, Cornwall

British Library Cataloguing in Publication Data
A catalogue record for this book is available
from the British Library

Library of Congress Cataloging in Publication Data
A catalog record for this book has been requested

ISBN 0–415–29678–1

Contents

Preface

Unsatisfied with quantitative comparisons of figures on trade and financial flows as a means of contrasting contemporary globalization with earlier historical periods, globalization is theorized in this book as a new stage of capitalism. With that aim the chapters interweave threads from three fields: the history of economic thought, economic history and international political economy.

A brief survey of economists' debates over globalization in Chapter 1 is followed by three chapters, each of which takes nineteenth-century ideas and theories as their starting points and gradually develops these ideas' relevance for our understanding of contemporary globalization. They are organized around three central concepts: international trade (Chapter 2), the combination of free trade with international movement of capital (Chapter 3), and the interconnection and internationalization of the three circuits of capital: trade, finance and production (Chapter 4).

Since the internationalization of trade, finance and production is neither linear nor symmetrical – and because globalization is after all a child of the capitalist economic system – globalization is then conceived as a new stage of capitalism in the next two chapters. Chapter 5 takes up three theories of stages – long waves, the Regulation approach, Social Structures of Accumulation – that were developed in the 1970s. After a delineation of their convergences and divergences a synthesis of these three theories is proposed. The final chapter brings all the threads together and also discusses three scenarios for the future development of the global economy.

Although I am of course solely responsible for the final result and for any mistakes, this work owes a great deal to many colleagues, comrades, friends and adversaries from various walks of life. Since the mid-1990s both academic interest and social movements have fuelled and crossfertilized my fascination for the development and consequences of economic globalization. I find this a fruitful combination, since scientific puzzles about the driving forces behind and dynamics of globalization are equally relevant to the question how a different world can be envisaged. This dual source of inspiration has also allowed me to write and lecture for and discuss with varied audiences, and test and debate ideas and hypotheses with both academics and people involved in social movements.

Lectures and discussions at numerous sessions of the International Institute for Research and Education (IIRE) in Amsterdam gave me an invaluable opportunity to exchange perspectives on globalization with social movement activists from every part of the world. The annual conferences of the European Association for Evolutionary and Political Economy (EAEPE) in Lisbon (1998), Prague (1999), Berlin (2000) and Sienna (2001) were a chance to present to heterodox economists papers that have found their way into this book. The weekly meetings of the Amsterdam Research Group in History and Methodology of Economics were always agreeable and stimulating, and I have learned a great deal in exchanges there with Adrienne van den Bogaard, Marcel Boumans, Hsiang-Ke Chao, Joshua Cohen, Carla van El, Ewald Engelen, Edith Kuiper, Harro Maas, Mary Morgan, Geert Reuten, Peter Rodenburg and Jack Vroman, who participated in (a number of) these sessions while I was present. Finally, the annual meetings of the network of European Economists for an Alternative Economic Policy in Europe are always a source of inspiration, since they bring together colleagues with a similar interest in policy-relevant analyses of the development of the world economy and Europe's place in it.

The many talks, lectures, panel discussions and workshops on globalization that I have given since 1996 – at universities and other educational institutions, for different social movements, for Association for Taxation of Financial Transactions in the Interests of the Citizen (ATTAC), or for trade union groups – forced me to (re)formulate ideas and concepts more clearly, and participants' reactions and comments during these activities often gave me food for further thought. Some of these meetings I will never forget because they were special. The debate with Alfred Kleinknecht and Wim Boerboom, organized by the trade union magazine Solidariteit (Solidarity) in 1996, was not only an educational and pleasant confrontation between three views on globalization, but also taught me that you always have to bring your overhead sheets, since Wim even brought a portable projector. The economists' seminars at the Ernest Mandel Study Centre were an occasion for exceptionally stimulating exchanges with like-minded economists from several other countries. My presentations at shop steward trainings of the Transport Union FNV were memorable because discussions with the participants went in so many directions that I never managed to finish even half of the three hour presentation that I had prepared for the three hours scheduled. And the alternative conference for a different Europe that was held in Amsterdam during the June 1997 EU summit, where I participated in two panel discussions, was memorable not only because of the many people from all over Europe who were present, but also because of the creative atmosphere which gave us the feeling – at least for a few days – that change was in the air.

My thanks to Mark Blaug, Massimo De Angelis, Klaus Dräger, Peter Drucker (also for his careful correction of my English), Rob Gerretsen, Michel Husson, Joost Kircz, Alfred Kleinknecht, Francisco Louça, Terry McDonough, Mary Morgan, Angelo Reati, Tony Smith, Rob van Tulder, referees of the *Journal of Economic Issues*, and referees of *Science and Society*, who commented on one or more drafts of chapters and/or suggested complementary literature. And a special thank you to Geert Reuten, for his invaluable help by reading and commenting on all the different drafts and versions that I have produced over the years.

An abridged version of Chapter 2 has been published in the *Journal of Economic Issues*, volume XXXIV, number 3 (September 2000), pp. 655–677. It is reprinted here with the permission of the copyright holder, the Association for Evolutionary Economics. An expanded version of a section of Chapter 6 is published in *Science & Society* vol. 65, no. 4, pp. 484–491. An earlier version of Chapter 3 is forthcoming in *Science & Society*. Earlier versions of Chapters 3, 5 and 6 were presented during annual conferences of the European Association for Evolutionary Political Economy (EAEPE) in Lisbon (1998), Berlin (2000) and Sienna (2001) respectively, and an earlier version of Chapter 6 was also presented during the annual meeting of the Society for the Advancement of Socio-Economics (SASE) in Amsterdam (2001).

1   Approximating globalization

Although *globalization* is a relatively new concept, it has already provoked all
kinds of analyses and discussions, and has given rise to a rich mosaic of theories
and diagnoses. Academics from different disciplines, policymakers and Non-
Governmental Organizations (NGOs) continue to study and debate, sometimes
passionately, the extent to which globalization really exists and is or is not something new. Innumerable books, research papers, and articles have been written
about globalization's causes, dynamics, consequences, and future. And all over
the world conferences and seminars are being organized to study and debate the
impact and effects of globalization, the need for and conceivability of regulation,
and/or the rationales for resistance to globalization's outcomes.[1]

Although analyses, opinions and debates about globalization have gone in
many directions, we will see in this chapter that since about the turn of the millennium this fascinating pandemonium has begun to give way to a consensus on
some important questions.

1.1   ECONOMISTS ON GLOBALIZATION

Globalization has not left economic science untouched. There is an ongoing
debate among economists, especially among trade and labor market specialists,
about the extent to which increased inequality in developed countries can be
explained by economic globalization.[2] Economists have debated whether we
should talk about *regionalization* or *triadization* rather than globalization, if we
look at actual developments in the world economy.[3] The question whether the
nation-state is (virtually) dead as an instrument of economic policy has been
taken up by many economists.[4] And last but not least, economists have studied the
question to what extent big companies have become 'footloose.'[5] But in comparison with the animated discussions in some other disciplines, the interest globalization has caused among economists is more modest.

Economists' most important contributions on globalization have, however,
been made in debates about just how new contemporary global economic integration is.[6] In this discussion, which has been rather important especially during
the 1990s, one can – a bit schematically – distinguish three currents of opinion.

Economists such as former US Secretary of Labor Reich (1992) and Japanese business guru Ohmae (1995) have argued that globalization is a definite trend that is changing everything, and against which nation-states or trade unions can do very little or even nothing. Partially, in reaction to these claims, economists such as Hirst and Thompson (1996) and Ruigrok and van Tulder (1995b) have strongly questioned the importance, novelty and effects of globalization. Among other things these authors have argued that the world economy was at least as internationalized at the end of the nineteenth century as it is today.[7] Finally, economists such as Altvater and Mahnkopf (1996) and Boyer and Drache (1996) have defended a third position, which can be summed up in the proposition that globalization is an exaggeration. These economists have argued that the world economy is changing significantly, with important implications for the organization and functioning of the world economy, but that we are (still?) far from a truly globalized economy, and that many of the claims of globalization ideologues are untenable.[8]

The importance attached by economists to this question seems to a large extent explicable by the fact that two central features of the current international regime – free trade and free capital flows – were also characteristic of the previous period of increasing internationalization, that is during the decades before the First World War.[9] Many economists will sympathize with the statement by Sachs and Warner (1995: 61), 'The world economy at the end of the twentieth century looks much like the world economy at the end of the nineteenth century. A global capitalist system is taking shape, drawing almost all regions of the world into arrangements of open trade and harmonized economic institutions.'

The First World War put an end to a long period of increasing internationalization of trade and financial flows. It then took approximately 60 years before the world economy's pre-First World War level of openness to trade was reached again, and before financial flows were once again as liberalized as they had been in the years before the First World War.[10] One way to interpret the increasing internationalization of the world economy since the mid-1970s is therefore to see this globalization process as the termination of a 60-year-long protectionist detour, and a return to free trade and free capital flows that was long overdue.

Most economists seem to hold such a view implicitly or explicitly, i.e. that globalization is nothing new, and to subscribe to the belief expressed by Higgott (1999: 26) that the 'argument for liberalization and open markets as generators of wealth has been won at both *intellectual* and *evidentiary* levels' (emphasis added). But is this really the case?

As far as free trade is concerned, the intellectual case for free trade goes back a long way to the theorem of comparative advantage that, as will be recapitulated in Chapter 2, is generally credited to David Ricardo (1817). Although this theory has been challenged from different angles since its inception, it remains to this day the dominant approach in mainstream economic thought. Most economists maintain that '(u)nder a system of free trade there would be conflicts in economic interests Neither among different nations Nor among the corresponding classes of different nations' (Schumpeter, 1919: 100).

Much more controversial among economists, however, is the intellectual case for the combination of free trade and free capital flows.[11] Ricardo was of the opinion that the theory of comparative advantage will not hold if capital is mobile, because in that case specialization will be determined by absolute and not by relative costs. And Keynes, one of the principal architects of the Bretton Woods agreement, defended the principle that finance should be primarily national (cf. Chapter 3).

Moreover, precisely at the time when economies have reached unprecedented levels of international integration, doubts about the consequences of increasing economic internationalization have also been recurring with new strength at the evidentiary level. At the end of the twentieth century, in the slipstream of the failures and successes of globalization, doubts and criticisms about the consequences of international trade and international capital flows are – once again – increasing.

During the Asian crisis, which began in Thailand in July 1997, the renowned free-trade economist Bhagwati (1998) attacked, for example, the fundamental idea that 'free capital mobility among all nations was exactly like free trade in their goods and services.' Bhagwati forcefully argues that 'the claims of enormous benefits from free capital mobility are not persuasive' but a myth, 'created by what one might christen the Wall Street–Treasury complex, following in the footsteps of President Eisenhower, who had warned of the military-industrial complex.'[12] And to give another example, Rodrik (1997a: 72–75), self-proclaimed 'neoclassical economist', has heavily criticized mainstream economics for its myopia, ignorance and arrogance: 'International economists in particular have been too Panglossian about the consequences of globalization. (...) (E)conomists could play a much more constructive role if they were to recognize that the tensions between social stability and globalization are real. (...) (E)conomists must demonstrate more modesty, less condescension, and a willingness to broaden their focus.'[13]

1.2 PARTIAL CONSENSUS, NEW QUESTIONS

Few – if any – observers and analysts will disagree with the statement that at the end of the twentieth century many views on globalization had changed – sometimes drastically – and that skepticism about the effects and future of globalization had reached broader layers of academics, policymakers and NGOs. Two partially related developments stand out as major contributors to this shift in opinions.[14]

The first and most important factor was the – totally unexpected – outbreak of the crisis in several countries in East Asia in 1997, which were until then considered a model for underdeveloped countries.[15] This crisis fundamentally altered perceptions and expectations of globalization, not only because of its depth and severe social effects, but also because of the subsequent extension of crises and instability to other parts of the world.[16] In addition, the Asian crisis was a sharp warning about the dangers posed by the instability of the globalized financial markets – grossly underestimated, at least until then – and about the structural weaknesses of the 'international financial architecture.'[17]

Second, international mobilizations by social movements and NGOs against (the consequences of) globalization, as in 1999 in Seattle (during the WTO summit) and in 2000 in Prague (during the annual meeting of the IMF and World Bank), have had a huge impact on public opinion and international organizations.[18] These campaigns have attracted so much publicity and popular support that leading politicians and editorialists in the business press and newspapers have repeatedly expressed fears of what they call a 'backlash against globalization.'[19] *Business Week* (2000a), to give an example, editorialized that '(u)nless measures are taken now, with the world economy in a strong upswing, the backlash will become much, much worse once the economic cycle begins to turn down.' And *The Economist* (2000b: 103), noting that the protestors 'enjoy the sympathy of many people in the West' and reflect 'popular concern about the hard edges of globalization', warned that 'global economic integration may be at greater risk than many suppose.'[20] The doubts expressed in these and other popular publications seem exemplary of a more general feeling that the perspectives for globalization are not preordained. World Bank economist Williamson (1997: 117), for example, raised the question whether the world economy will 'once again retreat from globalization as the rich OECD countries come under political pressure to cushion the side effects of rising inequality.'[21]

I submit that in the course of these developments, and as a result of the work and debates of academics from various disciplines, a consensus has begun to develop on some important questions, which were still heavily contested before the events in Asia. This partial convergence of opinions can be summarized in the following three points.

Important changes are indeed transforming the global economy. A number of researchers and policymakers have challenged this statement over the years from several angles, and until the end of the 1990s several of them would continue to argue that globalization does not exist, is a myth, or – in the words of Meiksins Wood (1997) – downright 'globaloney.' But since the Asian crisis even former skeptics such as Krugman write and talk unrestrainedly about 'globalization', and very few observers now seem to deny that today's global economy differs in fundamental ways from previous periods.[22] That does not mean that there are no disagreements left.[23] There definitely are, and they are discussed vehemently. But the scope of this debate has been narrowed down somewhat.

Globalization is not caused by technology. Although nobody denies that technological developments play an important enabling role in processes of globalization, very few contemporary analysts or observers claim that globalization is brought about by 'some natural or technologically driven phenomena' (Kitson and Michie, 2000: 14). To talk about a 'backlash against globalization' would be senseless if globalization was to be understood as the automatic outcome of exogenous technological processes, since that would imply that globalization is irrevocable. As Frankel (2000: 6–7) argues: '(T)here is a tendency to see globalization as irreversible. But the political forces that fragmented the world for 30 years (1914–1944) were evidently far more powerful than the accretion of technological progress in transport that went on during that period. The lesson is that there is nothing inevitable about the process of globalization.'[24]

Globalization has not reduced inequality of income and wealth. Since the outbreak of the Asian crisis and its aftershocks, a growing number of researchers and observers have become aware of the fact that social differences are globally increasing in a double process of polarization, within countries and among countries. This is not to suggest that this social polarization only began with the Asian crisis in 1997. Even before its outbreak UNCTAD General Secretary Ricupero noted for example:

> The big story of the world economy since the early 1980s has been the unleashing of market forces.... The 'invisible hand' now operates globally and with fewer countervailing pressures from governments than for decades. Many commentators are optimistic about the prospects for faster growth and for convergence of incomes and living standards which greater global competition should bring. However, there is also another big story. Since the early 1980s the world economy has been characterized by rising inequality and slow growth.
>
> (UNCTAD, 1997: 5)

Data to support this analysis have been presented for example by the UNDP (1998: 29), which notes that 20 per cent of the world's population living in the richest countries increased its income from 30 times the poorest 20 per cent's income in 1960 to 82 times the poorest 20 per cent's income in 1995. World Bank economist Milanovic calculated in a study covering 85 per cent of the world's population from 91 countries that the richest 50 million people in the world earn as much as the poorest 2.7 billion (Elliot and Denny, 2002). And to give another example, Weller *et al.* (2001: 7) argue that the 'distribution of world income between counties grew unambiguously in the 1980s and 1990s', with the effect that the rich countries have gotten richer and the poor countries have gotten poorer:

> The median per-capita income of the world's richest 10% of countries was 76.8 that of the poorest 10% of countries in 1980, 119.6 times greater in 1990, and 121.8 times greater in 1999. The ratio of the average per capita income shows a similar, yet more dramatic, increase.[25]
>
> (Weller, Scott and Hersh 2001: 7)

In sum, there is a growing sense that a central feature of today's globalized world economy is 'the egregious and historically unprecedented degree of global inequality – in income and wealth, and life chances broadly construed. Though inequality between the North and the South is particularly extreme, there are stark (and rapidly deepening) inequalities within each of these regions as well' (DeMartino, 2000: 218).[26] This sentiment contrasts of course sharply with the beliefs and expectations many economists, policymakers and opinion leaders have expressed about the effects of globalization.

Over the years, academics and policymakers have challenged these statements about globalization to varying extents, but around the turn of the millennium they have nevertheless become accepted rather widely. Future research programs of globalization will therefore (partially) chart new directions. Three broad puzzles appear key in this next round of analyses and debates. The first obvious question is what is driving globalization, if not the development of technology itself? The second related issue is just as clear-cut, since the moment we note that globalization is not irreversible the question arises whether globalization will persist and deepen, and under what conditions? Finally, a third question follows from the realization that globalization has not so far decreased social differences. Do we just need more patience, because – as some hold – at least in the long run income and standards of living will converge? Or is it rather the case that policy interventions and institutional changes are necessary because global markets will not turn out to be benevolent even in the long run, and if so what kind of interventions and where?

1.3   CONCLUSION

To sum up, around the turn of the millennium a consensus on globalization began to take shape, which can be summarized in three points. (1) Important changes are transforming the global economy. (2) Globalization is not caused by technology. (3) So far globalization has not decreased inequality of income and wealth. New contributions in what will become the next round of analyses and debates about globalization will most likely start from and build on these partial results.

   Clearly, the questions that are now posed call for thorough analyses of the dynamics of globalization and of the conflicts it gives rise to. Future discussions on these and related topics will not be less intense or passionate than during the first round of discussion. In fact, the reverse is much more likely. Not only has it become clearer for all sides in the globalization debate over the years what the stakes are; in addition, more academics, policymakers, and NGOs have become familiar with and/or interested in (part of) the debate. Finally, as has been argued, the partial consensus – that important changes are transforming the global economy, that globalization is not caused by technology, and that globalization has not decreased social differences – has narrowed down the number of issues to be studied and debated.[27]

NOTES

1 As an indication, Ruigrok and van Tulder (1995a: 139) note that some 670 articles were published in the year 1990 in prominent business and economic journals with 'global' or 'globalization' in their titles, up from only 50 in 1980. Hay and Marsh (1999: 5) note in a special issue of a young journal which reflects this increased interest that debates about and efforts to conceptualize globalization have given new oxygen to some academic circles:

International political economy (IPE), whether as a concept, object of analysis or mode of enquiry, is currently undergoing something of a renaissance. Indeed, perhaps more academics from a wider variety of "disciplinary" traditions would claim today that they were exponents and indeed advocates of international political economy than ever before. That this is so reflects one key aspect of globalization – the proliferation and global diffusion of ideas of, and about, globalization and the centrality to such ideas of claims about the international or global political economy.

2 See, e.g. Brainard and Riker (1997), Burtless (1995), Freeman (1995), Galbraith *et al.* (1999), Krugman (1995), Mishel *et al.* (2001), Richardson (1995), Sachs and Warner (1995) and Wood (1994, 1995).
3 See, e.g. Hirst and Thompson (1996), Kleinknecht and ter Wengel (1998) and Ruigrok and van Tulder (1995b).
4 See, e.g. Baker *et al.* (1998) and Weiss (1996).
5 See, e.g. Ruigrok and van Tulder (1995b) and Doremus *et al.* (1998).
6 See, e.g. Altvater and Mahnkopf (1996), Baker *et al.* (1998a, b), Chesnais (1997a, b), Feenstra (1998), Giussani (1996), Gordon (1988), Irwin (1996a, b), Kleinknecht and ter Wengel (1996a, b, 1998), Krugman (1995), Mahnkopf (1999), Mensink and van Bergeijk (1996), Ohmae (1995), van Paridon (1996), Reich (1992), Ruigrok and van Tulder (1995a), Went (1996a, b, 1997) and Williamson (1998).
7 Going back in time much further, Frank (1998: 38 and 53) quite correctly argues against the misguided idea 'that our world is only now undergoing a belated process of "globalization,"' 'the widespread neglect and even frequent denial of the existence' of a world market. But as will be demonstrated later, it is quite possible to agree with these statements and at the same time distinguish different levels and forms of internationalization in different historical periods. See Ellman (2001) for a discussion of Frank's world system theory.
8 Held *et al.* (1999) have christened these three positions as the hyperglobalist thesis, the skeptical thesis, and the transformationalist thesis.
9 One big difference between then and now that is not taken up in this work is that at that time labor 'flowed across national frontiers in unprecedented quantities' (Williamson, 1996), while today 'globalization at the policy level does not include the movement of labor. In the case of migration of people, in many respects what is going on is counter-globalization.' (Sutcliffe, 1998: 326; Sassen, 1996; See also Sassen, 1996).
10 On the world economy's openness to trade see Kitson and Michie (1999: 49). On the (il)liberality of international financial flows see Adam (1998: 559).
11 The classical defense of free capital flows is 'The Case for Flexible Exchange Rates' by Friedman (1953: 157–203); a recent update is DeRosa (2001). See Patomäki (2001: 226–229) for a critique.
12 See also 'Why Free Capital Mobility May Be Hazaradous to Your Health' (Bhagwati, 2000: 14–19).
13 See also Rodrik (1998, 1999). Higgott (1999: 26) judges in the same vein that 'when it comes to an examination of the impact of globalization, economics is an excessively optimistic science.'
14 The fact that only these two developments are discussed is not to suggest, let alone claim, that they are exclusively responsible for the alterations under discussion. But they are, in the opinion of the present author, the most important factors. Other contributing elements are illuminating reports by several UN organizations, most importantly the International Labor Organization (ILO), the United Nations Conference on Trade and Development (UNCTAD) and the United Nations Development Programme (UNDP).
15 On this crisis see, e.g. Bello (1998) and Jomo (1998).
16 On this see, e.g. Krugman (1999), Michie and Grieve Smith (1999) and UNCTAD (2000a).

17 On this see, e.g. Aglietta and Moatti (2000), Eatwell and Taylor (2000) and Eichengreen (1999).
18 On the importance of this factor, *Business Week* (2000c: 42) wrote:

> 'Yet it would be a grave mistake to dismiss the uproar witnessed in the past few years in Seattle, Washington, DC and Prague. Many of the radicals leading the protests may be on the political fringe. But they have helped to kick-start a profound rethinking about globalization among governments, mainstream economists, and corporations, that, until recently, was carried on mostly in obscure think tanks and academic seminars. This reassessment is badly overdue.'

19 Similarly, Soros (1998) warned, in the midst of the Asian crisis, of the 'disintegration of global capitalism.' After the effects of the crisis on the world economy as a whole turned out to be less severe than he feared at the time, he withdrew this prediction, arguing that he had 'goofed' under the impact of events.
20 Naomi Klein, a well-known representative of the new movement against contemporary globalization, argues in her bestseller *No Logo*, which has been described by *The Observer* (London) as the *'Das Kapital* of the growing anti-corporate movement':

> When I started this book, I honestly didn't know whether I was covering marginal atomized scenes of resistance or the birth of a potentially broad-based movement. But as times went on, what I clearly saw was a movement forming before my eyes. (...) This emerging movement even has a victory under its belt: getting the Multilateral Agreement on Investment taken off the agenda of the Organization of Economic Co-operation and Development in April 1998. As the *Financial Times* noted with some bewilderment at the time: "The opponents' decisive weapon is the Internet. Operating from around the world via web sites, they have condemned the proposed agreement as a secret conspiracy to ensure global domination by multinational companies, and mobilized an international movement of grassroots resistance." The article went on to quote a World Trade Organization official who said, "The NGO's have tasted blood. They'll be back for more." Indeed they will.
>
> (Klein, 1999: 443)

21 Kanbur, former director of the World Bank's Development Report on Poverty, who resigned from the World Bank after a conflict on policies to reduce poverty, reflects as follows:

> The end of history lasted for such a short time. If the early 1990s raised hopes of a broad based consensus on economic policy for growth, equity and poverty reduction, the late 1990s dashed them. The East Asian crisis and the Seattle debacle saw to that. In the year 2000, the governors of the World Bank, whose mission is eradicate poverty, could meet only under police protection, besieged by those who believe instead that the institution and the policies it espouses cause poverty. And the street demonstrations in Prague, Seattle and Washington D.C. are one of a spectrum of disagreement, which includes vigorous debates in the pages of the leading newspapers, passionate involvement of faith based organizations, and the genteel cut and thrust of academic discourse.
>
> (Kanbur, 2001: 2)

22 'It is a bit hard to remember what the world looked like before globalization', wrote Krugman (1999: 16) after the Asian crisis. Compare this with his skeptical position in Krugman (1995).

23 When it comes to policy conclusions Kitson and Michie (2000: 13) are, for example, of the opinion that there is much exaggeration regarding globalization. Also, many authors argue quite correctly that we are (still) very far from a real 'globalized economy' (see, e.g. Hirst and Thompson, 1996, 1997; Frankel, 2000; Rodrik, 2000).

24 In an editorial that was published in the week of the protests in Prague against the IMF, *The Economist* (2000a: 17) similarly noted: 'If technological progress were the only driver of global integration, the anti-capitalist threat would be less worrying. (...) Again the protestors are absolutely right: governments are not powerless.' And *Business Week* states:

> The downside of global capitalism is the disruption of whole societies, from financial meltdowns to practices by multinationals that would never be tolerated in the West. Industrialized countries have enacted all sorts of worker, consumer and environmental safeguards since the turn of the century, and civil rights have a strong tradition. But the global economy is pretty much still in the robber-baron age. If global capitalism's flaws aren't addressed, the backlash could grow more severe.
>
> (*Business Week*, 2000c: 43; see also Prakash, 2001)

25 These facts are echoed in the popular business press, where *The Economist* (2000a: 17) has argued that protestors against globalization 'are right that the most pressing moral, political and economic issue of our time is third-world poverty.'

26 In that same vein, Rowthorn and Kozul-Wright argue that 'there are serious doubts about the empirical evidence on fast growth and convergence with the world economy becoming more open', since

> there has been a persistent slowing down of the world economy as it has become more closely integrated over the past two decades. Moreover, this slowdown in growth has been accompanied by increasing volatility of growth performance. (...) Perhaps most significantly, the pattern of economic growth since the late 1970s has coincided with ever larger income gaps not only across countries but also within them.
>
> (Rowthorn and Kozul-Wright, 1998: 9–10)

On the increase in social inequality see, e.g. also Faux and Mishel (2000), Galbraith *et al.* (1999), Kaplinksy (2001), Maddison (1999), Sutcliffe (2001) and Wade (2001).

27 We can borrow an observation from Kanbur (2001: 6) on debates about poverty reduction: 'It is almost as if the battle is more intense because it is now focused more sharply on fewer and fewer remaining issues.'

2 The genesis and contemporary comeback of the theory of free trade

One of the central aspects of today's economic globalization is increasing free trade. The arguments for such a policy go back two centuries, to the time when Smith and Ricardo armed advocates of free trade with the theorem of comparative advantage. Since then they have been 'winning every battle in the textbooks' (Pen, 1967). And today opponents of protectionist policies and proponents of globalized free trade are once again claiming victory.[1] However, public anxiety about globalization and free trade is rising. In some policy circles and NGOs proposals are being discussed for new forms of protectionism, so as to re-empower the local and regional in the face of the social and ecological consequences of free trade and increased capital mobility.[2] Moreover, research on technology and economic development is putting in question the fashionable idea that, as far as policy choices are concerned, national states are virtually dead in today's global economy.[3]

This chapter discusses old and new analyses of free trade and protectionism. The retreat from mercantilism began in countries such as England and France in the late eighteenth century, so Section 2.1 deals with the genesis of classical trade theory. Section 2.2 discusses the heroic assumptions of this free trade theory, and the gap between theory and real-world developments. Section 2.3 takes up major criticisms already raised at the time, especially from a national and class conflict perspective. In Section 2.4 we take a look at important contemporary criticisms of the free-trade paradigm.

2.1 THE FIRST VICTORY OF FREE TRADE

'Since the early nineteenth century, comparative advantage has been the bedrock on which all subsequent developments in the theory of international trade have rested' (Maneschi, 1998: 10).[4] As every student in economics is supposed to know, Adam Smith and David Ricardo were the first to make a coherent case for the principle of free trade. Important elements of free-trade doctrine were already present in the mercantilist period.[5] But the classical economists supplied the coherent framework that is still with us today.

In his authoritative study of theories of international trade Viner (1955: 108) concludes that 'all the important elements in Adam Smith's free-trade doctrine had been presented prior to the *Wealth of Nations.*' But there is 'little evidence that these early expositions had much influence', and they were often 'to be found only in isolated passages not wholly consistent with the views expounded in the surrounding text.' Although 'certain elements of doctrine tending to lead to free-trade views were fairly widely prevalent' (Viner, 1955: 92) and 'calls for greater liberty in commerce flourished among intellectuals in France and Britain', the idea of free trade 'did not have a particularly strong economic basis and was sometimes founded upon a vague cosmopolitanism that had little economic content and therefore could be easily dismissed' (Irwin, 1996b: 73–74). Among the ideas that were already floating around and which were important for the successful formulation of the free-trade doctrine, Viner (1955: 92–107) mentions: the quantity theory of money and the criticism and qualifications of the balance-of-trade doctrine; the general agreement that the profit motive was the controlling factor in economic behavior; the concept of 'economic man'; the argument that regulation of trade by government went counter to human nature and could not prevail over the power of the profit motive, while such regulation also faced such problems as the regulators' incompetence and the unavailability of unbiased advisers; the 'elaborate reasoning' in Mandeville's *Fable of the Bees* 'in support of individualism and laissez faire, resting on his famous argument that "private vices" such as "avarice" and luxury were "public benefits"'; and 'some of the specific economic arguments for unrestricted trade' as stated or approximated by writers such as Houghton (in 1677), Barbon (in 1690) and Davenant (in 1697).[6] As is clear from this incomplete enumeration, Smith did not base the development of his free-trade doctrine only on economic ideas in the narrow sense, but drew on more general philosophical ideas as well. Both Irwin (1996b: 62–63) and Viner (1955: 109) even conclude, 'perhaps somewhat surprisingly', that 'the moral philosophy that emerged in the eighteenth century enlightenment' was more important for Smith's approach to free trade than 'the earlier English economic literature.'[7]

Adam Smith's 'stupendous accomplishment' was that he 'achieved what others before him had failed to do: present a systematic, coherent framework for thinking about the economics of trade policy', by providing 'a more soundly based economic logic to accompany the philosophically derived compatibility of private interests and public benefits' (Irwin, 1996b: 73–74). The key argument that Smith advances for free trade is directly linked to the plea for the division of labor that opens book I of *The Wealth of Nations.* 'The greatest improvement in the productive powers of labour, and the greater part of the skill, dexterity, and judgment with which it is any where directed, or applied, seem to have been the effects of the division of labour', Smith (1776: 13) writes. He argues that '(i)t is the maxim of every prudent master of a family, never to attempt to make at home what it will cost him more to make than to buy', illustrating the argument with his famous example:

> The taylor does not attempt to make his own shoes, but buys them of the shoemaker. The shoemaker does not attempt to make his own cloaths, but employs

a taylor. The farmer attempts to make neither the one nor the other, but employs those different artificers. All of them find it for their interest to employ their whole industry in a way in which they have some advantage over their neighbours, and to purchase with a part of its produce, or what is the same thing, with the price of a part of it, whatever else they have occasion for.

(Smith, 1776: 456–457)

Extrapolating from individuals to countries, Smith appeals to the commonsensical thought that '(w)hat is prudence for every private family, can scarce be folly in that of a great kingdom', to state the case for free trade. He succeeded in defending free trade not as important for a particular industry or class, but as a general interest. Directly challenging mercantilist doctrines, Smith (1776: 457) argued that the 'importation of gold and silver is not the principal, much less the sole benefit which a nation derives from its foreign trade', because there are two other major benefits that can be gained from trade: 'It carries out that surplus part of the produce of their land and labour for which there is no demand among them, and brings back in return for it something else for which there is a demand.' And by 'opening a more extensive market for whatever part of the produce of their labour may exceed the home consumption, it encourages them to improve its productive powers, and to augment its annual produce to the utmost, and thereby to increase the real revenue and wealth in the society.'

After Smith the case for free trade was further developed and strengthened by the theory of comparative costs or comparative advantage. This finishing touch to free-trade doctrine is attributed to David Ricardo.[8] He introduced in 1817 in Chapter 7 of his *Principles of Political Economy and Taxation* the idea that even countries that are superior in producing *all* goods in comparison with potential trading partners will benefit from trade: 'This explicit statement that imports could be profitable even though the commodity imported could be produced at less cost at home than abroad, was, it seems to me, the sole addition of consequence which the doctrine of comparative costs made' (Viner, 1955: 441).

Ricardo basically went one step further than Smith, because he took the fact into consideration that productivity levels differ from one country to another. By incorporating that aspect in his argument he succeeded even better than Smith in showing that free trade is in the interest of *every* country, because there is always something that can be traded. Ricardo set out the case for countries specializing in the production of goods in which their opportunity costs were lowest with his famous example of the trade in wine and cloth between England and Portugal:

England may be so circumstanced, that to produce the cloth may require the labour of 100 men for one year; and if she attempted to make the wine, it might require the labour of 120 men for the same time. England would therefore find it her interest to import wine, and to purchase it by the exportation of cloth.

To produce the wine in Portugal, might require only the labour of 80 men for one year, and to produce the cloth in the same country, might require the labour of 90 men for the same time. It would therefore be advantageous for her to export wine in exchange for cloth. This exchange might even take place, notwithstanding that the commodity imported by Portugal could be produced there with less labour than in England. Though she could make the cloth with the labour of 90 men, she would import it from a country where it required the labour of 100 men to produce it, because it would be advantageous to her rather to employ her capital in the production of wine, for which she would obtain more cloth from England, than she could produce by diverting a portion of her capital from the cultivation of vines to the manufacture of cloth.[9]

(Ricardo, 1817: 134–135)

Like Smith before him, Ricardo (1817: 128) argued that free trade will 'very powerfully contribute to increase the mass of commodities, and therefore the sum of enjoyments.' The resulting greater abundance of commodities for lower prices is advantageous for the whole community and trade is therefore beneficial to countries. This argument is usually presented in the canonical justifications for (the advantages of) free trade; but in addition to this motive Ricardo gives a second justification for foreign trade when he argues that it may increase the profit rate. This argument is very important for Ricardo, because like other classical economists he was convinced that there is a tendency for the average rate of profit to fall:

It is quite as important to the happiness of mankind, that our enjoyments should be increased by the better distribution of labour, by each country producing those commodities for which by its situation, its climate, and its other natural or artificial advantages, it is adapted, and by their exchanging them for the commodities of other countries, as that they should be augmented by a rise in the rate of profits.

(Ricardo, 1817: 132)

Ricardo went to great lengths to make clear that trade in itself does not lead to a higher profit rate. He even opens his chapter on foreign trade by opposing that specific idea: 'No extension of foreign trade will immediately increase the amount of value in a country.'[10] He saw such an increase in the profit rate only as a possibility under very specific circumstances. Because there is an inverse relationship between wages and profits, 'the rate of profit can never be increased but by a fall in wages,' he spells out. And the consequence is that 'there can be no permanent fall of wages but in consequence of a fall of the necessaries on which wages are expended' (Ricardo, 1817: 132). Only when trade leads to a decrease in the price of, for example, food or cloth for the working class, he argued, can wages go down and will profits rise. Ricardo generally considered the fall of the rate of profit unavoidable, because of the decreasing quality of the land that would have to be cultivated to be able to feed the increasing population, which would lead to increasing food prices for the workers. But trade in his view could therefore partially counter the fall of the rate of profit.

For our further discussion it is important to emphasize once again that Smith and Ricardo did not propagate free trade for general cosmopolitan or altruistic reasons, but because they considered the extension of international exchange of goods to be more in the interest of nations than protectionism. In fact, they held that there is no contradiction between the national interest and free trade.

2.2   HEROIC ASSUMPTIONS AND LIMITATIONS

Since the genesis of the classical theory of free trade, two major types of criticisms have been raised against its theoretical and empirical underpinnings. The first questions the heroic assumptions that have to be fulfilled to make the theory of comparative advantage work, while the second observes that real-world developments do not match the theory's predictions and expectations. These objections are reviewed in this section.

2.2.1   Heroic assumptions

Although he does not formulate them explicitly, many assumptions underlie Ricardo's free-trade theory. Without any further elaboration he assumes that all income in a country is expended to buy goods; that there is never any reduction of demand because money is saved; that full use is being made of productive capacity and of the factors of production (which adapt instantly to changes in demand); that countries always have or are headed rapidly towards a balance of trade; and that markets adapt quickly and are therefore perfectly flexible. Frey and Weck-Hannemann show that all these assumptions can be challenged when they attempt to solve the riddle of why protectionism has existed in all periods and countries when economic theory argues so convincingly that free trade maximizes a country's economic welfare and leads to the most efficient allocation of resources:

> (T)he assumptions underlying the pure theory of international trade do not fully obtain in reality. In particular, it should not be assumed that markets are perfect: real economies are subject to imperfect competition which distorts relative prices, and there are non-negligible costs of information, transaction and bargaining. Markets are thus not perfectly flexible, and it proves to be difficult, and sometimes impossible, to undertake the redistributions necessary to compensate the losers from a (potentially) Pareto-optimal trade-liberalizing measure.[11]
>
> (Frey and Weck-Hannemann, 1996: 154–155)

For Viner (1955: 444) 'it is more or less obvious' that Ricardo based his analysis on assumptions, 'which, in conformity with his usual practice, he never expressly states.' These are in his opinion: 'ample time for long-run adjustments; free competition; only two countries and only two commodities; constant labor costs as output is varied; and proportionality of both aggregate real costs and

supply prices within each country to labor-time costs within that country.'
Emmanuel also lists a number of assumptions:

> (C)onstant costs, equality in potential of production and consumption in the
> two countries concerned, wages everywhere equal to the subsistence min-
> imum, identical techniques, identity in respect of money and incomes, identity
> in balance of payments and trade balance, full employment of the factors.
>
> (Emmanuel, 1972: ix)

All these assumptions have been discussed and rejected.[12] But when a theory's
assumptions do not state necessary conditions for the theory to hold, '(s)howing
that the theory's assumptions are false (...) does not imply that the theory is
false' (Vromen, 1995: 29).[13] To effectively challenge Ricardo's theory it would
therefore be necessary to discredit a sufficient and necessary assumption.

However, there is an additional assumption in Ricardo's theory that has not yet
been mentioned, which he does emphasize himself as a necessary condition for
the theory of comparative advantage to work. To the question what would be the
most advantageous if the production of both wine and cloth required less labor in
Portugal than in England, Ricardo replies:

> It would undoubtedly be advantageous to the capitalists of England, and to
> the consumers in both countries, that under such circumstances, the wine and
> the cloth should both be made in Portugal, and therefore that the capital and
> labour of England employed in making cloth, should be removed to Portugal
> for that purpose. In that case, the relative value of these commodities would
> be regulated by the same principle, as if one were the produce of Yorkshire,
> and the other of London; and in every other case, if capital freely flowed
> towards those countries where it could be most profitably employed, there
> could be no difference in the rate of profit, and no other difference in the real
> or labour price of commodities, than the additional quantity of labour
> required to convey them to the various markets where they were to be sold.
>
> (Ricardo, 1817: 136)

If capital is mobile, Ricardo posits here, the theory of comparative costs will not
hold, because in that case international specialization will be determined by
absolute costs, like specialization in one country.[14] As this would erase his free trade
principle, it is only logical that Ricardo expresses the conviction – and hope –
that this will not happen:

> Experience, however, shows, that the fancied or real insecurity of capital,
> when not under the immediate control of its owner, together with the natural
> disinclination which every man has to quit the country of his birth and con-
> nexions, and intrust himself with all his habits fixed, to a strange government
> and new laws, check the emigration of capital. These feelings, which I should
> be sorry to see weakened, induce most men of property to be satisfied with a

low rate of profits in their own country, rather than seek a more advantageous employment of their wealth in foreign nations.

(Ricardo, 1817: 136–137)

This argument is rather remarkable when we consider today's world economy, in which financial flows are largely unregulated and financial markets are so heavily integrated that a tempest in one part of the world almost automatically conjures up storms in other parts. Even more important, multinationals organize the conception, production and sales of their products worldwide, and therefore increasingly resort to foreign direct investments and outsourcing. The capitalism of Ricardo's time must certainly have been different from today's capitalism:

It is becoming exceptionally clear that this is also a question of the *culture* of capitalism. The type of 'nativist' position that Ricardo expresses is no longer in keeping with the conditions of casino capitalism and its world of financial derivatives. His simple assumptions about capitalists' attachment to their own culture are no longer viable.

(Altvater and Mahnkopf, 1996: 206)

But the truth of the matter is that even in Ricardo's day this assumption did not hold. Adam Smith already had a different opinion when he wrote his *Wealth of Nations*:

A merchant, it has been said very properly, is not necessarily the citizen of any particular country. It is in a great measure indifferent to him from what places he carries on his trade; and a very trifling disgust will make him remove his capital, and together with it all the industry which it supports, from one country to another.

(Smith, 1776: 426)

Williams (1929: 209) comments that precisely because of this instability of mercantile and industrial capital, Smith, 'who was a nationalist of nationalists, objected to the encouragement of international trade and industries dependent thereon; in a "natural" order capital would go first into agriculture at home and become planted in the soil.' More importantly, Williams also notes that Smith was not the only one; there was 'general recognition among writers and statesmen (…) that the same profits motivation which moved goods could move also the labor and capital requisite to produce them effectively.' Williams cites, for example J.S. Mill, who wrote about the West Indies:

All the capital employed is English capital; almost all the industry is carried on for English uses…. The trade with the West Indies is therefore hardly to be considered as external trade, but more resembles the traffic between town and country, and is amenable to the principles of the home trade.

(Williams, 1929: 206–207)

This does not mean, however, that the rate of profit on capital was becoming equal in all countries. As Mandel (1972: 353) argues, the hypothesis of international equalization of profit rates 'presupposes perfect international mobility of capital – in effect, the equalization of all economic, social and political conditions propitious to the development of modern capitalism on a world scale.' This was not the case at the time, nor is it today, as can easily be seen from the divergent rates of return on capital from country to country or the correlation between savings and investment ratios.[15]

In sum, we have seen that Ricardo based his theory of comparative advantage on a number of (not explicitly stated) assumptions, many of which have been challenged since then. He himself presented the premise that there be no cross-border factor mobility as critical for his theory. But economic writers among his contemporaries noted that even then capital and labor were in fact internationally mobile to a certain extent.

2.2.2 Apparent refutations

The second category of criticism concerns the gap between the world as described or predicted by free trade theory and the rather different reality. In a speech in Brussels in 1848 Marx, for example, used the case of the West Indian colonies to criticize the classical theory:

> (W)e are told that free trade would create an international division of labour, and thereby give to each country the production which is most in harmony with its natural advantages. You believe perhaps, gentlemen, that the production of coffee and sugar is the natural destiny of the West Indies. Two centuries ago, nature, which does not trouble herself about commerce, had planted neither sugar-cane nor coffee trees there. And it may be that in less than half a century you will find there neither coffee nor sugar, for the West Indies, by means of cheaper production, have already succesfully combated this alleged natural destiny of the West Indies. And the West Indies, with their natural wealth, are already as heavy a burden for England as the weavers of Dacca, who also were destined from the beginning of time to weave by hand.
>
> (Marx, 1848: 252)

Altvater and Mahnkopf refer to the same historical example and extend the conclusion that can be drawn from it to countries that have industrialized more recently:

> If the theory of comparative advantage had held true, then India's cotton and silk manufactures would have made life difficult for the rising British textile industry in the early nineteenth century, and England would have had to specialize in sheep herding and whiskey distilleries. Other late-industrializing countries (like Japan and South Korea) would also have remained

agricultural countries if they had not steered their economic development towards industrialization by political means, quite contrary to the principle of specialization upheld by Ricardo's theorem.

(Altvater and Mahnkopf, 1996: 207)

In a remarkable dissertation in 1970, Sideri investigated the structure and dynamics of the trade between England (cloth) and Portugal (wine), Ricardo's famous example. The Anglo-Portuguese commercial treaties of 1642, 1654, 1661 and 1703 (the Methuen Treaty) are a good example of the division of labor between two countries in accordance with the principle of comparative advantage. But Sideri finds that the actual outcome was not what the theorem predicts. He argues that 'the negative effects of this kind of international division of labour on Portugal's economy (...) contradict Ricardo's tenet that foreign trade based on the doctrine of comparative advantage was beneficial for all trading partners.' These negative effects on the Portuguese economy were 'mainly the result of the "type" of international division of labour (...) which was forced on Portugal that, at the end of the 17th century, really produced both wine and cloth.' Portugal's manufacturing sector had been sacrificed to the production of wine. Its terms of trade deteriorated, which 'emphasizes the impact of the specialization in primary goods on the economic structure of the country which has accepted such an international division of labour' (Sideri, 1970: 3–7). The conclusion Sideri draws puts the debate between proponents of free trade and protectionism in a different perspective:

> In an international system, that is a system composed of nations, the relations among those elements are bound to be pervaded by power both as ends and a means. Mercantilism and free trade are not basically different, but both are the manifestation of and the instrument by which power is exercised. Free trade is 'the mercantilism of the strongest power, and it leads to imperialism almost as surely as a thought-out commercial policy'.

(Sideri, 1970: 6)

More generally, when it comes to international trade one cannot help observing that historically there is 'a complete divorce between thought and praxis.' Leaving aside interludes, 'the normal practice of the world, since the early Middle Ages and even since the Greco-Roman period, to go no further back, has been and still remains protectionism.' This has been the case although 'year after year, decade after decade, imperturbably and tireless, the postmercantilist economists, from François Quesnay and Adam Smith onward, went on demonstrating the errors of protectionism and the advantages of free trade' (Emmanuel, 1972: xiv). As Guttmann argues:

> Even though free trade has been the orthodox view among most economists since the days of Smith and Ricardo, in practice very few countries actually followed this prescription. By and large only the strongest industries in the

most powerful countries favored such a policy, and in each case they did so to exploit their competitive advantage over others. Between the Congress of Vienna (1814–1815) and World War I (1914–1918) only Great Britain, then the world's domestic economic power, was firmly committed to free trade; other economies remained strongly protectionist. The United States converted to free trade only after it emerged as the new superpower at the end of World War II, and other industrial countries gradually followed suit.[16]

(Guttmann, 1994: 325–326)

Also, it is no coincidence that Ricardo's theory of free trade originated in England:

as a liberal critique of aristocratic privileges in early-nineteenth-century England, where the landed gentry wanted to protect English agriculture while emerging industrial capitalists wanted freedom to exploit trade opportunities. The doctrine served Britain well in the mid-nineteenth century, at the height of British hegemony.

(Kuttner, 1992: 116)

Based on his inquiry into the economic and power relations between England and Portugal at the genesis of classical free trade theory, Sideri therefore concludes:

(W)hen the international division of labour resulting from the classical but 'highly simplified model' (...) is analyzed in a more realistic setting which includes international power relations, socio-political national structures, and type of trade, then Ricardo's 'welfare proposition that trade is beneficial', in other words that 'a poor country does better to trade with a rich country', appears mainly as a long term generalization of what is correct for the most powerful manufacturing countries. Consequently, the free trade policy when utilized to produce a country's specialization in primary products really becomes, as a great Portuguese scholar and politician remarked, 'a chain prepared for the simple ..., an excellent doctrine for the strong against the weak'.

(Sideri, 1970: 215)

As Kuttner argues, even a cursory look at the behavior of policymakers in the United States immediately confirms this judgment. In the nineteenth and early twentieth centuries the US was much more protectionist, 'as early American manufacturers realized that they could not initially compete with cheaper British imports (this is the famous "infant industry" argument)'. But today, among influential economists and in the US diplomatic corps, 'you find an almost universal devotion to the theory of comparative advantage as politically and scientifically essential.' For Kuttner the reason for this change is no secret: 'Though the United States itself was relatively mercantilist in the nineteenth century, the Ricardian view has been internalized and treated as gospel since 1945 precisely *because it is so congruent with the logic of American hegemony*' (Kuttner, 1992: 117 emphasis in original).

In sum, serious doubts have been raised about the empirical validity of the classical free trade theory, and about the claim that free trade is advantageous for all countries. The next section reviews two critiques of the comparative advantage theorem that may help us understand these apparent refutations.

2.3   NOT A HARMONIOUS WORLD REPUBLIC: TWO EARLY CRITIQUES

Smith and Ricardo argued the case for free trade from what today would be called a 'win–win perspective': there are no losers, everybody gains. They therefore consider international economic relations as 'essentially harmonious' (Gilpin, 1987: 188) and beneficent for all, as long as trade is allowed to take its 'natural or spontaneous course' (Mill, 1844: 21). Characterizing free trade as natural or spontaneous often has an ideological function, as Manoïlesco, Romania's minister of industry and trade, noted in 1931 in his attempt to formulate a general theory of protectionism:

> Free-trade looks scientific because it pretends to derive from a certain determinism which was in fashion at the beginning of the [nineteenth] century, and was then taken for science. The discoveries of great naturalists, and especially those of Darwin, had spread the conviction that nature is governed by a certain automatism, thanks to which living beings – after a series of struggles against their environment – always reach a state of equilibrium in which the preservation of the species is maintained. The same conception was adopted for economic phenomena by free-traders and generally by the Liberal school. (...) Free-trade, in recommending the specialising of each country in the articles in which it presents the greatest superiority in comparison with other countries – thus, just those products favoured by nature – seems to believe in a natural harmony of the interests of all countries. This natural harmony appeared simple and automatic. It was to function of itself with no interference of men or of State politics.
>
> (Manoïlesco, 1931: 58, 212)

In *The National System of Political Economy* (1841), his most important work on free trade and protectionism, Friedrich List reproached free trade theorists for assuming a state of affairs which is not (yet) present:

> It assumes the existence of a universal union and a state of perpetual peace, and deduces therefrom the great benefits of free trade. In this manner it confounds effects with causes. (...) That, however, under the existing conditions of the world, the result of general free trade would not be a universal

republic, but, on the contrary, a universal subjection of the less advanced nations to the supremacy of the predominant manufacturing, commercial, and naval power, is a conclusion for which the reasons are very strong and, according to our view, irrefragable.

(List, 1841: 102–103)

The case for free trade is of course part of the general case for free markets (Krugman, 1986: 10) and of the laissez-faire case for the least possible government intervention in economic life.[17] In an earlier work, List (1837: 70) had already commented: 'The cosmopolitan theorists do not question the importance of industrial expansion. (...) They consider that government action to stimulate the establishment of industries does more harm than good.'

According to Keynes (1926: 34) the fact that the principles of laissez-faire have been 'confirmed in the minds of sound thinkers and the reasonable public' is partially due to 'the poor quality of the opponent proposals – Protectionism on one hand, and Marxian Socialism on the other.' Kahan also mentions List and Marx as the main critics of classical economics, and notes an interesting similarity:

(I)t may be observed that Marx, who was trained in the German philosophy but embraced the classical economics, displayed in his economic writing some affinity with the criticisms brought by the historical school against classical economics. Consider the phrase 'the capitalist system represents the relation between producers as the exchange of commodities': substitute 'national interests' for 'class interests' in the Marxian analysis and you have, prima facie, an echo of some of the criticism leveled against the classical school mentioned above.

(Kahan, 1968: 22)

We now turn to these criticisms, and will see that List and Marx, each from a different perspective, challenge the assumption that the world is 'a harmonious world republic.'[18]

List: nations are not individuals

List, whose work obviously 'bears the mark of the country in which the author wrote and the times in which he lived, as well as his own personality' (Manoïlesco, 1931: 240), published his *National System of Political Economy* in 1841, seven years after the foundation of the German Zollverein.[19] In this book List strongly opposes what he calls the 'bottomless cosmopolitanism' of the free trade school and develops his alternative 'system,' which has as its distinguishing characteristic: 'NATIONALITY. On the nature of *nationality*, as the intermediate interest between those of *individualism* and of *entire humanity*, my whole structure is based' (List, 1841: xliii). For List, the system of the classical school suffers from three main defects:

(F)irstly, from boundless *cosmopolitanism*, which neither recognises the principle of nationality, nor takes into consideration the satisfaction of its interests; secondly, from a dead *materialism*, which everywhere regards chiefly the mere exchangeable value of things without taking into consideration the mental and political, the present and the future interests, and the productive powers of the nation; thirdly, from a *disorganising particularism* and *individualism*, which, ignoring the nature and character of social labour and the operation of the union of powers in their higher consequences, considers private industry only as it would develop itself under a state of free interchange with society (i.e. with the whole human race) were that race not divided into seperate national societies.

(List, 1841: 141)

The fundamental methodological problem, List raises with the classical school, is that the generalization from individuals to nations is unacceptable, because 'the interest of individual merchants and the interest of the commerce of a whole nation are widely different things.' List was not the only one criticizing this philosophical starting point, as can be seen from the *Statement of Some New Principles on the Subject of Political Economy* published in 1834 by Rae:

My main object, in this book, is to show that the notion of the exact identity of the causes giving rise to individual and national wealth, on which the reasonings and arguments of Adam Smith all along depend, is erreonous, that consequently the doctrines he has engrafted on it, cannot be thus maintained, and are inconsistent with facts admitted by himself.[20]

(Rae, 1834: 8)

The reason, why it should be 'evident' that nations are not individuals, is formulated by List when he deals with the behavior of the merchant who:

may be accomplishing his purpose (viz. gain of values by exchange) at the expense of the agriculturists and manufacturers, at the expense of the nation's productive powers, and indeed of its independence. It is all the same to him; and according to the character of his business and occupation, he need not trouble himself much respecting the manner in which the goods imported or exported by him act on the morality, the prosperity, or the power of the nation. He imports poisins as readily as medicines. He enervates whole nations through opium and spirituous liquors. Whether he by his importations and smugglings brings occupation and sustenance to hundreds of thousands, or whether they are thereby reduced to beggary, does not signify to him as a man of business, if only his own balance is increased thereby. Then if those who have been reduced to want bread seek to escape the misery in their fatherland by emigrating, he can still obtain profit by the business of arranging their emigration. In the time of war he provides the enemy with arms and ammunition. He would, if it were possible, sell fields and meadows to foreign countries, and when he had sold the last bit of land would place himself on board his ship and export himself.

(List, 1841: 209)

It is no coincidence that List opens his *The National System of Political Economy* with a book about the history of Italy, England, the Netherlands and seven other countries, and only introduces his theory in the second book, after that description. He does so because he wants to show that nations have their own specific histories, which have to be taken into account. Nations find themselves in different phases of development, and List (1841: 143) takes for granted that all nations 'have to pass through the following stages of development: original barbarism, pastoral condition, agricultural condition, agricultural-manufacturing condition, and agricultural-manufacturing-commercial condition.' As Freeman (1997: 24) notes, 'the racialist and colonialist overtones' in List's book 'were in strong contrast to the internationalist cosmopolitan approach of the classical free-trade economists', but 'despite these unattractive features of his outlook, he clearly anticipated many contemporary ideas.' And Levi-Faur (1997: 159), noting that List 'emphasized the importance of human capital in economic development', argues that 'List should be considered one of the founders of human capital theory and deserves more appreciation in this regard than he has received.' Today, when the World Bank emphasizes the need for intangible investments in knowledge List's criticism of Smith sounds surprisingly modern:

If we continue to consider the example of the pin manufacture adduced by Adam Smith in illustration of the advantages of division of labour, and seek for the causes of the phenomenon that ten persons united in that manufacture can produce an infinitely larger number of pins than if every one carried on the entire pin manufacture seperately, we find that the division of commercial operations without *combination of the productive powers towards one common object* could but little further this production. In order to create such a result, the different individuals must co-operate bodily as well as mentally, and work together. (...) The popular school, because it has regarded the division of operation alone as the essence of this natural law, has committed the error of applying it merely to the separate manufactory or farm; it has not perceived that the same law extends its action especially over the *whole manufacturing* and *agricultural power*, over *the whole economy of the nation*.

(List, 1841: 122)

The problem of the classical school is therefore for List, that it confounds individuals' accumulation of wealth with the development of nations' productive capacity. From this observation he concludes that the state has an important role to play in coordinating and carrying out industrial and economic policies, and that unrestricted free trade as propagated by the classical school should be opposed.[21]

In reality, List was only a moderate protagonist of import restrictions, and he was certainly not against free trade in general.[22] In fact, Manoïlesco criticized him exactly for that reason:

> But List did not found a theory of the protectionist phenomenon. It is sufficient to observe that actual protection far exceeds the framework in which List explained and justified it. Protection is therefore quite other, with a much wider extension than List believed it to be. List never contested free-trade. He did not refute free-trade arguments one by one. He did not build up a proper system of a general and permanent character, which may constitute a complete answer to free-trade. (...) Instead of a theory of generality, he put forward a theory of exceptions. He craved for protectionism only a purely provisional rôle, dependent upon numerous conditions and restrictions; and, what is more serious, he presented protection to public opinion as a sacrifice, a necessary evil, whose only excuse is of being temporary.
>
> (Manoïlesco, 1931: 240–241)

List's basic argument is that nations have to protect themselves temporarily against imports from countries that are further developed, as long as they need the time and means to develop themselves to the highest possible stage of development. Linked to the colonialist overtones in his work and his rather mechanical stagist view of how nations develop, he qualified his defense of protectionism even further. List (1841: 247) considered the famous 'infant industry argument' only applicable to the industrial development of bigger countries already close to the last of his development stages, and not to agriculture or smaller or less developed countries.[23] There is no need to emphasize that this approach reflects List's experiences in the US, and his preoccupation with turning Germany into a leading world power.

Marx: free trade is freedom of capital

We now turn to Marx, who had quite different reasons to be skeptical about free trade. In September 1847 an economists' congress was organized in Brussels to push for free trade. Georg Weerth, the only critical speaker, called it scandalous that no attention was paid to the misery that free trade caused for workers. Karl Marx, who was also invited to the congress, wanted to support that point of view but did not get the floor and was told that the speakers' list was full (McLellan, 1975: 207–211). He subsequently had his remarks published in a small Belgian paper and delivered a public speech 'On the question of free trade' before the Democratic Association of Brussels on January 9 of the following year.

Clearly the criticism Marx raised There at the age of 29 and 20 years before the publication of his *Capital*, has a different status than the critique of List or of the older Marx, since it was a political speech and Marx had not yet extensively studied capitalism. But nonetheless the speech contains some interesting thoughts that are worth recapitulating.

Unlike List, Marx criticizes free trade not from a national but from a class point of view, claiming that free trade is 'the freedom of capital to crush the worker.' In contrast to List, Marx does not support what he calls the 'conservative' protectionism 'of our day.' For Marx, the debate about free trade was neither timeless nor about principles in general. He discussed the reasons for and consequences of free trade 'under the present condition of society', that is in early capitalism. In that context he summarizes his criticism as follows:

> It is freedom of capital. When you have overthrown the few national barriers which still restrict the progress of capital, you will merely have given it complete freedom of action. (...) Gentlemen! Do not allow yourselves to be deluded by the abstract word *freedom*. Whose freedom? It is not the freedom of one individual in relation to another, but the freedom of capital to crush the worker.
>
> (Marx, 1848: 250–251)

Before he arrived at this conclusion, Marx discussed the arguments that were being used in the major political fight of that time over the Corn Laws. As Parry and Steiner (1998: xiv) note the repeal of these laws in 1846 'was an event of enormous significance in the history of international trade, in the development of institutions of international regulation, in the realignment of political parties and interests in Britain, and in the emergence of new modes of political action (...). With the repeal of these laws, Britain entered a period of free trade that lasted until the early part of the twentieth century. Trade was also liberated in Europe in the latter half of the nineteenth century with free-trade agreements being signed between Britain and France in 1860, France and the Zollverein (a group of independent German states) in 1862, and France and other European states later (Rodgers, 1998: 203). At that moment in history, English manufacturers opposed protectionism and defended free trade, because imports would make food cheaper (making lower wages possible), while the landlords wanted to maintain limitations on food imports. Just as they do today, supporters of free trade argued that protectionism was contrary to everybody's interests. But as Marx (1848: 238–239) noted, 'the people for whom cheap food is to be procured at all costs are very ungrateful.' Why this ingratitude? '(A)ll this hypocrisy was not calculated to make cheap bread attractive to the workers.'

Marx also took up Ricardo's argument that free trade can lead to an increase of the profit rate if it leads to cheaper foodstuffs for the workers. He argued that English workers were not impressed by the 'missionaries' preaching 'the gospel of free trade', the distribution of 'thousands of pamphlets to enlighten the worker upon his own interests', and the 'vast administrative system for the conduct of the free trade movement':

> The English workers have very well understood the significance of the struggle between the landlords and the industrial capitalists. They know very well that the price of bread was to be reduced in order to reduce wages, and that

the industrial profit would rise by as much as rent fell. Ricardo, the apostle of the English free-traders, the most eminent economist of our century, entirely agrees with the workers upon this point. (...) So long as the price of corn was higher and wages were also higher, a small saving in the consumption of bread sufficed to procure him other enjoyments. But as soon as bread is very cheap, and wages are therefore very cheap, he can save almost nothing on bread for the purchase of other articles.

(Marx, 1848: 240–241)

After having discussed various arguments free-trade protagonists put forward, Marx sums up the argument for free trade: 'Free trade increases productive forces. If industry keeps growing, if wealth, if the productive power, if, in a word, productive power increases, the demand for labor, the price of labor, and consequently the rate of wages, rise also.' He agrees with the thesis that free trade is beneficial for the accumulation of capital, but he does not accept that this growth of capital leads to higher wages:

The growth of productive capital implies the accumulation and the concentration of capital. The centralization of capital involves a greater division of labour and a greater use of machinery. The greater division of labour destroys the especial skill of the labourer; and by putting in the place of this skilled work labour which any one can perform, it increases competition among the workers. (...) Thus, as productive capital grows, competition among the workers grows in a far greater proportion. The reward of labour diminishes for all, and the burden of labour increases for some. (...) The progress of industry creates less expensive means of subsistence. Thus spirits have taken the place of beer, cotton that of wool and linen, and potatoes that of bread. Thus, as means are constantly being found for the maintenance of labour on cheaper and more wretched food, the minimum of wages is constantly sinking. If these wages began by making the man work to live, they end by making him live the life of a machine. His existence has no other value than that of a simple productive force, and the capitalist treats him accordingly.[24]

(Marx, 1848: 243–250)

It is therefore clear for Marx that 'either we must reject all political economy based upon the assumption of free trade, or we must admit that under this free trade the whole severity of the economic laws will fall upon the workers.' He considers this rejection all the more necessary since free trade also leads to increasing exploitation on an international scale:

We have shown what sort of brotherhood free trade begets between the different classes of one and the same nation. The brotherhood which free trade would establish between the nations of the earth would hardly be more fraternal. To call cosmopolitan exploitation universal brotherhood is an idea that could only be engendered in the brain of the bourgeoisie. All the destructive phenomena which unlimited competition gives rise to within one country are reproduced in more gigantic proportions on the world market.

(Marx, 1848: 251)

For Marx, as will by now be clear, there is no timeless or principled choice for either free trade or protectionism but only one criterion on which proposals for policies have to be judged: 'What influence will the adoption of free trade have upon the condition of the working class?' (Marx, 1848: 249) The same question must also be raised in relation to protectionism, which he opposed (Marx, 1848: 253) based on his concrete analysis of the consequences of either policy.[25] For Marx in that particular historical period free trade was to be preferred over protectionism for one reason: because he expected such a policy to facilitate the replacement of capitalism by socialism.

In sum, we have seen in this section that at the time of the first victory of free trade List and Marx challenged for different reasons the implicit assumption in the comparative advantage theorem of a 'harmonious world republic.' While List emphasized the specific place and role of nations and their conflicts, Marx focused on the divergent consequences of free trade for different social classes and their struggles.

2.4   RESURGENT DOUBTS ABOUT FREE TRADE IN THE GLOBALIZED ERA

In his survey on the methodology of economics, Blaug (1992: 239) argues that the central weakness of modern economics is 'reluctance to produce the theories that yield unambiguously refutable implications, followed by a general unwillingness to confront those implications with the facts.' Few economic theories fully meet falsificationist standards, but even within an instrumentalist framework this poses a problem. The theorem of comparative advantage seems a clear case in point.

The fact that many unrealistic assumptions underlie the classical free trade theory is not an argument against it, instrumentalists hold. In Friedman's (1953: 15) words, 'the relevant question to ask about the "assumptions" of a theory is not whether they are descriptively "realistic," for they never are, but whether they are sufficiently good approximations for the purpose in hand.'[26] So how should we judge a theory's robustness? Friedman argues that such a question can only be answered 'by seeing whether the theory works, which means whether it yields sufficiently accurate predictions.' But when a theory's predictions are refuted, rather than conclude that the theory is incorrect, many economists try to find other evidence that does affirm their theory. As we have seen, serious doubts have been raised about the empirical validity of the comparative advantage theory's prediction that all countries will benefit from free trade. Ricardo's theory has even been refuted by his own example of British–Portuguese trade. Nevertheless this empirical weakness has not diminished support for the comparative advantage theorem among most economists and policymakers and powerful international institutions and organizations. Despite all the evidence, there is now even less room than before for a 'more pragmatic, country-by-country approach, with room for neomercantilist regimes until such countries are firmly on the convergence track' (Scott, 2001: 176). The classical free trade theorem is upheld as *the* way to go forward, for each and every country, under all circumstances.[27]

Today, according to the dominant discourse about globalization, states are withering away and being replaced by a unified global economy and cosmopolitan institutions of government. The dominant economic theory also holds fast to the blissful expectation that increased internationalization of economies will lead to a convergence of incomes and development levels. It seems that we are finally entering the 'harmonious world republic' that is assumed in classical trade theory.

Free trade is an essential element of today's dominant economic approach, fostering increasing economic globalization. At the end of 1997, to give an example, Director General Ruggiero of the World Trade Organization (WTO) welcomed the agreement that had just been concluded on international trade in financial services. Celebrating the, what he called a 'golden year' for the WTO, he spoke about a 'landmark in the history of trade liberalization', following agreements earlier that year to free trade in information technology products and liberalize telecommunications services. To give another example, OECD Secretary General Johnston (1996: 4), argued that 'all trade' offers 'mutual benefit.'[28]

Bhagwati explicitly argues that the increased internationalization and interdependence of economies in this era of globalization in no way lessens the fundamental importance of comparative advantage theory. To make the classical theory suitable for today's reality, he introduces the concept of 'kaleidoscopic comparative advantage.' By so doing he wants to give 'meaning to the notion that globalization of the world economy has led to fierce competition: slight shifts in costs can now lead to shifting comparative advantage, which is therefore increasingly volatile.' Today's comparative advantage is kaleidoscopic, Bhagwati argues, because 'firms are increasingly tempted to look over their foreign rivals' shoulders to see if differences in their domestic policies and institutions are giving them that fatal extra edge in competition which then amounts to *unfair trade*. But although 'the substantial sense of *economic insecurity*' is reinforced and 'the *decline in real wages* of the unskilled' is probably reinforced, the same comparative advantage paradigm still holds. Bhagwati (1997: 266–282) argues therefore that we 'need to reject the folly of including a Social Clause and eco-dumping varieties of trade and environmental agendas into the world trading regime', and have to unite the nations of the world behind the vision and objective of 'worldwide free trade.'

What Bhagwati and other contemporary proponents of free trade do not attempt to address is the additional problem that globalization has created for redistribution of the gains of trade to the less-well off. In what quantities and how the welfare gains of free trade are divided *among* countries is an open question in free trade theory, and the standard remedy to the inequalities caused by international trade *inside* countries is to require that the winners share some of their gains with the losers through some form of compensation. The latter is becoming more difficult, Rodrik (1997: 53, 64) argues, because globalization 'results in increased demands on the state to provide social insurance while reducing the ability of the state to perform that role effectively', i.e. 'reduces the ability of governments to spend resources on social program.' Only true believers in the comparative advantage theorem can dismiss this novel corollary of globalization as irrelevant for the general applicability of their article of faith.

Statements like the ones just cited do not mean that the comparative advantage theorem is still central in dominant trade theory. It is closer to the truth to say that the principle of comparative advantage is once again dominant. Krueger recapitulates that '(i)deas with regard to trade policy and economic development' have 'changed radically' in comparison with the 1950s and 1960s.[29] In those days

> there was a broad consensus that trade policy for development should be based on 'import substitution'. By this was meant that domestic production of import-competing goods should be started and increased to satisfy the domestic market under incentives provided through whatever level of protection against imports, or even import prohibition, was necessary to achieve it. It was thought that import substitution in manufactures would be synonymous with industrialization, which in turn was seen as key to development. The contrast with the views today is striking. It is now widely accepted that growth prospects for developing countries are greatly enhanced through an outer-oriented trade regime and fairly uniform incentives (primarily through the exchange rate) for production across exporting and import-competing goods.
>
> (Krueger, 1997: 1)

For Krueger it is still 'almost incredible that such a high fraction of economists could have deviated so far from the basic principles of international trade.' She therefore tries to answer the question 'how the principle of comparative advantage could have been so blithely abandoned' (Krueger, 1997: 11). Her reply is that good theory was often misapplied; that too much research was devoted to 'finding exceptions to the proposition that comparative advantage should form the basis of trade policy'; that good theory was misused because 'many good theory papers are written where the authors assume that their audience will consist entirely of other theorists'; and that theorists who assert that rents *might* be captured from infant industries by strategic trade policy 'are simply providing a carte blanche for policy makers and bureaucrats to intervene in whatever ways they like, and this will simultaneously be seized upon by special interests to bolster their causes' (Krueger, 1997: 17–19).

The received opinion is that the failure of import substitution is now clear to everybody, and that 'there is no question of "going back" to the earlier thinking and understanding of the process' of international trade because 'the principle of comparative advantage has worn out again' (Krueger, 1997: 2). The same euphoric conclusion can be found in Irwin's widely acclaimed intellectual history of free trade:

> The case for free trade has endured (...) because the fundamental proposition that substantial benefits arise from the free exchange of goods between countries has not been overshadowed by the limited scope of various qualifications and exceptions. Free trade thus remains as sound as any proposition in economic theory which purports to have implications for economic policy is ever likely to be.
>
> (Irwin, 1996b: 8)

Once again, and perhaps this time with even more force than before, the principle of comparative advantage is being promoted as generally applicable, as a general law for all times and situations.[30] Free trade is proclaimed to have won its second victory. If we all stick to the principle of comparative advantage from now on, 'hand in hand, in sacred partnership, the nations of the world' will be on their way towards 'a truly golden Age with worldwide free trade' (Bhagwati, 1997: 283). But will they?

Free trade based on the theory of comparative advantage is extremely popular among economists and policymakers, but in the rest of the world support for this policy is much less general. Referring to a 'sudden interest' in 'national development policies' by List, Drucker (1997: 167) prophesizes that '(t)he international economic policies likely to emerge over the next generation will be neither free-trade nor protectionist.' According to Krugman (1987: 536), 'the case for free trade is currently more in doubt than at any time since the 1817 publication of Ricardo's *Principles of Political Economy*.' And Rodrik (1999: 74) challenges the one-sidedly negative view of import substitution industrialization (ISI) in mainstream economics, arguing that such policies 'apparently worked well in a broad range of countries until at least the mid-1970s. (...) Had the world come to an end in 1973, ISI would never have acquired its dismal reputation.'[31] At the end of the twentieth century, doubts about free trade are therefore not just persistent, but once again increasing. To understand why, we will briefly review four contemporary criticisms of the free trade paradigm.

2.4.1   Shaped advantage

A criticism of free trade with influence on a broader group of economists and policymakers has emerged in the work of Krugman.[32] The 'New View' on trade challenges the traditional theory, arguing 'that the extreme pro-free-trade position – that markets work so well that they cannot be improved on – has become untenable' (Krugman, 1986: 15). *Arbitrariness, history* and *initial conditions*, says Krugman, are factors that comparative advantage theories do not adequately take into account:

Why are aircraft manufactured in Seattle? It is hard to argue that there is some unique attribute of the city's location that fully explains this. (...) In many of the new models of trade, the actual location of trade is to some degree indeterminate. Yet what the example of Seattle suggests, and what is explicit in some of the models, is a critical role for history: Because Seattle (or Detroit or Silicon Valley) was where an industry initially got established, increasing returns keep the industry there.

(Krugman, quoted in Kuttner, 1992: 120)

New trade theories stress that most international markets are characterized by imperfect competition, economies of scale and externalities. In oligopolistic markets it is not excluded that 'excess profits' can be earned, because barriers such as exclusive patent rights, trade barriers or economies of scale can make it risky or impossible for new firms to enter the market. New trade theorists form a heterogeneous group, inspired by Smith, Rae, Mill and List.

This new trade theory was later joined by the new endogenous growth theory, 'which also took its cue from advances in the theory of industrial organization, modeling growth in the presence of increasing returns to scale, R&D and human capital formation' (Maneschi, 1998: 223).[33] As Maneschi (1998: 225) notes, '(T)he new growth theory had the salutary effect of drawing attention to the lack of convergence between developed and developing countries, and highlighting the need to explore new ways to transform comparative advantage so that laggard countries can compete in an increasingly globalized world economy.'

'God-given natural phenomena such as climate' do not determine comparative advantage, Maneschi and his co-thinkers reason. Accepting this conclusion has practical implications. Moreover, it means that interventions by governments

in the form of export subsidies or import restrictions can play the role of cost-reducing technological innovations by the firm and give it the initial advantage required to establish its 'comparative advantage' in the chosen field. Such interventions can also determine the thrust of scientific and technical innovations and with them the whole culture.[34]

(Streeten, 1996: 358)

As Albo (1997: 15–17) notes, the case for shaped advantage that flows from this analysis 'can be bolstered once the general equilibrium model of individual agent market exchanges is let go, and alliances of competing states and firms are explicitly allowed to shape the "path-dependency" of economic outcomes.'

Although the New View 'has blown a big hole in the traditional theory of comparative advantage', Kuttner argues, the advocates of the theory themselves are generally hesitant to advocate industrial policies.

A typical New View scholarly article, especially when written by economists wishing to keep their neoclassical union cards, takes care to include the disclaimer that even if profit shifting or other benign interventions are possible in theory, they are often implausible in practice.

(Kuttner, 1992: 121)

As an example he cites Krugman, who argues:

> To abandon the free trade principle in pursuit of the gains from sophisticated intervention could open the door to adverse political consequences that would outweigh the potential gains. It is possible, then, both to believe that comparative advantage is an *incomplete* model of trade and to believe that free trade is the right policy.

(Kuttner, 1992: 121)

Two reasons are given for opposing government interference with trade: it is difficult to decide which industries governments should select to subsidize, and there will be pressures on political decision-makers by industries that want to be recognized as strategically important. But as Kuttner correctly notes, the 'New View' still fundamentally alters the trade debate, 'for it removes the presumptions that nations like Japan, which practices strategic trade, cannot, by definition, be improving their welfare. Orthodox economists must now concede that advocates of industrial policy are not economic illiterates after all.' The fact that for many economists '(u)nder real-world political pressures, the allure of strategic trade policy fades quickly' (*The Economist*, 1997a: 100), does not diminish the pertinence of this critique.[35]

2.4.2   Not convergence but more inequality

A major claim of proponents of globalization is that increased internationalization of the world economy will lead to a convergence between rich and poor countries. No less an authority than Pritchett (1995), senior economist at the World Bank, concluded, however, that convergence 'just hasn't happened, isn't happening, and isn't going to happen without serious changes in economic policies in developing countries.' This conclusion is based on extensive research, which shows:

> Divergence in relative productivity levels and living standards is the dominant feature of modern economic history. In the last century, incomes in the 'less developed' (or euphemistically, the 'developing') countries have fallen far behind those in the 'developed' countries, both proportionately and absolutely. I estimate that from 1870 to 1990 the ration of per capita incomes between the richest and the poorest countries increased by roughly a factor of five and that the difference in income between the richest country and all others has increased by an order of magnitude.

(Pritchett, 1997: 3)

Many other studies come to the same pessimistic conclusions. After a survey of studies about the supposed convergence of productivity levels and living standards, Boyer concludes for example:

> (S)tatistical evidence does not confirm any general and secular trend toward economic convergence in productivity levels and standards of living. Such convergence is restricted to the small club of nations that have been able to invest sufficiently in productive investment, infrastructure, and education. The poorest countries (for example, in Africa) have been left out of the process of economic development.
>
> (Boyer, 1996: 57)

In the same vein, the UNDP's (1998: 29) *Human Development Report* notes that 20 per cent of the world's population living in the richest countries increased its income from 30 times higher than the poorest 20 per cent in 1960 to 82 times higher in 1995. The two billion poorest people in the world, living on 350 US dollars or less per year, saw their share in the world's global product decline from 4.2 per cent in 1980 to 2.5 per cent in 1997. And to give one final example, Bairoch and Kozul-Wright (1996: 18–19) argue that while 'globalization is expected to release a new growth dynamic in the world economy', with the 'greatest impact on the growth potential of developing countries', in reality 'the world economy has been on a visibly slower growth path over the past two decades and (...) most of the available evidence points to divergence, not convergence among countries.'[36]

We can therefore only conclude that the promise that more free trade in the globalized economy will lead to more equality and to convergence between rich and poor countries has not been kept. Social differences are not only increasing among countries, but also within countries.[37] Most economists that have addressed this issue do not consider globalization an (important) explanation for increased social inequality – the consensus opinion is that it accounts at most for a minor part of the aggravated income differences.[38] But a remarkable study by Dani Rodrik of the Institute for International Economics (IIE) in Washington goes against this consensus. He argues that within the models and assumptions of orthodox neoclassical economics, increased trade in a globalized economy can indeed have labor-market consequences. Such trade does often exert pressure toward arbitrage in national norms and social institutions. In addition, it undermines the postwar social bargain between workers and employers, reduces the ability of governments to spend resources on social programs, and makes it more difficult to tax capital (Rodrik, 1997a).[39]

The arguments raised by Rodrik point to important new effects of globalization on the functionality of the comparative advantage theorem. Economic globalization undermines full employment and makes it more difficult to tax capital and maintain social programs. Key assumptions of the comparative advantage theorem do not hold, insofar as it becomes more difficult – or even impossible – to compensate losers of free trade (e.g. workers in a company that has to close shop because of cheaper imports, which in itself can be beneficial for the whole population) with new jobs or social benefits.

Prebisch, former Director of the United Nations Economic Commission for Latin America and one of the main theoreticians of import-substitution industrialization, argued in 1959 that a 'dynamic economy' has to absorb the redundant labor that is continually emerging as a result of technical progress.

> In addition, there is a second form of manpower that has to be so absorbed. There are indeed vast numbers of marginal workers of low productivity rendering poorly paid personal services, as well as people engaged in other forms of precarious employment or disguised unemployment of a precapitalist character who should be moved to new jobs.
>
> (Prebisch, 1959: 255)

In this article Prebisch discussed policies to allow for the future development of the underdeveloped countries. It is ironic that in the contemporary globalized economy we can see in developed countries, where flexibility, job insecurity and low-paid jobs in personal services are on the rise, the reverse happening of what he at the time analyzed in developing countries. This partial 're-underdevelopment' of developed countries can be seen as a consequence of increased opportunities for capital to move around the world, and of rapidly changing comparative advantages. At the same time, the possibilities of absorbing redundant labor through stable, well-paid jobs are decreasing, as a consequence of reduced economic growth, less government spending, and technological developments.

2.4.3   The ecological price

With fewer limitations on cross-border trade, companies and traders can shop all over the world for parts, labor to produce products, economies of scale and bigger markets. Free trade thus leads to more transportation of goods. So, Daly argues,

> by making supplies of resources and absorption capacities anywhere available to demands everywhere, free trade will tend to increase throughput growth and with it the rate of environmental degradation. It will greatly reduce the control local communities have over their local environments as well as their livelihoods.[40]
>
> (Daly, 1995: 325)

Not only does free trade lead to more transportation and therefore more pollution, but a world market for toxic waste has also come into existence. As Bellamy Foster (1994) records, between 1989 and 1994 there were more than 500 attempts to send over 200 million tons of waste from the 24 rich countries in the OECD to 122 other countries. Many of these countries hardly have a choice when they can get money in exchange for accepting such waste. The government of

Guinea-Bissau, for example, accepted the dumping of 15 million tons of toxic waste in exchange for 600 million dollars, which is four times the national income. 'We need the money', was the argument of the minister of trade and tourism.

This case is a good example for Daly's claim that the logic of free trade hinders real solutions to waste problems by promoting static efficiency:

> In other words, free trade in toxic wastes promotes static efficiency by allowing the disposal of wastes, wherever it costs less, according to today's prices and technologies. A more dynamic efficiency would be served by outlawing the export of toxins. That step would internalize the disposal costs of toxins to their place of origin – to both the firm that generated them and the nation under whose laws the firm operated. This policy creates an incentive to find technically superior ways of dealing with toxins or of redesigning processes to avoid their production in the first place.
>
> (Daly, 1996: 238)

In neoclassical models free trade leads to upward harmonization of standards, and falling wages or unsustainable environmental norms are temporary phenomena. Multinationals, for example, are expected to implement the higher norms they have to abide by in their – more regulated – mother countries in the rest of the world as well, and are thus expected to play a 'civilizing' role in the developing world. The problem with such assumptions is, however, that the world is not a harmonious world republic. Conflicting interests exist. Wealth and power are very unevenly divided, and profit-maximizing companies have an incentive to try to evade or weaken regulations. In addition, national governments are often unable to oblige the beneficiaries of trade 'to invest sufficient amounts to assure "clean and safe" production processes while compensating the losers (peasant communities and poor urban neighborhoods) for their sacrifices' (Barkin, 1998: 38).

2.4.4 The demise of a development model

In December 1994 a heavy crisis broke out in Mexico, the country that had been perceived until then as 'the Rolls Royce' among emerging markets. Mexico, the first Third World country to enter the OECD in 1994, formed a free trade zone with the USA and Canada in 1994 and 'adopted a more laissez-faire approach to the surge in foreign capital. In fact, the Mexican capital account has been dramatically liberalized since the mid-1980s, partly in connection with Mexico's signing of the North American Free Trade Agreement (NAFTA)' (Agosin and Ffrench-Davis, 1996: 179).

When the peso collapsed the IMF had to help the invisible hand, and put together a 50 billion-dollar support package in a 'financial operation Desert Storm' (*Business Week*, 13-2-1995) to avoid the total collapse of the Mexican economy, which could have had a major impact on the rest of the world. In Mexico itself the immediate effect of the peso crisis was a big increase in unemployment and rise in inequality. And because financial markets are so much integrated today, there was also an unprecedented spillover – the 'tequila effect' – from Mexico to Brazil, Argentina, Nigeria, Bulgaria, Russia and other countries. This Mexican crisis has therefore often been presented as the 'first crisis of the 21st century' or the 'first crisis of globalization.'

In the months following the Mexican crisis, commentators and analysts from international organizations warned of more crises, although nobody knew when or where. Sooner than many expected it became clear that the next Mexicos were to be found in Asia, where from mid-1997 onwards one Tiger economy after the other fell into deep crisis. The crisis itself and its effects have since spread to other continents, showing the contagious character of economic troubles in the globalizing world economy.[41]

The globalization of the Southeast Asian crisis was a very unwelcome shock to protagonists of free trade and financial liberalization, who had presented these Asian economies' development as ultimate proof that their policies work. In Krueger's account of why import substitution strategies were defeated and policies based on the theorem of comparative advantage reign supreme once more among trade economists and policymakers, for example, the Asian experience is very important:

> At the same time as evidence of the high costs of import-substitution regimes was accumulating, another important development occurred. Starting first in Taiwan, several East Asian economies began growing rapidly under policies diametrically opposite to those prevalent under import substitution. (...) (T)he East Asian experiences demonstrated, as nothing else could have, the feasibility and viability of alternative trade policies. (...) They also showed that rates of growth well above those realized even in the most rapidly growing import-substitution countries such as Brazil and Turkey could be realized.
>
> (Krueger, 1997)

In the light of such ideas it is no accident that the IMF and World Bank did not foresee the crisis in Asia. Less than 3 months before the crisis in South Korea broke out, the IMF wrote in its annual report: 'Directors welcomed Korea's continued impressive macroeconomic performance (and) praised the authorities for their enviable fiscal record.' And while the country was on the verge of a financial collapse, the IMF 'strongly praised Thailand's remarkable economic performance and the authorities' consistent record of sound macroeconomic policies' (Sachs, 1997). And the World Bank

> published in April 1997 a list of countries whose capital markets were strong enough to support a high degree of financial integration with the rest of the world: South Korea, Malaysia, Thailand, 'with Indonesia and the Philippines not far behind', Chili, Mexico, 'with Brazil also ranking well'. The east Asian crisis began a few months later.
>
> (Wade in the *Financial Times*, January 9, 2002)

The same indestructible confidence in free trade and financial liberalization was expressed in Fund negotiators' demands on countries that needed financial support. Asian countries in crisis were instructed to do more of the same: export more, reduce import restrictions and get rid of restrictions on financial flows.[42] A couple of years later, in an article on Argentina, Palast (2002) characterized the learning capacity of the IMF and World Bank as follows: 'They learn the way a pig learns to sing: They can't, they won't and, if they try, the resulting noise is unbearable.'

But despite what official institutions say and do, this crisis's economic and social consequences, its contagion to other countries, and the effects on the world economy as a whole, have meant that the dominant paradigm has once more come under serious attack.[43] And Eichengreen (1999: 9) can therefore hardly be accused of exaggerating when he compares the importance of the Asian crisis 'for those concerned with the operation of international financial markets' with 'what the collapse of the Eastern Bloc was to Sovietologists. It has forced old models of the international financial architecture to be abandoned and prompted some radical new thinking.'[44]

2.5 SUMMARY AND CONCLUSION

Adam Smith and David Ricardo were the first to make a coherent case for the principle of free trade. Important elements of the free-trade doctrine were already present in the mercantilist period. But the classical economists provided the framework that is still with us today. Smith, directly challenging mercantilist doctrines, succeeded in defending free trade not as important for a particular industry or class, but as in the general interest. Extrapolating from individuals to countries, he appealed to the commonsensical thought that what is good for every private family must also be good for countries as a whole. After Smith the case for free trade was further developed and strengthened by the theory of comparative costs, or comparative advantage. This finishing touch to the free-trade doctrine is attributed to David Ricardo. He went one step further than Smith, because he took the fact into consideration that productivity levels differ from one country to the next. By incorporating that aspect in his argument Ricardo succeeded even better than Smith in showing that free trade is in the interest of *every* country, because there is always something that can be traded. Both Smith and Ricardo propagated free trade, not for general cosmopolitan or altruistic reasons, but because they considered the extension of international exchange of goods to be more in the interest of nations than protectionism. In fact, they held that there is no contradiction between the national interest and free trade.

Since the genesis of the classical theory of free trade, two major types of criticisms have been raised against its theoretical and empirical underpinnings. The first questions the heroic assumptions that have to be fulfilled to make the theory of comparative advantage work, while the second observes that real-world developments do not match the theory's predictions and expectations. In addition, we have seen that at the time of free trade's initial victory List and Marx challenged – for different reasons – the comparative advantage-theorem's implicit assumption of a 'harmonious world republic.' While List emphasized the specific place and role of nations and their conflicts, Marx focused on the divergent consequences of free trade for different social classes and their struggles.

The final section showed that despite the weak underpinnings of free trade based on the principle of comparative advantage, the doctrine is once again dominant. But the Ricaradian theorem is also seriously challenged. Once again, and perhaps this time with even more force than before, the principle of comparative advantage is being promoted as generally applicable, as a general law for all times and situations. But although free trade based on the theory of comparative advantage is extremely popular among economists and policymakers, in the rest of the world support for this policy is much less solid. Four critiques of the free trade paradigm were discussed. New trade theories justify interventions by governments because history matters and advantages can be created. Contrary to the belief and promise of globalization ideologues, we have not seen a convergence of income and productivity levels, but persistent or even increasing divergences and increasing inequality. The ecological costs of free trade, rapidly increasing in the globalizing economy, are not taken into account in the standard theories and models. And the economic collapse of Asian countries, which were until recently considered a success of paradigmatic policies, challenges policies promoting free trade and financial liberalization. For all these reasons the claim that globalization is promoting a 'harmonious world republic' cannot be maintained.

NOTES

1 See, e.g. IMF (1997a), Irwin (1996b) and Krueger (1997).
2 See, e.g. Husson (1996), Lang and Hines (1993) and Mander and Goldsmith (1996).
3 See, e.g. Boyer and Drache (1996), Freeman (1997) and Weiss (1998).
4 'The basic case for free trade has changed little over the past two centuries', DeMartino notes:

> Since David Ricardo introduced the concept of comparative advantage in the early nineteenth century, the notion that free trade benefits all countries has been a central tenet of orthodox theory. Even most heterodox economists have accepted the basic logic involved in this proposition. Nevertheless, the concept of comparative advantage is at the center of the contemporary controversy over free trade.
>
> (DeMartino, 2000: 195–197)

5 Incidentally, that is also true for many arguments used to defend protectionism (Viner, 1955: 73).
6 As Viner sets out:

> The concept of the 'economic man', instead of being, as is often alleged, an intervention of the nineteenth-century classical school, was an important element in the mercantilist doctrine. Between the attitudes of the two schools toward the 'economic man' (...) there was this important difference, however, that the classical

economists argued that men in pursuing their selfish interests were at the same time, by a providential harmony of interests, either rendering the best service of which they were capable to the common good or at least rendering better service than if their activities were closely regulated by government, whereas the mercantilists deplored the selfishness of the merchant and insisted that to prevent it from ruining the nation it was necessary to subject it to rigorous control.

(Viner, 1955: 93)

7 Maneschi (1998: 18) underlines this point when he argues: 'Starting with Adam Smith, the classical economists frequently merged the positive and normative aspects of trade.'

8 Irwin (1996b: 91) finds the credit given to Ricardo exaggerated. 'Yet Ricardo's mere three-paragraph discussion was poorly expressed, awkwardly placed in the chapter, and failed to bring out the essence of the theory.' And John Chipman (1965: 480) is even of the opinion that Ricardo's 'statement of the law is quite wanting, so much so as to cast some doubt as to whether he truly understood it.' According to William Thweatt (1976), James Mill was actually responsible for Ricardo's three-paragraph example.

9 Here and elsewhere I refer to the first edition of any work. The edition quoted from can be found in the bibliography. In this case citations are from the third (1821) edition.

10 The point cannot be taken up here, but it should be noted that Marx did not agree. In the third volume of *Capital* (1894: 344–347) he argued that there are mechanisms through which foreign or colonial trade increases the rate of profit in industrial countries (see also Mandel, 1964). If true, this would of course further strengthen the argument that trade can lead to an increase in the profit rate.

11 This is these authors' second possible explanation for the 'glaring gap between theory and reality.' First they dispose of the other option, which is that 'policymakers are misinformed and/or of limited intelligence and therefore do not know the welfare-increasing effect of unilateral tariff reductions.'

12 A concrete example of the importance of these assumptions is a paper that was presented in the preparation of the WTO-summit (Quatar, November 2001) with a calculation of the benefits of trade liberalization. Dorman (2001) argues that the underlying assumptions with which Brown, Deardorff and Stern come to the conclusion that complete elimination of all trade barriers in the world would add $1.9 trillion (about 5 per cent) to the worlds GDP by 2005 are unreliable.

13 Or as Leamer (1995: 2) notes, 'textbook writers remind us that theories are neither true nor false. Theories are sometimes useful and sometimes not so useful.'

14 Williams challenges also this assumption:

Indeed, it is not Ricardo's immobility premise that stands most in need of defence, but rather his mobility premise, the assumed free movement of factors within countries. Perhaps no reminder is necessary that this assumption, no less than the other, is essential for the validity of the comparative cost principle.

(Williams, 1929: 197)

15 See, e.g. the often cited paper by Feldstein and Horioka (1980).

16 Bairoch is even more outspoken:

There is no doubt that the economic liberalism imposed on the Third World in the nineteenth century is one of the main factors that explains its delayed industrialization...It would be difficult to find factual examples – at least in nineteenth-century economic history – that are in more flagrant contradiction with the dominant theory, which holds that protectionism has a negative impact. Protectionism, if not a source of industrialization and economic development, has always accompanied them.

(Bairoch, 1993: 79–81)

17 According to List (1904: 208), 'Laissez faire, laissez passer' is 'an expression which sounds no less agreeably to robbers, cheats, and thieves than to the merchant, and is on that account rather doubtful as a maxim.' Freeman (1997: 27) reminds us that List, emphasizing 'the role of the state in co-ordinating and carrying through long-term policies for industry and the economy', often 'took issue with Jean-Baptiste Say, his favorite target in his polemics with the classical school, who had argued that governments did not make much difference, except in a negative way.'

18 As an aside we note that Marx and List occasionally crossed each other's paths. List 'was offered the post of editor of the *Rheinische Zeitung*, a new liberal paper which was being established in Cologne. But he declared that ill-health prevented him from accepting the post – which eventually went to Karl Marx' (Henderson, 1983: 85). Later, in 1845, Marx accepted Engels' proposal that he write a critique of List's theory, but the project never materialized (McLellan, 1975, 166). As for their influence, List's biographer notes that his most important book, *The National System of Political Economy*, 'has been more frequently translated than the works of any other German economist, except Karl Marx' (Henderson, 1983, 214).

19 Archibugi and Michie note:

> It is no coincidence that List was German. At the beginning of the nineteenth century, German cultural life was dominated by the philosophy of history, which had as its main concern the explanation and prediction of the rise and fall of nations. Influenced by the rise of American society, in which he lived for several years, List tried to provide an economic explanation for the changing positions of nations in history. (...) Today, economists remember List as a fierce opponent of the theory of free trade as advocated by Adam Smith and his followers. (...) But in List's native town of Reutlingen, he is remembered as the pioneer of railways: he spent a large part of his life urging the princes who ruled 'the Germany of one hundred homelands' to develop transportation. He understood that infrastructure, which in his day meant, above all, the railways, was a fundamental component of any strategy for economic growth since it allowed commodities, individuals and information to circulate.
>
> (Archibugi and Michie, 1997a: 6–7)

And Freeman (1997: 25) reminds us that it was 'thanks to the advocacy of List and like-minded economists as well as the long-established Prussian system, that Germany developed one of the best technical education and training systems in the world' (see also Warren James, 1965).

20 Rae's biographer notes:

> There was nothing essentially new in Rae's argument. The same general ideas had been argued by the Earl of Lauderdale in his *Public Wealth* in 1804 and by Jeremy Bentham in his letter to Adam Smith on projects in arts written in 1787. Rae quotes from both these authors and was probably familiar with their criticisms.
>
> (Warren James, 1965: 144)

21 As we have already seen Rae drew the same policy conclusions in 1834. Warren James notes:

> The implications of this view for economic policy were immediately clear. It was a cardinal requirement of policy to foster invention and to facilitate the transference of inventions from one country to another. This view further justified the intervention of the state in helping new industries by protective duties, bounties

and other financial encouragements. Moreover, Rae believed that it was desirable for the state to encourage and support financially industrial research which would lead to new inventions. Rae's essential criterion for assessing economic policy as well as social behaviour was the effect on the accumulation of capital.

(Warren James, 1965: 144)

22 On this see, e.g. Irwin (1996b) and Levi-Faur (1997).
23 As Manoïlesco argued:

The best proof of his empiricism and of his arbitrary affirmations is the fact that, generally speaking, he is against all protection for agriculture. Now, there is no reason whatever to exclude a priori a certain branch of production from protection.

(Manoïlesco, 1931: 246)

24 Reminiscent of the way economists argue today that unemployment and other social problems are no more than temporary consequence of free trade, because in the long run everybody will benefit, Marx (1848: 245) writes: 'We know beforehand the reply of the economists. The men thus deprived of work, they say, will find other kinds of employment.'
25 Bairoch propagates a similar approach:

If I had to sum up the essence of what economic history can contribute to economic science, I would say that there are no economic 'laws' or rules that are valid for all historical periods or for each of the different economic systems.

(Bairoch, 1993: 224)

26 In fact, in what Samuelson later called 'the extreme version of the F-twist', Friedman even argues that it is not only not necessary for assumptions to be realistic, but that it is an advantage if they are not. As Blaug says, the weakness of this method

is that of black-box theorizing that makes predictions without being able to explain why the predictions work: the moment the predictions fail, the theory has to be discarded in toto because it lacks an underlying structure of assumptions, an *explanans* that can be adjusted and improved to make better predictions in the future. It is for this reason that scientists usually do worry when the assumptions of their theories are blatantly unrealistic.

(Blaug, 1992: 99)

See also Hodgson (1988: 27–50).
27 As Scott proposes:

Poor nations should be allowed to do what today's rich countries did to go ahead, not to be forced to adopt the laissez-faire approach. Insisting on the merits of comparative advantage in low-wage, low-growth industries is a sure way to stay poor.

(Scott, 2001: 176)

28 The same type of argument is regularly presented to the public by the British weekly *The Economist* as being based on 'the fundamental insight of the theory of comparative advantage' (The Economist, 1997a: 100), which is 'one of the subtlest but most

powerful deductions in economic theory' (*The Economist*, 1996: 65). This last article concludes with the statement that worries about unfair North–South trade and complaints about exploitation of workers in the South can best be answered by pointing out that '"fair" or not, trade raises incomes in both countries. Victims of injustice and exploitation should always be so lucky.' The last sentence is symptomatic for the self-aggrandizing moral claim by contemporary advocates of free trade that their opponents do a disservice – deliberately, or through lack of knowledge – to those they want to defend. A less subtle variant of this argument was presented as follows in an editorial in The Financial Times (10-9-1997): 'The self-fulfilling prophecies of protectionist scaremongers must be ignored. They are without merit, not just analytically, but morally.'

29 See, e.g. Dos Santos (1970, 1978) and Prebisch (1959). Prebisch, in particular, former Director of UNCTAD, had an important influence on developing countries for a whole period; but Irwin (1996b) does not even mention him in his 'intellectual history of free trade.' This neglect is no accident, as Rodrik (Rodrik 1997b: 1) testifies in the opening remarks of his Prebisch Lecture:

> Let me begin with a confession: until about a month ago, when I began to prepare for this lecture, I had not actually read any of Raul Prebisch's writings. I was of course familiar with many of Prebisch's ideas – his intellectual leadership at ECLA and UNCTAD, the so-called Prebisch-Singer thesis on the deterioration of the terms of trade for primary products, and his advocacy of import protection as a way of speeding up industrialization. But like most development economists of my generation, I knew Prebisch second hand and mostly as a label associated with a particular type of development strategy.
>
> (Rodrik, 1997b: 1)

30 Although Krueger (1997: 19) still sees risks ahead. 'No matter how careful economists are, special interests always will seize their research results in supporting their own objectives', she writes, and 'there always will be politicians formulating, and non-economists administering, policies.'

31 For a more differentiated evaluation of import substitution strategies see also e.g. Bruton (1998) and Coutrot and Husson (1993).

32 See, e.g. Nelson (1999).

33 For a review of endogenous growth theory see Blaug (2000).

34 Bernstein notes another, comparable problem in an article on shoe manufacturer New Balance:

> Now some trade experts are wondering if the seemingly iron law of comparative advantage always holds. The theory rests on the assumption that a low-skilled U.S. job shifted offshore would have remained low-skilled had it stayed home. But if U.S. companies could raise the skill level for such work and perform the task more efficiently, as New Balance does, the gains from shifting production would diminish. If the work can be upgraded, 'it's not so obvious which countries should do the exporting,' says Robert C. Feenstra, a trade economist at the University of California at Davis. 'Our predictions about trade patterns get a little hazy when this happens; economists haven't really worked it out.'
>
> (Bernstein, 2001)

35 Archibugi and Michie (1998) present a useful review of literature on the evolutionary institutional economics of technical change.

36 See, e.g. also Rowthorn and Kozul-Wright (1998).

37 See also Weller *et al.* (2001).
38 See, e.g. Garretsen and Peeters (1999) and Slaughter and Swagel (1997).
39 According to mainstream economic theory underdeveloped countries should see an increase in income for the most abundant production factor as a result of more trade, but Tanksi and French show that this is not what happened in Mexico:

> (T)he Heckscher-Ohlin theorem predicts that with increasing trade based on comparative advantage, Mexico's national income should be redirected away from the scarce factor of production (capital) and toward the abundant factor (labor, or low skilled workers), as the demand for their services increases. Hence, workers incomes should increase relative to returns to capital. In Mexico, however, we have seen practically the opposite: increasing concentration of income controlled by capital, along with relatively stagnant wages, benefits, and employment for manufacturing workers. Part of the explanation for this rests with one of the assumptions underlying the theory of comparative advantage, i.e. that full employment exists in each of the trading countries (...). This assumption does not coincide with reality in the case of Mexico.
>
> (Tanksi and French, 2001: 705)

In the same vein, Rodrik (1999: 20) argues that the distributional evidence from Latin America contradicts the prediction of the Stolper–Samuelson theorem that the removal of trade restrictions increases the real return to a country's relatively abundant factor of production and reduces the real return to the scarce factor.

40 Morris provides an often quoted fascinating example of what this may lead to:

> A few years ago, I was eating at a restaurant in Saint Paul, Minnesota. After lunch I picked up a toothpick wrapped in plastic. On the plastic was the word "Japan". Now Japan has little wood and no oil. Yet in our global economy, it is deemed efficient to send little pieces of wood and some barrels of oil to Japan, wrap the one in the other and send them back to Minnesota. This toothpick may embody 50,000 miles of travel. Meanwhile, in 1987, a Minnesota factory began producing millions of disposable chopsticks a year for sale in Japan. In my mind's eye, I see two ships passing one another in the northern Pacific. One carries little pieces of Minnesota wood bound for Japan; the other carries little pieces of wood from Japan bound for Minnesota. Such is the logic of free trade.
>
> (Morris, 1996: 222)

41 See, e.g. IMF (1999a) and World Bank (1999a, 1999b).
42 Not everybody agreed with such prescriptions; influential economists like Krugman and Sachs voiced their dissent. The *Financial Times* therefore noted in an editorial:

> The International Monetary Fund has become the world's economic fireman. (...) In carrying out its job, the IMF reflects the technocratic approach of the finance ministries and central banks that govern it. But its power has bred protests, not just from borrowers, but also from respected professional economists.
>
> (*Financial Times*, 17 December 1997)

43 See, e.g. Bello (1998), Corsetti *et al.* (1998), Jomo (1998), Krugman (1998, 1999), Radelet and Sachs (1998), Rodrik (1999), Rude (1998), Sharma (1998), Soros (1998), United Nations Economic Commission for Latin America and the Caribbean (1998) and Wade and Veneroso (1998a, 1998b).

44 This is not to suggest that things have really changed since this discussion began, because they have not. As Soederberg notes, while the so-called New International Financial Architecture (NIFA)

> is often presented as a shift toward a compromise between financial stability and deregulation (the Third Way), it remains oriented toward preserving the imperative of free capital mobility rather than implementing profound political changes in the functioning and regulation of global financial flows. This position is clearly reflected in Washington's tenacious resistence to universal capital controls. The big winners of maintaining the imperative of capital account liberalization are unmistakably global financial players and the United States.
>
> (Soederberg, 2001: 453)

3 The combination of free trade and free capital flows: theories of imperialism

In analyses and debates about whether economic globalization is an old or new phenomenon, comparisons with the period 1870–1913 play an important role. Not only are those years closer in time than the preceding free trade era of laissez-faire, but this second period of free trade has more similarities with the current period. Then as now, international trade was increasing and capital flows were internationalizing.[1]

It is rarely noticed that this comparison can be pushed even further. The combination of free trade and free capital flows is characteristic both of contemporary economic globalization and of the international regime before the First World War. The establishment of this even closer resemblance seems at first to lend strength to claims that globalization is not at all a novelty, or even that it is a return to earlier modes of functioning of world capitalism.

While the social, political and economic consequences of and driving forces behind the increasing international interconnectedness of economies are being debated heatedly today, the same was also true at the beginning of the twentieth century. At the time, the causes, dynamics and possible future development of capitalism were broadly discussed in terms of imperialism. This chapter lays out similarities and differences between that period and today's globalization.

3.1 ONCE AGAIN THE COMBINATION

The combination of free trade and free movement of capital is characteristic of contemporary economic globalization. Even a cursory look at developments since the end of the 1970s shows how much the global economy has changed. Rodrik (1999: 8–9) argues that at the end of the twentieth century 'we have the widest-ranging trade liberalization the world has ever witnessed', and that 'the volume of international trade increased at twice the rate of growth of world output from 1985 to 1994.' UNCTAD (1999: 7, 55) points out that for 'the world as a whole, the ratio of foreign direct investment (FDI) stock (inward plus outward) to GDP has increased steadily since 1980', as more and more countries 'adopt FDI-specific regulatory frameworks to support their investment-related objectives'. Radice (1999: 20) notes that in Third World countries 'there have been almost universal moves to liberalize controls on trade and FDI, including controls on for-eign ownership of banks and other financial institutions, and of minerals, energy, transport and communications companies.' And Baker *et al.* (1998b: 9–15) char-acterize the growth of gross capital flows as 'dramatic', pointing to the 'great expansion of international lending' and 'explosion of secondary market trading in stock, bond, foreign exchange, and derivative markets since the demise of Bretton Woods and the emergence of deregulated domestic financial markets.'[2] In their view two 'quite dramatic changes' stand out: 'The first is the rise in the propor-tion of manufacturing exports among the less-developed countries. The second is the explosion of short-term capital movements.'

The rationale given in economic theory for financial deregulation is founded on a conception of how financial intermediaries and markets operate. Coggins (1998: 35–62) shows that arguments in support of free capital flows are grounded in main-stream neoclassical analyses of the firm – which are also presumed to hold for depository financial firms (DFFs) – and of the functioning of financial markets.[3] He identifies 12 assumptions behind this thinking, including: 'financial markets are robust and stable,' 'market signals are accurate and trustworthy,' 'market partici-pants have adequate information,' 'DFFs do not have extensive externalities,' and 'well-run DFFs operate with longer-run planning horizons.' Alternative, heterodox perspectives pose challenges to all these assumptions. Concretely: 'financial mar-kets are fragile and unstable,' 'market signals are often inaccurate and unreliable,' 'market participants must cope with uncertainty, the unknowable, unpredictable future,' 'DFFs have extensive externalities,' and 'because of competitive pressures, DFFs adopt shorter-run planning horizons to succeed' (Coggins, 1998: 63–127).

Not only is financial deregulation debatable in itself. In addition, it is import-ant to point out that an international regime characterized by the combination of free trade and free international capital mobility, which is currently often pre-sented as 'natural' or 'economically commonsensical', has not always been the practice, and that its supposed merits have also been challenged within economic theory. As UNCTAD researcher Felix puts it:

> Is free international capital mobility compatible with free trade and stable exchange rates? The answer of the architects of the Bretton Woods system, who filtered the inter-war experience through the then burgeoning Keynesian theoretical paradigm, was a firm no. The current answer of the chief surviv-ing Bretton Woods institution, the International Monetary Fund, and of the G-7 monetary authorities, who filter post-World War II experience through the New Classical Macroeconomics paradigm, is yes. Their efforts to stabil-ize the volatile international monetary system is premised on the compatibil-ity, indeed the desirability, of combining free international capital mobility with stable exchange rates and free trade.
>
> (Felix, 1995: 1)

It is no accident that Felix cites Keynes as describing 'proposals to stabilize exchange rates and promote free trade without limiting international capital mobility' as 'exercises in squaring the circle.' Keynes would have looked at the offspring of the postwar economy, 'the global financial markets and the theology of free trade, with a very cold eye,' notes Longworth. He quotes Keynes' now famous passage:

> I sympathize, therefore, with those who would minimize, rather than those who would maximize, economic entanglement between nations. Ideas, knowledge, art, hospitality, travel – these are things which should of their nature be international. But let goods be homespun whenever it is reasonable and conveniently possible: and above all, let finance be primarily national.
>
> (Longworth, 1998: 47)

Keynes was one of the principal architects of the Bretton Woods agreement of 1944. During the negotiations US representative White promised 'to respect the priority the British attached to full employment', although controls on international capital movements were 'contrary to White's early vision of a world free of controls on both trade and financial flows' (Eichengreen, 1996: 96–98). Clearly, the US did not subscribe to 'the darker Keynesian view of the behavior of financial markets, in which volatility is largely endogenously generated because the bandwagon overbidding and herd-like dumping of financial assets results from rational individual behavior under uncertainty' (Felix, 1998: 196). But the outcome of Bretton Woods was explicit, as Boughton notes:

> (T)he truth is that the founding fathers were downright bullish on capital controls. (...) As drafted at Bretton Woods, Section 1(a) of article VI read: 'A member may not make net use of the Fund's resources to meet a large or sustained outflow of capital, and the Fund may request a member to exercise controls to prevent such use of the resources of the Fund. If, after receiving such a request, a member fails to exercise appropriate controls, the Fund may declare the member ineligible to use the resources of the Fund.'
>
> (Boughton, 1997: 10)

After the Second World War, capital controls were broadly considered necessary as a means to give governments a degree of control over their national economies and allow the implementation of national policy goals (Eichengreen, 1996). The background is the basic macroeconomic policy 'trilemma' that a country can only have two of the following three features: a fixed exchange rate, full capital mobility and monetary policy independence (Wyplosz, 1998: 4). This means that countries combining a more or less fixed (or pegged) exchange rate with free movement of capital, as is common today and was common before the First World War under the gold standard, are forced to give up control over domestic macroeconomic objectives, such as full employment, thus either inducing capital formation or dampening inflation in developing countries (Bruton, 1998: 907).[4] Capital controls, Eichengreen argues,

48 *Theories of imperialism*

loosened the link between domestic and foreign economic policies, providing governments room to pursue other objectives like the maintenance of full employment. (...) By limiting the resources that the markets could bring to bear against an exchange rate peg, controls limited the steps that governments had to take in its defense. For several decades after World War II, limits on capital mobility substituted for limits on democracy as a source of insulation from market pressures.

(Eichengreen, 1996: 5)

Obstfeld (1998: 8) argues that '(t)he broad trends and cycles in the world capital market over the last century reflect changing responses to the fundamental policy trilemma'.

There is general agreement that the periodization of the level of international capital mobility shows a U-shaped pattern:

Before World War I, controls on international financial transactions were absent and international capital flows reached high levels. The interwar period saw the collapse of this system, the widespread imposition of *capital controls*, and the decline of international capital movements. The quarter-century following World War II was then marked by the progressive relaxation of controls and the gradual recovery of international financial flows. The latest period, starting with the 1970s, is again one of high capital mobility.[5]

(Eichengreen, 1996: 3)

Although today national economies are increasingly linked and interwoven, the idea that capital controls are an essential (though insufficient) policy tool to safeguard economies from becoming a plaything of financial markets has largely disappeared since the beginning of the 1980s.[6] A real paradigm shift has taken place in major international organizations' policy orientation. Writing from the inside about the IMF's history, Boughton notes that by 1994, 'the long-simmering debate over the wisdom of capital controls has been completely overtaken.' Echoing the often-heard argument that technological developments leave no other choice, he infers that

no country can share in the benefits of international trade unless it allows capital to move freely enough to finance that trade, and modern financial markets are sophisticated and open enough that capital transactions can no longer be compartmentalized as trade-related or speculative.

(Boughton, 1997: 8)

The IMF itself is of course the best example of how far this mutation has gone. The Fund's Interim Committee decided unanimously in April 1997 to amend the Fund's Articles so that capital controls would henceforth only be allowed temporarily in exceptional situations (*IMF Survey*, May 12, 1997).[7] Nor is the IMF the only powerful international organization pushing in this direction. After difficult negotiations and substantial pressure on hesitant governments, more than a 100 countries signed a pact under the aegis of the World Trade Organization (WTO) to liberalize trade in banking, insurance and other financial services in December 1997. And secret negotiations by the OECD to formulate a Multilateral Agreement on Investment (MAI), which would have institutionalized the global right of capital to move freely in and out of countries, only failed because NGOs managed to mobilize broad resistance to such an agreement in various parts of the world, and because doubts about such a far-reaching treaty were present even in governmental circles in OECD member states like France.

In sum, a central feature of contemporary economic globalization is the combination of free trade and free capital flows as an international regime and on the level of policy descriptions. Since a similar international regime was characteristic of the decades before World War I, it may be illuminating to investigate that era's debates about the consequences of and driving forces behind the increasing international interconnectedness of economies.

3.2   CLASSICAL IMPERIALISM

At the beginning of the twentieth century an extensive discussion took place about important changes that were taking place in the character and functioning of capitalism. The emergence of big conglomerates and monopolies, the increasing weight of finance capital, the importance of capital exports as a means of raising the profit rate in addition to international trade, and the accompanying drive for – or inevitability of – imperialist policies by national states were recognized and discussed in different parts of the world, in different groups and milieux. This section reviews some of these debates.

The English sociologist and economist Hobson, who published his extensive study of imperialism in 1902, was one of the first analysts to distinguish imperialism from colonialism, a much older phenomenon:

> First – Almost the whole of this imperial expansion was occupied with the political absorption of tropical or subtropical lands in which white men will not settle with their families. Second – Nearly all the lands were thickly peopled by 'lower races.' Thus the recent imperial expansion stands entirely distinct from the colonization of sparsely peopled lands in temperate zones, where white colonists carry with them the modes of government, the industry and other arts of the civilization of the mother country. The 'occupation' of these new territories was comprised in the presence of a small minority of white men, officials, traders, and industrial organisers, exercising political and economic sway over great hordes of population regarded as inferior and as incapable of exercising any considerable rights of self-government, in politics or industry.
>
> (Hobson, 1902: 27)

For Hobson (1902: 94–109), imperialism 'implies the use of the machinery of government by private interests, mainly capitalists, to secure for them economic gains outside their country'. The economic root of imperialism is 'the desire of strong organized industrial and financial interests to secure and develop at the public expense and by the public force private markets for their surplus goods and their surplus capital. War, militarism, and a "spirited foreign policy" are the necessary means to this end.'

For his classical treatise *Imperialism, the Highest Stage of Capitalism* (1917), the Russian socialist leader Lenin made extensive use of Hobson's monumental work. Lenin came up with the following – now famous – definition of imperialism:

> (W)ithout forgetting the conditional and relative value of all definitions in general, which can never embrace all the concatenations of a phenomenon in its full development, we must give a definition of imperialism that will include the following five of its basic features:
>
> (1) the concentration of production and capital has developed to such a high stage that it has created monopolies which play a decisive role in economic life; (2) the merging of bank capital with industrial capital, and the creation, on the basis of this 'financial capital', of a financial oligarchy; (3) the export of capital as distinguished from the export of commodities acquires exceptional importance; (4) the formation of international monopolist capitalist associations which share the world among themselves, and (5) the territorial division of the whole world among the biggest capitalist powers is completed. Imperialism is capitalism at that stage of development at which the dominance of monopolies and finance capital is established; in which the export of capital has acquired pronounced importance; in which the division of the world among the international trusts has begun, in which the division of all territories of the globe among the biggest capitalist powers has been completed.
>
> (Lenin, 1917: 83)

For Lenin, domination by monopolistic associations of big employers is imperialism's principal feature.[8] In its economic essence imperialism 'is monopoly capitalism', he writes, identifying four principal manifestations of monopolies:

> Firstly, monopoly arose out of the concentration of production at a very high stage. (...) Secondly, monopolies have stimulated the seizure of the most important sources of raw materials. (...) Thirdly, monopoly has sprung from the banks. (...) Some three to five of the biggest banks in each of the foremost capitalist countries have achieved the 'personal link-up' between industrial and bank capital. (...) A financial oligarchy, which throws a close network of dependence relationships over all the economic and political institutions of present-day bourgeois society – such is the most striking manifestation of this monopoly. Fourthly, monopoly has grown out of colonial

policy. (...) To the numerous 'old' motives of colonial policy, finance capital has added the struggle for the sources of raw materials, for the export of capital, for spheres of influence, i.e., for spheres for profitable deals, concessions, monopoly profits and so on, economic territory in general.

(Lenin, 1917: 114–115)

As the emphasis he puts on the increasing weight and power of finance capital shows, Lenin leans heavily on the famous 1910 study *Das Finanzkapital* by the German economist Hilferding, later finance minister under the Weimar Republic. Industry's increasing dependence on bank capital means for Hilferding that the finance capitalist increasingly concentrates 'his control over the whole national capital by means of his domination of bank capital.' Capital export makes it possible for the first time 'to overcome the harmful effects of a protective tariff on the rate of profit', and the fact that new markets are no longer simply outlets for goods but also spheres for the capital investment brings about a change in the political behavior of capital-exporting countries. Direct rule over the area where capital is invested becomes more important, and capitalists with interests in foreign countries therefore call for a strong state to protect their interests all over the world

> and for showing the national flag everywhere so that the flag of trade can also be planted everywhere. Export capital feels most comfortable, however, when its own state is in complete control of the new territory, for capital exports from other countries are then excluded, it enjoys a priviliged position, and its profits are more or less guaranteed by the state. Thus the export of capital also encourages an imperialist policy.
>
> (Hilferding, 1910: 322)

Both Hilferding and Lenin hold that capital, under the leadership of finance capital, has become the conqueror of the world, in an expansionist policy to colonize new foreign markets. One of their main opponents on this issue was German socialist leader Kautsky. Like Lenin, Kautsky originally considered war, militarism, imperialism and capitalism as closely linked; but by 1912 his position had changed radically (Geary, 1987: 53). Kautsky then argued that imperialist expansion was related to the interests of *pre-industrial* elites and high finance, and started defending the idea that finance capital only plays a secondary role in the imperialist phase of capitalism. The most important fraction of capital became industrial capital for Kautsky. He argued that other options were available to industry to guarantee the necessary agrarian hinterland for raw materials and foodstuffs than colonization of agrarian territories and war (Salvadori, 1979: 187).

Later Kautsky concluded that the interests of all sections of capital would be best served by free trade and improved communication, and therefore not by colonial wars but by peace. He considered it likely that capitalist nations would recognize this common interest, and therefore envisaged in 1914 the possibility of a peaceful 'ultra-imperialism', in which capital based in different countries would cooperate to organize its worldwide domination:[9]

> From the purely economic standpoint (...) it is not excluded that capitalism may live through another new phase, the transference of the policy of cartels to foreign policy, a phase of ultra-imperialism, which of course we must fight against just as energetically as we fought imperialism. Its dangers would lie in a different direction, not in that of the armaments race and the threat to world peace.
>
> (Kautsky, 1915: 90)

Kautsky (1915: 90–91) maintained that imperialism is a 'political system', that is neither 'an economic phase' nor 'advanced capitalism of a higher stage', but 'a particular kind of capitalist policy, just like Manchesterism, which it replaces.' There are clear similarities with the position of Hobson, who also maintained that imperial expansion is not indispensable to create the necessary outlets for expanding industry, and argued for an alternative policy on the basis of an under-consumptionist analysis:

> It is not inherent in the nature of things that we should spend our natural resources on militarism, war, and risky, unscrupulous diplomacy, in order to find markets for our goods and surplus capital. An intelligent progressive community, based upon substantial equality of economic and educational opportunities, will raise its standard of consumption to correspond with every increased power of production, and can find full employment for an unlimited quantity of capital and labour within the limits of the country which it occupies. Where the distribution of incomes is such as to enable all classes of the nation to convert their felt wants into an effective demand for commodities, there can be no over-production, no under-employment of capital and labour, and no necessity to fight for foreign markets.[10]
>
> (Hobson, 1902: 86–87)

Kautsky's position faced harsh criticism from Lenin (1917: 85–86), who argued that Kautsky 'detaches the politics of imperialism from its economics' and did not understand that imperialism 'strives to annex *not only* agrarian territories, but even most highly industrialised regions'. Contrary to what Kautsky alleges, Lenin argues, the 'characteristic feature of imperialism is *not* industrial but *financial* capital'. It is remarkable that not only Marxists made this analysis. Lenin quotes, for example, a statement by Cecil Rhodes, a British financial magnate who led colonial expeditions in southern Africa at the turn of the century:

> I was in the East End of London [a working class quarter] yesterday and attended a meeting of the unemployed. I listened to the wild speeches, which were just a cry for bread! bread! and on my way home I pondered over the scene and I became more than ever convinced of the importance of imperialism. (...) My cherished idea is a solution for the social problem, i.e., in order to save 40,000,000 of the United Kingdom from a bloody civil war, we colonial statesmen must acquire new lands to settle the surplus population, to

provide new markets for the goods produced in the factories and mines. The Empire, as I have always said, is a bread and butter question. If you want to avoid civil war, you must become imperialists.

(Rhodes, quoted in Lenin, 1917: 74)

Rhodes was far from the only pro-capitalist defender of imperialism. Conservative and liberal advocates of imperial expansion such as Otto von Bismarck and the French politician Jules Ferry also stressed its economic necessity (Geary, 1987: 47). Nor were such insights limited to Europe. Parrini and Sklar (1983) suggest that the 'Hobson–Lenin theory of imperialism' has 'pro-capitalist American origins', and that their thinking was already published and in place in the years 1896–1901 by 'some neglected turn-of-the-century American economists, who influenced or participated in the formation of US foreign policy'.

Arthur Twining Hadley (Yale), Jeremiah W. Jenks (Cornell) and financial authority and journalist Charles A. Conant 'took the lead among American thinkers in laying the theoretical foundations for the break with the classical model of the competitive market'. They identified the role of monopolies and international investment at an early stage and argued that 'the condition for a viable national corporate investment was its globalization in an international investment system.' In their view, the economic, political, social, and cultural requirements for such an international system 'lay at the heart of modern capitalist imperialism, the root cause of which was surplus capital in the highly developed industrial societies.' According to Parrini and Sklar (1983: 569), Conant held state intervention to be necessary 'on behalf of an international investment system and imperialism in foreign affairs.' He also 'frankly affirmed' imperialist relations with the world's non-industrial societies 'as necessary, unavoidable, in the national interest, and, being developmental and "civilizing," as enlightened and progressive'.

These ideas had a major influence on US government policies. Conant and Jenks served on the three-member Commission for International Exchange (CIE), established in 1903 by President Roosevelt, to develop plans to integrate China and other non-industrial countries on silver standard currencies into an international investment system based on the gold standard. This commission played an important role in formulating the so-called Open Door Policy, which was implemented by the McKinley–Roosevelt and later administrations. Pointing to capital seeking investment but failing to find a profitable rate, the CIE concluded that finding outlets for this capital was in some respects 'more important than increasing the annual exports of manufacturing countries'. It was therefore considered necessary to construct an international monetary and investment system, which was presented as providing 'common benefits for all'. But this idea was clearly based on the assumption 'that the stability, growth, and prosperity of the American economy depended on its ability to expand freely into, and exercise a controlling voice in, the international economy'.

In sum, at the beginning of the twentieth century, when free trade and free capital flows were characteristic of the international economic regime, the evolution of capitalism into an imperialist system was widely discussed in different parts of the world by various groups and milieux. Important characteristics that were being discussed were the emergence of big conglomerates and monopolies, the increasing weight of finance capital, and imperial policies by national states. As Kemp argues:

> To claim that 'imperialism' was not a necessary stage in capitalist develop-ment is to imagine that the colossal development of the productive forces which took place in the nineteenth century could have proceeded without the bringing into being of a world-wide economy dominated by the leading capitalist powers. It is to imagine that somehow the characteristics of early industrial capitalism could have become permanent, without the growth of combines and monopolies, as an atomized collection of owner-financed firms. It is to assert that there was no relation between the politics of states and the dominant economic interests within them. It is to assume that the powerful economic forces released by capitalism were kept in tow by oldline statesmen, demagogues and ideologues. It is to argue (...) that the characteristics of 'imperialism' were atavistic survivals foreign to the true nature of capitalism, adopted by the bourgeoisie only as the result of a betrayal.
>
> (Kemp, 1967: 165–166)

Financial capital was generally seen as the main driving force behind these imperialist state policies. But there were major disagreements about the weight of this sector within the whole of capital. Linked to that question, controversy existed about the (im)possibility of capitalist development without militarism and war, such as the ultra-imperialism suggested by Kautsky, and the ideas about substan-tial equality of economic and educational opportunities propagated by Hobson.

3.3   A RETURN TO CLASSICAL IMPERIALISM?

For both supporters and opponents of imperialism, free trade and international capital mobility were essential instruments to stabilize and extend worldwide capitalism at the beginning of the twentieth century. Since then many things have changed in the structure and organization of the global economy, but after a long detour such policies are dominant again today, and are strongly advocated by major international organizations, university and think-tank figures, and OECD governments. There is little or no room left for any other policies. And as was recently demonstrated again in Asia, globalized financial markets, the IMF and like-minded organizations, and national business elites prevail on unwilling or hesitant governments to comply with the dominant paradigm.[11]

The way these policies are defended is also reminiscent of earlier times. Today, free trade and free capital movement are supposed to lead to an optimal alloca-tion of capital, goods and services, and should therefore bring about a better life for everybody. In a similar vein, classical economists such as J.S. Mill, Torrens and Wakefield once advocated colonization 'based on the classical principles of free trade and the free movement of resources' as a means 'to ensure continued improvements in living standards for all people, both at home and in the colonies' (Hodgart, 1977: 3–4). As we have seen in the previous section, proponents of imperialist policies as essential to guaranteeing capitalist stability and growth also presented their policies at the beginning of the last century as beneficial for all, civilizing and progressive.

Numerous empirical studies nonetheless give cause for serious doubts about such claims.[12] As UNCTAD Secretary General Ricupero testifies in his overview of its 1997 Trade and Development Report:

> The big story of the world economy since the early 1980s has been the unleashing of market forces. (...) The 'invisible hand' now operates globally and with fewer countervailing pressures from governments than for decades. (...) Since the early 1980s the world economy has been characterized by rising inequality and slow growth. Income gaps between the North and South have continued to widen. (...) Polarization among countries has been accompanied by increasing income inequality within countries. (...) In almost all developing countries that have undertaken rapid trade liberaliza-tion, wage inequality has increased.
>
> (UNCTAD, 1997: 2–10)

Ricupero notes that these facts fly in the face of the many optimistic commen-taries about the prospects for faster growth and convergence of incomes and liv-ing standards that global competition should bring about:

> These trends are rooted in a common set of forces unleashed by rapid liber-alization that make for greater inequality by favouring certain income groups over others. (...) Capital has gained in comparison with labour, and profit shares have risen everywhere. (...) In the North there has been a remarkable upward convergence of profits among the major industrial countries. (...) A new rentier class has emerged worldwide with the substantial expansion of international capital flows and the hike of interest rates.
>
> (UNCTAD, 1997: 6)

How should this change in the prevailing view of the incompatibility of free trade and free capital flows be interpreted? Not only empirical evidence but also theoretical arguments for the gains from free trade and free movement of capital are – to put it mildly – weak.[13] Objections such as the one expressed by Keynes in 1942 to Harrod still appear to be valid:

> Freedom of capital movement is an essential part of the old *laissez-faire* system and assumes that it is right and desirable to have an equalization of interest rates in all parts of the world. It assumes, that is to say, that if the rate of interest which promotes full employment in Great Britain is lower

than the appropriate rate in Australia, there is no reason why this should not be allowed to lead to a situation in which the whole of British savings are invested in Australia, subject only to different estimations of risk, until the equilibrium rate in Australia has been brought down to the British rate. In my view the whole management of the domestic economy depends upon being free to have the appropriate rate of interest without reference to the rates prevailing elsewhere in the world. Capital control is a corollary to this.

(Keynes, 1980: 149)

In fact, there is evidence that this criticism of freedom of capital movement is even more cogent now than it was then. Calvo and Mendoza (1997: 27–28) conclude that 'the global economy is inherently more volatile than a world economy with limited capital mobility' and that this 'global market volatility can induce large social costs.' Wyplosz (1998: 2) argues that 'financial market liberalization is the best predictor of currency crises. This has been true in Latin America in the 1980s, in Europe in the early 1990s and in Asia in 1997.' As for its social effects, research shows that '(d)eveloping countries that liberalized and globalized were subject to larger swings in inequality than countries that did not. (...) In most cases, identifiable liberaliza-tions are followed by rising inequality in wages' (Galbraith *et al.*, 1998: 6). One of the reasons for this, Felix (1998: 209) says, is that 'liberalization of international capital movements has forced macroeconomic policy to react primarily to signals from the financial rather than from the job market. (...) Economists defending the position that liberalizing and globalizing financial markets has improved economic welfare now avert their eyes from the adverse real economic trends.'[14] Finally, Obstfeld (1998: 1) notes that '(r)egional financial crises seem to have become more frequent, and the domestic impact of global financial developments has grown – to the alarm of many private citizens, elected officials, and even economists.'

One of these economists is Bhagwati (1998), who calls the idea, that full capital mobility is inevitable and desirable, 'a myth'. He argues that 'claims of enormous benefits from free capital mobility are not persuasive', and that 'none of the proponents of free capital mobility have estimated the size of the gains they expect to materialize, even leaving out the losses from crises that can ensue'. Bhagwati, former economic policy adviser to GATT's director general, also reminds us that countries as different from each other as China, Japan and those in Western Europe have all achieved their highest growth rates without capital account convertibility. In the same vein, Rodrik (1998) finds, on the basis of data from almost 100 countries, that between 1975 and 1989 free capital mobility had no significant impact on countries' economic fortunes. He concludes, 'The greatest concern I have about canonizing capital-account convertibility is that it would leave economic policy in the typical "emerging market" hostage to the whims and fancies of two dozen or so thirty-something country analysts in London, Frankfurt and New York.'

Today's heavy-handed promotion of the combination of free trade and free capital flows cannot be attributed to demonstrated economic advantages. Based on written commentaries and analyses produced by large multinational banks and on interviews with major decision-makers at these and other private sector financial institutions, Rude shows that since the East Asian financial crisis even participants in the financial markets tend to agree:

> The severity of the financial implosion that took place in East Asia has prompted many market participants to question the stability of today's globalized financial system. Market participants have not only lost faith in the prospect of continued robust growth, therefore, but in the merits of financial market liberalization and globalization, indeed, in the viability of free, unregulated international capital markets as well.
>
> (Rude, 1998: 4)

Like previous changes of monetary regimes, the most recent shift has to be interpreted as the outcome of political changes. Eichengreen argues that the gold standard could only be maintained before World War I because

> the insulation enjoyed by the monetary authorities allowed to commit to the maintenance of gold convertibility. (...) The extension of the franchise and the emergence of political parties representing the working classes raised the possibility of challenges to the single-minded priority the monetary authorities attached to convertibility. Rising consciousness of unemployment and of trade-offs between internal and external balance politicized monetary policy.[15]
>
> (Eichengreen, 1996: 42–43)

The main factor in this most recent change is the global shift in the relationship of forces between capital and labor that has taken place since the mid-1970s. The increase of unemployment in the OECD countries after the long post-war expansion ended and the disappearance of full employment as a policy goal; a number of setbacks and defeats of national and socialist movements and projects in Third World countries; and the collapse of the former Soviet bloc in Eastern Europe have all worked to the benefit of capital.[16]

These changes have resulted in a substantial increase in capital's share of income in all parts of the world, and – more generally – in a political, social and economic agenda in which the interests of capital take pride of place. Bhagwati (1998) argues that the current myth of enormous benefits from free capital mobility has been created by 'the Wall Street–Treasury complex, following in the footsteps of President Eisenhower, who had warned of the military-industrial complex'. Wade and Veneroso (1998b: 35) argue that the 'US has a powerful national interest in establishing the free movement of capital worldwide – there is probably no more important foreign economic policy issue for the US than this.' Gowan (1997) concludes that the 'new monetary and financial regime' is 'not in the least a spontaneous outcome of organic economic or technological processes, but a deeply political result of political choices made by successive governments of one state: the United States'.

In sum, the break with the policies that prevailed during the first three decades after World War II reflects a profound change in the relationship of forces between capital and labor.[17] Just as at the beginning of the last century, the interests of First World capital can be identified as the motor force behind the current global drive towards free trade and unrestricted capital movement.[18]

But today's promotion of free trade and free capital flows, two important economic arms of imperialism at the beginning of the last century, hardly proves that globalization is a mere repetition or continuation of this earlier period of capitalism. Although there are important similarities, significant changes have to be taken into account. They can be summarized in three points.

First, while Lenin, Hilferding and Hobson noted the existence of capital flows from imperialist countries to other dominant countries, in their time such inter-penetration of capital was a minor tendency.[19] The main trend was the centralization of capital on a national level, 'transforming thousands and thousands of scattered economic enterprises into a single national capitalist, and then into a world economy' (Lenin, 1917: 32). At the time there was a general consensus that – because the finance capitalist 'increasingly concentrates his control over the whole national capital by means of domination of bank capital' – the struggle was intensifying among nations on behalf of their respective capitals 'to incorporate parts of the world market into the national market, through a colonial policy which involves the annexation of foreign territories' (Hilferding, 1910: 225, 325).

The structure of the world economy has changed considerably since then, however, and inter-OECD investments have become much more important. As early as the end of the 1960s Magdoff (1969: 62) saw that 'the internationalization of capital among the giant firms is of a much higher order today than was the case 50 years ago when Lenin wrote his work on imperialism.' Around the same time, Mandel (1972: 64) pointed out that the rise of new industries in metropolitan countries and the fear of liberation movements in the Third World had led after the Second World War to 'an abrupt change in the pattern of long-term capital export. In contrast to the period from 1880 to 1940, capital now no longer mainly moved from the metropolitan countries to the underdeveloped ones. Instead, it chiefly went from some metropolitan countries to other imperialist countries.' So what 'marks the post-war period is the predominance of the interpenetration of trade and investment within the advanced capitalist countries compared to the orientation towards formal and informal colonies in the inter-war period' (Fine *et al.*, 1999: 68). These facts underscore the point made by Blaug (1968: 271) in his discussion of Marxist theories of imperialism, that the idea that colonies are indispensable to advanced capitalist countries is a myth.[20]

This trend has only intensified in the ensuing decades, as can be seen among other things from the multiplication of regional trade blocs and customs unions since the beginning of the 1980s, most spectacularly the European Union. Such developments are an important reason why critics of globalization argue that regionalization (or triadization) is a better term to characterize the dominant trend in the world economy, because it expresses where the biggest share of trade and capital flows come from and go to. It is, as Radice (1999: 5) points out, 'undoubt-edly the case that trade and investment flows are concentrated among the advanced industrial countries; (...) this is hardly surprising, since they constitute the largest and richest markets in a world where most economic activity is now based on production for sale at a profit.' In a similar vein, it is scarcely surprising that in the real world of transport and other distance costs – including those arising from cultural differences, protectionism, etc. – businesses will look first to neighbouring countries for markets, labour, capital, or production sites. Hence higher levels of trade, capital flows, etc. will be found between adjacent territories such as Canada and the USA. In the colonial era, trade and capital flows were less geographically regional, simply because the political systems of colonialism were designed to reduce those 'distance costs' for the merchants and financiers of the colonial power (and greatly increase them, of course, for those of other powers).

(Radice, 1999: 4–5)

Instead of the national cartels that competed for world markets at the beginning of the last century, many types of international investors, alliances and multinationals are now competing and cooperating with each other on the basis of various different strategies in both developed and developing countries. At the same time, the number of international organizations and panels charged with coordinating and regulating economic policies has increased dramatically. In these organizations the big countries work together, particularly to open up developing countries to trade and capital. None of this means that there is no longer any competition among imperialist countries; but such rivalries are fought out economically rather than militarily.[21] This can also be seen from the fact that the US, the world's main imperialist country, is no longer seriously preparing for a possible war with Japan or Europe.[22]

A second difference, linked to the previous one, concerns the role and structure of finance capital. The national bank-dominated financial systems that Hilferding and Lenin studied in their time have made way for a much more integrated world-wide financial system, where global norms are set for profitability.[23] Because of the disappearance of capital controls and immense expansion of financial markets, globalized financial markets, where a lot of speculation takes place, increasingly discipline investors and governments, and space for national differences is narrowing. As Plender puts it:

At the risk of some slight oversimplification, if a country tries artificially to reduce the financial returns available to depositors and investors, its exchange rate will collapse in the long run as domestic and international capital pours out in pursuit of higher returns elsewhere. Because governments and central banks will act to forestall the inflationary consequences of a collapsing exchange rate, they will, in normal circumstances, raise interest rates, thereby bringing their industries' cost of money back into line with the international norm.

(Plender, 1997: 97)

For some theoreticians this means that capitalism has entered a different phase since the beginning of the 1980s.[24]

There is a third difference of a more political character. Dominant countries no longer colonize parts of the world by military force, but promote the combination of democracy and a market economy. In fact, according to Robinson (1996a), it is polyarchy rather than democracy that is being established: 'Promoting polyarchy and promoting neo-liberal restructuring has become a singular process in US foreign policy.'[25] Robinson maintains that 'authoritarianism increasingly proved to be an untenable mode of domination and an unpredictable means of preserving asymmetries within and among nations as globalizing processes began to assert themselves.' He forcefully argues that this is a shift in the means of policy, not in its ends, which are still 'defense of the privileges of the Northern elites and their Southern counterparts in a highly stratified world system'.

In sum, as in the world economy at the beginning of the last century, which was widely characterized as imperialist, the interests of First World capital are the motor force behind the current global drive towards free trade and unrestricted capital movements. But that does not mean that economic globalization is just a repetition of this earlier period of capitalism. There are significant changes in the functioning of the world economy that we have to take into account, most importantly increased cross-border links and internationalization of capital. There are also essential differences in imperialist domination, which today is expressed mainly in economic and hardly at all in military rivalry among the main capitalist powers.

3.4   SUMMARY AND CONCLUSION

A key aspect of today's economic globalization is the emphasis on the combination of policies of free trade and free movement of capital, which seems to signify a return to the similar international regime that existed before World War I. But despite many similarities, economic globalization is not a repetition or continuation of this previous period of capitalism.

Policies in the pre-World War I era of imperialism were driven by the interests of nationally centralized capital under the control of bank-dominated finance capital, and resulted in national states' well-known imperial practices of incorporating foreign territories into their national markets to make possible increased exports of goods and capital. The interests of First World capital are also the driving forces behind the current economic globalization. But today's world economy is characterized by an increasing number of cross-border links among different countries, a higher level of internationalization of capital, an integrated worldwide financial system, and a greater role for international organizations and panels charged with coordinating and regulating economic policies. Consequently, domination is expressed today mainly in economic and hardly at all in military rivalry among the main capitalist powers.

NOTES

1 Data about trade and financial flows now and at that time are often compared, and used to make the point that economic globalization is nothing new (see, e.g. Hirst and Thompson, 1996; Kleinknecht and ter Wengel, 1998; Ruigrok and Van Tulder, 1995b). But such aggregated data risk missing qualitative differences, such as the ones described by the IMF:

The process observed before 1914 could hardly be called 'globalization,' however, since large parts of the world did not participate and also because the speed of transport and communication was such that it was much less feasible than it is today to organize markets, or to operate forms, at the global level. Furthermore, international financial markets today are characterized by much larger gross flows, with a much larger variety of financial instruments being traded across borders. Nevertheless, the trends we have been observing in recent decades are in a sense taking us back to the future.

(IMF, 1997a: 112)

The problematic character of these comparisons is further discussed in Went (1996b).
2 In its 1999 – triennial – Central Bank Survey of Foreign Exchange and Derivatives Market Activity, the BIS reports the growth of foreign exchange operations:

In terms of notional principal amounts, global turnover in traditional foreign exchange market segments (spot transactions, outright forwards, and foreign exchange swaps) reached an estimated daily average of $1.5 trillion in April 1998. This represented a growth of 26 per cent in the three-year period since April 1995, an apparent sharp slowdown from the 45 per cent rate of expansion of the 1992–95 triennium. However, adjusted for differences in the dollar value of non-dollar transactions, growth accelerated between the two periods, from 29 per cent to 46 per cent. Forward instruments (outright forwards and forex swaps) consolidated their dominant position with a market share of 60 per cent (up from 56 per cent in April 1995). At the time, the market continued to be dominated by inter-dealer business (63 per cent) and cross-border transactions (54 per cent).

(BIS, 1999: 1)

3 This view of markets is basically

in line with that espoused by Milton Friedman. According to Friedman, the voluntary exchanges, which take place under free markets, provide both the cooperation of agents and the coordination of market activities because the resulting market prices of such exchange serve as signals which create both the incentive and the information need to act. (. . .) Under these conditions, allowing all agents (individuals and institutions) a free pursuit of their own interest will optimize the institutional structures of society and maximize social welfare. With such a view of markets, it is natural for the Deregulationists to argue that free financial markets, through heightened market discipline, will deliver what is in both the individual and public interest – a safe and sound financial structure. This view of markets can be seen in the Deregulationists' discussion of free markets and the efficiencies and discipline they generate.

(Coggins, 1998: 41)

4 See, e.g. Bordo and Schwartz (1997) and Eichengreen (1996) on the history of and conditions for the functioning of the gold standard. As they spell out, trade and foreign borrowing were simplified when more and more countries adopted the same monetary standard. In the final years of the nineteenth century the system reached into Asia (Russia, Japan, India, Ceylon) and Latin America (Argentina, Mexico, Peru, Uruguay), while silver remained the monetary standard only in China and a few Central American countries (see also Eichengreen and Flandreau, 1996). It should not be forgotten, however, that the cooperation necessary to a gold standard functioned mainly to the advantage of North Central Europe, led by England, the main economic power, and Germany, and that

peripheral countries' problems did not threaten systemic stability. Europe's central banks were thus less inclined to come to the aid of a country in, e.g. Latin America.

5 See also Bordo and Schwartz (1997).

6 In a typical editorial, the *Financial Times* (April 18, 1998) argues that everybody has to understand that 'at the national level, the emerging global standard consists of liberal trade and open financial markets'. This 'global standard' has been promoted and imposed in all corners of the world by international organizations and lobby groups, business elites, multinationals and traders on financial markets. It is therefore hardly surprising that US Treasury Secretary Rubin urged, e.g. 'African governments to open goods and financial markets and embrace globalization even at the risk of political difficulties' (*Financial Times*, July 15, 1998).

7 Wade and Veneroso characterize this revision of the IMF's constitution – its articles of agreement – as one of the most irreversible measures to establish free capital movement worldwide:

> The proposed revision of Article I, which describes the *purposes* of the Fund, says that promotion of the orderly liberalization of capital is one of the Fund's main purposes. The revision to Article VIII, which describes the *jurisdictions* of the Fund – and hence the matters subject to sanctions of a legal character – says that the Fund shall have the same jurisdiction over the capital account of its members as it has over the current account. This means, in effect, that the Fund shall oversee and approve any capital account restrictions. Moreover, the language *requires* countries to commit themselves to open the capital account.
>
> (Wade and Veneroso, 1998b: 34)

8 In describing imperialism interchangeably as the 'highest', a 'special', and 'the latest' stage or 'epoch' of capitalism, Lenin's theory can be seen, as McDonough (1995) shows, as ancestor of later theories of capitalist stages, such as the regulation approach and long waves theories (see also Chapter 5).

9 This theory of a peaceful imperialism, to be achieved by the workers movement in cooperation with progressive elements of the bourgeoisie, was widely held within the Second International. This is one reason why Kautsky and many others in this movement were unprepared when war broke out in August 1914 (Geary, 1987).

10 Lutz (1999: 81) argues that Hobson 'with a prophetic voice' already warned that production risked to be moved to cheaper areas without 'common economic rules of international conduct contributory to a more equal and more equitable apportionment of work and its product over the whole area of the world market.'

11 See, e.g. Bello (1998), Bullard (1998), Wade (1998) and Wade and Veneroso (1998a).

12 See, e.g. Galbraith *et al.* (1998), Galbraith and Jaiquing (1999), Pritchett (1996), Rodrik (1999) and UNDP (1997).

13 As has been argued in our discussion of free trade, Ricardo himself argued that capital immobility is a necessary condition for his theorem of comparative advantage to work. See also Bhagwati (1998) and Rodrik (1998) on free capital flows, and Bruton (1998) on import substitution policies and 'export fetishism'.

14 See also, e.g. Aglietta and Moatti (2000), Eatwell and Taylor (2000) and Eichengreen (1999).

15 Others have called this monetary laissez-faire, 'by which they mean limited government intervention' (Flandreau *et al.,* 1998: 129).

16 The debt crisis in Latin America in the 1980s has been used to strangle import substitution strategies and open up debtor countries to international capital:

> In the terminology of Hyman Minsky, Volcker's monetary policy transformed Mexico into a Ponzi financial unit. This ushered in Mexico's debt crisis, and the subsequent demands by the U.S. government, the Bretton Woods institutions, and

their private sector allies among the multinational banks and corporations that
Mexico undertake a program of free-market restructuring. Two main tenets of the
free-market restructuring program were for the state to sell a substantial share of its
assets to the private sector and to substantially reduce regulations on capital inflows
and foreign direct investment.

(Pollin, 1998: 225–226)

17 The combination of free trade and free capital flows is a break with the Bretton Woods
regime for First World countries, while an orientation towards free trade and export-
led growth constitutes an additional break (with the import substitution strategy) for
the Third World. See, e.g. Gowan (1998) and Rodrik (1999).
18 This time with even more pernicious consequences: 'Walter Wriston, ex-CEO of
Citicorp, chortles that the globalized financial markets now hold macroeconomic policy in a tighter grip than under the gold standard', Felix (1998: 209) notes for example.
19 As to the earlier period Hilferding noted, e.g. that

the United States exports industrial capital to South America on a very large scale,
while at the same time importing loan capital from England, Holland, France, etc.,
in the form of bonds and debentures, as working capital for its own industry.

(Hilferding, 1910: 326)

20 Blaug (1968: 271) also argues that it is not helpful to cling to the myth 'that developed
countries are rich *only* because they plundered Asia and Africa' (emphasis added).
Stated like this not many Marxists – or others – will disagree, but the opposite statement (which Blaug does *not* make) would not be correct either. As Mandel argues, differences between metropolitan and colonial rates of profit were a source of colonial
surplus profits during the classical imperialist period:

International movements of capital constantly reproduce and extend the international productivity differential which is characteristic of the history of modern
capitalism, and are in turn further determined by this differential. In the closing
decades of the 19th century there still existed large reserves of unutilized raw
materials and labour-power not yet drawn into the production of surplus-value.
These reserves combined with the availability of substantial excesses of capital in
the earliest industrialized countries to create a growing export of capital from the
metropolitan countries to the colonies and semi-colonies.

(Mandel, 1972: 343–376)

Subsequently, Mandel shows that colonial surplus profits were the chief form of
metropolitan exploitation of the Third World at that time, and unequal exchange a
secondary form. The proportions changed after the Second World War; since then
unequal exchange has become the main form of colonial exploitation, while the direct
form of colonial surplus profits now plays a secondary role. See also Frank (1998).
21 The collapse of the former Soviet bloc facilitated this change, but steps in this direction
were already being taken after the Second World War, as Magdoff argues:

While the imperialist powers did not give up the colonies gladly or easily, the
main purposes of colonialism had been achieved prior to the new political
independence: the colonies had been intertwined with the world capitalist
markets; their resources, economies, and societies had become adapted to the
needs of the metropolitan centers. The current task of imperialism now became to
hold on to as many of the economic and financial benefits of these former
colonies as possible. And this of course meant continuation of the economic and

financial dependency of these countries on the metropolitan centers. Neither in the period right after the Russian Revolution nor in our own day does the central objective of extending and/or defending the frontiers of imperialism signify the elimination of rivalries among the imperialist powers. However, since the end of the Second World War this central objective has dominated the scene because of the increasing threat to the imperialist system and because of the greater unity among the powers imposed by United States leadership.

(Magdoff, 1969: 40–41)

22 See Achcar (1998).
23 As Plender notes:

Today the cost of capital will tend to equalize between countries after allowing for risk, which means, among other things, that German and Japanese companies now have to meet a global profit criterion. If they fail to do so, their stock markets will in the end fall, thereby raising the cost of equity capital. Because of this they have already been forced to adopt more flexible labour-market policies, including the Anglo-Saxon practice of downsizing.

(Plender, 1997: 57)

On the consequences for workers see, e.g. Coutrot (1998), Moody (1997) and Sennett (1998).
24 One of the more prolific researchers defending such a position is the French economist François Chesnais:

For the time being I will designate this … by the somewhat complicated name of 'global accumulation regime dominated by finance', or 'financialized global accumulation regime', stressing its very marked rentier characteristics. (…) Born from the impasses to which the 'thirty glorious years' of prolonged accumulation led (…) this mode is based on transformations of the 'wage relation' and a very sharp increase in the rate of exploitation (…) but its functioning is governed mainly by operations and choices of forms of finance capital that are more concentrated and centralized than in any previous period of capitalism.

(Chesnais, 1997: 62–63)

See also Chesnais (1994, 1996a).
25 Robinson argues:

What US policymakers mean by 'democracy promotion' is the promotion of *polyarchy*, a concept which developed in US academic circles closely tied to the policymaking community in the United States in the post-World War II years. (…) Polyarchy refers to a system in which a small group actually rules and mass participation in decision-making is confined to leadership choice in elections carefully managed by competing elites. (…) Democracy is limited to the political sphere, and revolves around process, method and procedure in the selection of 'leaders'. This is an *institutional* definition of democracy. (…) A caveat must be stressed. US preference for polyarchy is a general guideline of post-Cold War foreign policy and not a universal prescription. Policymakers often assess that authoritarian arrangements are best left in place in instances where the establishment of polyarchic systems is an unrealistic, high-risk, or unnecessary undertaking.

(Robinson, 1996a: 49, 112)

4 The circuit of social capital

The internationalization of trade and finance is generally taken into account in measuring or comparing degrees of economic globalization, but there is a third component that also has to be considered. This necessity can be illuminated by introducing the concept and dynamics of the circuit of social capital, an analytical tool that Marx first used to make sense of the movements of capital.

Section 4.1 defines the meaning of circuits of capital. Section 4.2, then, deals with the (asymmetrical) internationalization of circuits of capital.

4.1 THREE CIRCUITS OF CAPITAL

In mainstream economics 'capital' is usually analyzed in one dimension: that of 'physical capital' in neoclassical economics, or of 'money capital' in financial economics. Volume II of Marx's *Capital*, which appeared posthumously in 1884, edited by Engels from Marx's manuscript, is divided into three main parts. In the first part, Marx analyzes the metamorphosis capital undergoes in its circuit, as money capital, production capital and commodity capital.[1] The notion that capital assumes three different forms – and mutates from one to another – is a major contribution. In Marx's own words:

> It should generally be noted (...) that the economists are much inclined to forget not only that a part of the capital needed in a business is constantly passing alternately through the three forms of money capital, productive capital and commodity capital, but that it is always different portions of this that possess these forms alongside each other, even if the relative magnitudes of these portions are in constant flux.
>
> (Marx, 1884: 333)

As Arthur states, the importance of the introduction of this idea

> cannot be overestimated. Whereas neoclassicals explicitly, and the classicals for the most part (if implicitly), as well as many Marxists, all deploy as a key analytical construct the notion of equilibrium, for Marx it is the concept of a

circuit that characterizes his grasp of capital. Furthermore, except in a special case, the circuit does not return to the beginning but is part of a spiral of accumulation, theoretically therefore much more appropriate to the study of the real world, which knows no equilibrium but is strongly marked by growth.[2]

(Arthur, 1998: 95)

Harvey (1986: 69–71) characterizes the circulation process that begins with money capital and ends with money capital plus profit as the 'paradigm form of circulation.' Marx 'depicted the process of expansion of value as passing through a sequence of metamorphoses – changes of state.' With money capital (M), brought into circulation to earn more money (M' = M + Δ*m*), the commodities (C), labor power (LP) and means of production (MP) are purchased as inputs for the production process (P) of commodities (C'), which have to be sold on the market.

Schematically, the circulation of capital can be summarized as follows:

$$M - C \{LP \ \& \ MP\} \ldots P \ldots C' - M' - C' \ \{LP' \ \& \ MP'\} \ldots P' \ldots C'' \ (\text{etc.})$$

At the end of the production process P...C', the capital value in the shape of commodities as outputs (C') is greater than the capital value in the shape of commodities that were used as inputs for the production process (C {LP & MP}...P, or C...P). Similarly, the capital in the shape of money at the 'end' (M') is greater than the capital in this shape at the 'start' (M).[3] Both M – C and C' – M' are transformations brought about by buying and selling, whereas the production process P involves a material transformation of the product.[4] As Foley describes it:

> We can think of the circuit of social capital as the combined circuits of all the individual capitals that make up the whole. Then it is natural to think of the capitalist production process as a closed circuit, with the different forms of capital – financial capital, production capital, and commercial capital – at the three main nodes.

(Foley, 1986: 66)

Because circulation is normally a continuous process we can break the overall circuit of social capital down into three circuits:[5]

$$M - C \{LP \ \& \ MP\} \ldots P \ldots C' - M' \quad (\text{circuit of money capital})$$

$$P \ldots C' - M' - C \{LP \ \& \ MP\} \ldots P \quad (\text{circuit of production capital})$$

$$C' - M' - C \{LP \ \& \ MP\} \ldots P \ldots C' \quad (\text{circuit of commodity capital})$$

Each of the three circuits 'describes the movement of an individual capital and an aspect, or component, of the circuit of total social capital' (Bryan, 1995a: 70).

Companies *can* specialize in one (or two) of the circuits, but there are also conglomerates that unify all three. Moreover, tendencies of specialization and of integration can be identified in different historical periods.[6] Because the conditions and concerns regulating the circulation of the three forms differ, there is reason for specialization.[7] Each of the phases of the process, for example, costs time: between the purchase of inputs for production and the emergence of finished products (*production lag*), before commodities are sold (*realization lag*), and before money is recommitted to the production process in the form of capital advances (*finance lag*). Merchant (or commodity) capitalists (C...C') therefore specialize in transforming commodities into money, money capitalists (M...M') in the circulation of money, and production capitalists (P...P') in production.[8] The three time lags are the *turnover times* of the phases of capitalist production.[9] Entrepreneurs in the different sectors obviously have an interest in reducing the time that their capital is tied up as much as possible, so that they can reinvest it more quickly and make more money.[10]

As a whole, to sum up, the process is a dynamic one, in which

> each of the nodes of the circuit of capital corresponds to a stock of value tied up in the form corresponding to that node; and between each of the nodes is a continuous flow of value moving from one form to the next. The flow between financial capital and production capital is the flow of capital outlays. The flow between production capital and commercial capital is the flow of finished commodities emerging from the production process. The flow between commercial capital and financial capital is the flow of sales of commodities.
>
> (Foley, 1986: 68)

When differentiating among the three forms, one should not lose sight of the whole. All three circuits, Arthur (1998: 110) argues, 'carry with them the possibility of some kind of reductionism. So the appropriate thing to say is that all three versions of the circuit express something valid but limited.'

4.2 THE ASYMMETRICAL INTERNATIONALIZATION OF THE CIRCUITS

From the – in itself rather non-controversial – notion that capitalism has always been international to some degree, it follows logically that statements about 'newer' or 'higher' levels of internationalization have to be carefully qualified.[11] The differentiation just sketched out among the three circuits of capital, which together form the total circuit of social capital, can be of great use for such refinements. This is all the more the case since there is no *a priori* reason to assume that the three circuits, each of which have their specific characteristics, will follow the same trajectory over time. Historically, in fact the three circuits have not internationalized uniformly or even together.

In a remarkable, rather neglected, contribution, Palloix (1977) points out the historically consecutive internationalization of trade, finance and production. He begins from the notion that commodity capital was the first circuit to be internationalized. After trade, finance was the next circuit to internationalize. Only more recently, Palloix argued, has production begun to internationalize as well.[12] Since he wrote this in 1977, the internationalization of production has accelerated immensely, as is documented, for example, in the *World Investment Report* series compiled and published annually by UNCTAD.

For Fine and Harris (1979: 151–152), writing at the end of the 1970s, the internationalization of production signified a qualitative shift towards a new stage of capitalism in which production capital in multinational or transnational companies (TNCs) is dominant.[13] But as we will see in Chapter 6, less than two decades later finance capital has become dominant.[14] This change of emphasis – i.e. from the dominance of production to the dominance of finance – in a relatively short interval underlines the danger of impressionistic generalizations, and most importantly the necessity of never losing sight of the whole circuit of social capital.

Bryan (1995a: 61), while noting the 'leadership of money within recent internationalization', comments, e.g. that it has 'become common to equate internationalization with the growth of TNCs [transnational companies].' But as he correctly points out, multinational companies should not be equated solely with the internationalization of the circuit of production capital, as they so often are:

> (T)he circuit of productive capital is just the circuit of industrial capital viewed from a particular perspective (that is, the circuit 'starts' and 'ends' with productive capital), but along the way, capital passes through all three forms. TNCs are engaged in the international movement of money and commodity capital, as well as the relocation of productive capital.
>
> (Bryan, 1995b: 427)

By arguing that TNCs are involved in all three circuits of capital, however, Bryan bends the stick too far in the other direction. There is no reason why companies operating internationally necessarily have to be engaged in international trade, international capital flows ánd international production.[15] Theoretically it is also possible to undertake just one or two of such cross-border activities, and in fact – as, for example, outsourcing of parts of the production chain by many companies shows – that is exactly what is often happening.

The point that multinationals cannot be equated with the internationalization of productive capital, however, is well taken. In statements such as the one criticized by Bryan, two dimensions that cannot be reduced to each other have often been confused. On the one hand, the extent to which circuits of capital transcend national borders is a measure of the level of internationalization of economic activities, with divergent implications for the possibility of influencing or regulating capital.[16] The number and economic weight of companies operating internationally, on the other hand, is rather a measure of the international concentration and centralization of capital. While the two are often linked, they cannot be reduced to each other. It would not make life easier for managers and shareholders, but it is quite possible for capital to become more concentrated and centralized internationally while international trade, capital flows or production are being severely curtailed.

4.3 SUMMARY AND CONCLUSION

Trade and capital flows are generally taken into account in comparisons of economic internationalization in different historical periods, but there is an important third component that has to be considered. As Marx laid out for the first time in his analysis of the circuit of social capital, capital assumes three different forms – commodity capital, money capital, and production capital – and mutates from one to the other.

The circuit of social capital can be thought of as the combined circuits of all the individual capitals that make up the whole. The capitalist production process is thus a closed circuit, which can itself be broken down into three circuits: the circuit of commodity capital, the circuit of money capital, and the circuit of production capital. Companies can specialize in one (or two) of the circuits, but there are also conglomerates that unify all three.

There is no *a priori* reason to assume that the three circuits, which each have their specific characteristics, will follow the same trajectory over time. Historically, in fact the three circuits have internationalized in a very uneven way. At the risk of schematizing too much, we can note historically increasing levels of internationalization of capital, through the sequential cross-border extension of the circuits of commodity capital, money capital, and production capital.

NOTES

1 On the background to this volume of *Capital* see Arthur and Reuten (1998b).
2 Arthur and Reuten compare the circuits of capital in the following way with the so-called 'modern orthodox economics':

> In the jargon of modern orthodox economics, by this Marx apparently takes the analysis into 'macroeconomics'. Indeed he does so, and Marx may therefore be considered a founder of a particular macroeconomics (...). Nevertheless to see merely that would be to miss important conceptual differences between Marx and modern orthodox economics, for much of *Capital II*, especially Part Two on the turnover of capital, would nowadays be classified as business economics. And to further complicate the comparison, much of that same part – together with the other two – would nowadays be classified as monetary economics.
>
> (Arthur and Reuten, 1998b: 5)

3 Since we are describing a circuit there is of course no 'start' and 'end.' We may envisage reference points however.
4 Marx defines the term 'circuit' as follows:

Let us now consider the total movement M – C...P...C′ – M′ (...). Here capital appears as a value that passes through a sequence of connected and mutually determined transformations, a series of metamorphoses that form so many phases or stages of a total process. Two of these phases belong to the circulation sphere, one to the sphere of production. In each of these phases the capital value is to be found in a different form, corresponding to a different and special function. Within this movement the value advanced not only maintains itself, but it grows, increases its magnitude. Finally, in the concluding stage, it returns to the same form in which it appeared at the outset of the total process. This total process is therefore a circuit.

(Marx, 1884: 132–133)

5 Arthur discovered a surprising feature of an earlier manuscript for Volume II of *Capital*. At one point Marx divided the circuit into four aspects:

In addition to the three with which we are familiar (. . .) he interposed a circuit he designated as that of 'the factors of the labour process' (. . .). More exactly, it is that of the commodities that in their use-value form serve as factors of the labour process, with their differentiation into means of production and labour power. In the first attempt at differentiating circuits he had not done this, stating quite clearly that there were three phases to be considered of 'the reproduction process'. This same view is resumed in Volume Two as we have it.' Arthur does not know when and why Marx dropped this experiment, but this may be discovered in the future as more drafts are published.

(Arthur, 1998: 119–120)

6 See also Reuten (2002).
7 Marx analyzes this in Parts 4 and 5 of Volume III of *Capital* (1894), where he develops 'capital in general' into the actual shapes of industrial capital (or production capital), merchant capital (or commodity capital) and money capital (or finance capital). See Reuten (2002) for a review of these texts and an exposition of the potential conflicts among these fractions of capital.
8 As van der Pijl notes,

one can hypothesize a specific phenomenology. The perspective of the trade, which prioritizes the profitable movement of goods and compares potential markets in terms of their capacity to absorb particular commodities; the *rentier* perspective of money capital, for which the money return is the sole decisive reference and which also, on account of its capacity to 'totalize' and arbitrate competing productive and commercial ventures, redistributes capital between them; and finally, the productive capitalist, concentrated on securing the specific human and material inputs of the next, expanded round of production.

(van der Pijl, 1998: 53)

See also van der Pijl (2001).
9 Marx develops the problems and consequences of these time lags and turnover times in detail in Part 2 of Volume II of *Capital* (1884), at the level of capital in general (see Smith, 1998).
10 '(C)apitalism is under the impulsion to accelerate turnover time, to speed up the circulation of capital and, consequently, to revolutionize the time horizons of development' (Harvey, 1995: 6).

11 Bryan, e.g. argues:

> International movement of capital, in the form of commodity trade and usury or credit, pre-dated and indeed was the precondition of the development of capitalism (...). Moreover, capitalist class relations have been internationalizing at least since the beginnings of European colonialism. Hence when internationalization is depicted as a distinct, recent development of capitalism, particularly in the period since the 1970s, there is need for clarification, for any perceived transformation should not be overstated. We must be aware that changes which may seem monumental at the time can appear much less decisive in retrospect. Moreover, there is the danger that the proclamation of internationalization as a 'new era' of capitalism can use newness (the image of a 'clean slate') as a means to avoid analyzing and explaining development within the "old".
>
> (Bryan, 1995a: 12–13)

12 See also Palloix (1975) and Mandel (1972). Since then many others have come to the same conclusion about this periodization, as, e.g. Fine and Harris:

> Thus commodity capital is the first form of capital to be internationalized, and this can be taken as the index of the first stage of the world economy. The development of the credit system which accompanies the predominance of the production of relative surplus value facilitates the internationalization of finance capital, and this may be considered as its second stage. The intensified production of relative surplus value gives rise to a third stage in which productive capital itself has internationalized with multinational corporations controlling production processes which cross national boundaries. At each of these three stages, the formation of the capitalists' class interest through the national state represents different internal conflicts as the external forces of competition are transformed.
>
> (Fine and Harris, 1979: 147–148)

13 The authors counterpose this dominance of production capital to the dominance of commodity capital and finance capital at the beginning of the 20th century.
14 See, e.g. Boyer (2000a), Chesnais (1997a, b), Gowan (1998), Huffschmid (1999) and Robinson and Harris (2000).
15 For the 'capital fractions approach' in International Political Economy, which is often associated with the 'Amsterdam Group', of e.g. van der Pijl and Overbeek, merchant houses, financial firms and industry are representatives or embodiments of commodity capital, money capital and productive capital, respectively (see Overbeek, 2000).
16 To give an example: one consequence of the increasing internationalization of production is that regulators, trade unions, consumers and non-governmental organizations have a much harder time monitoring – let alone influencing – the application of environmental and social standards during the production of goods.

5   Capitalism and stages of accumulation

This chapter proposes an approach to distinguishing different periods in the history of capitalism. While periodization is alien to conventional economic theory, non-mainstream economics has provided three theoretical frameworks: the Regulation approach, the Social Structure of Accumulation approach, and a variant of long wave theories. While there are differences among and within these approaches, it will be shown that they also complement each other and have much in common.[1] A body of joint features is outlined in this chapter that can be used as a heuristic device to analyze different stages in the long-run evolution of capitalism. This framework can then be used to analyze contemporary globalization and compare it with previous periods of intense economic internationalization.

Section 5.1 posits that capitalism can be analyzed at an intermediate level, which is more abstract and examines longer periods of time than detailed accounts, but is more concrete and examines shorter periods of time than capitalism's general laws of motion do. It argues that such intermediary analyses have to be broadly encompassing and integrate non-economic and external factors. Section 5.2 then deals with Kondratiev cycles, which are the best-known description of specific periods in the history of capitalism.[2] It argues that the deterministic role assigned to technological developments in these cycles is problematic, because technology in itself cannot explain contemporary globalization. Hence in Section 5.3 three non-deterministic theories of stages developed in the 1970s are introduced. The Regulation approach, the Social Structure of Accumulation approach and a variant of long wave theories all theorize that there is nothing automatic about the alternation of historical periods. Finally, building on these three heterodox theories, Section 5.4 develops a framework to analyze stages in the development of capitalism.

5.1   HOW TO ANALYZE CAPITALISM?

Most economic theories about capitalism's trajectory treat capitalist development from a long-term (structural) or short-term (business cycle) perspective. But between timeless general laws of motion of capitalist economies on the one hand

and empirical data about the ups and downs of trade flows and financial markets on the other, a third level of abstraction can be introduced. Such an intermediate level of analysis is more general and abstract than a detailed historical account of capitalist development, but more specific and concrete than an abstract theory of capitalism in general. Teeple sums up why working with this third time frame makes sense:

> The point is there is no such thing as capitalism pure and simple. Only in the most general, abstract sense is capitalism the same phenomenon down through the ages. If its fundamental characteristics are commodity production, production for profit, corporate private property, social labour, a world market, and the law of value, none of this says anything about their developmental stages or about how any of these properties manifest themselves in a given age or country.[3]
>
> (Teeple, 1999: 5)

While analyses of the characteristics of capitalism in general and of concrete data and processes are often necessary and fruitful, focusing on stages of capitalism can be helpful in understanding capitalist *development* and making possible a more qualitative comparison of different intervals.[4]

The instinctive rationale for an intermediate approach is that economic developments are neither accidental or random nor completely determined by general economic laws and tendencies. Different historical periods can be distinguished in the history of social formations.[5] While there is controversy about the causes, few people would deny that capitalism has taken different forms with specific characteristics:

> In fact, the existence and differentiation of long periods of structural evolution is intuitive and indeed accepted by most of the economic historians, although defined in several different ways: after the Industrial Revolution, the 'hungry forties', the Victorian boom, the Great Depression, the Belle Epoque and the revolution of steel and electricity, the crisis of the wars, the Fordist thirty golden years, and now the years of crisis – the rhythm of economic time is marked by the succession of those long expansions and depressions separated by deep structural changes. Those long periods represent distinct forms of organization of social relations, of science and technology, different cultural trends and political and social institutions.[6]
>
> (Louçã, 1997: xi)

Understanding different stages in the development of capitalism logically calls for broadly encompassing theories and analyses. In their important collective work on globalization, for example, Held, McGrew, Goldblatt, and Perraton argue that 'contemporary patterns of globalization constitute a distinctive historical form which is itself a product of a unique conjuncture of social, political, economic and technological forces' (1999: 429).[7] Most observers and scholars of contemporary globalization would agree readily, in light of the compelling magnitude of changes taking place in the global economy since the end of the 1970s. In his popular bestseller about globalization Thomas Friedman therefore takes economists to task who believe 'that you can explain the world with reference only to markets.' According to Friedman, 'in both journalism and academe, there is a deeply ingrained tendency to think in terms of highly segmented, narrow areas of expertise, which ignores the fact that the real world is not divided up into such neat little beats.' French economist Nicolas Beniès makes essentially the same point when he advocates 'a new theoretical framework' in which we can analyze the multidimensional character of the changes taking place in the global economy.[8]

But although many economists may recognize the importance of non-economic or external factors, in most cases actual investigation of such factors is left to sociologists and political scientists.[9] Conventional neoclassical theories are too limited: they restrict themselves to 'a clearly delimited, socially disembedded sphere of economic relations with a tendency towards general equilibrium' (Jessop, 1997: 504).[10] In addition, such theories generally discount or ignore time, on the assumption that all individuals have perfect knowledge of the future and actions of individuals cannot affect markets' overall development.

However, non-mainstream economics, not satisfied with such restrictions, has provided alternative frameworks that do incorporate broader social, political and institutional dimensions into economic analysis, with the explicit aim of understanding the specific characteristics and dynamics of historical periods. These approaches' methodological – and epistemological – point of departure is that contrary to the view of traditional neoclassical economics, institutions and social structure are important to the functioning of economic systems and therefore have to be integrated into analyses of capitalism.[11] As Guttmann argues in a well-phrased description, different institutional forms combine

> to determine the conditions that allow the economic system to reproduce itself in a stable manner and on an expanding scale. In other words, they regulate our economy by coordinating its decentralized decisions and integrating its separate activities into a unified structure capable of forward motion. (...) Different *modes of regulation* can be distinguished, depending on the prevailing set of monetary rules, corporate organization and competition, wage labor nexus, public policies, and international arrangements.
>
> (Guttmann, 1994: 56)

To sum up, a third time frame can be distinguished between day-to-day economic data and capitalism's general laws of motion, and can be used to analyze and compare the concrete forms capitalism assumes in different periods. Such intermediary analyses will necessarily be broadly encompassing, integrating non-economic and external factors.

5.2   KONDRATIEV CYCLES: IS TECHNOLOGY DRIVING HISTORY?

The best-known description of the existence of specific periods in the history of capitalism is the theory of Kondratiev cycles, which were discovered and discussed as early as the 1920s. The (possible) existence of such cycles became generally known in mainstream economics, thanks to Joseph Schumpeter, who was the first to call them 'Kondratiev cycles' in 1939.[12] Long (Kondratiev) cycles are 45–60 year cycles in economic activity, which according to Kondratiev are linked to social phenomena such as wars and revolutions, and are caused by the periodic renewal of basic capital goods. These periods (or stages) of capitalism are therefore to be differentiated from the successive stages of development countries will (have to) go through hypothesized by, for example, List (1841) and Rostow (1960).[13]

Each so-called Kondratiev wave (or K-wave) can schematically be divided into four phases: prosperity (with high growth), recession (with decelerating growth), depression (with near zero or negative growth), and recovery (with a modest growth rate). Furthermore, 'each wave tends to be associated with particularly significant technological changes around which other innovations – in production, distribution and organization – cluster and ultimately spread through the economy' (Dicken, 1998: 147). As new technologies are diffused they stimulate economic growth and employment, but at some point growth slackens because of the exhaustion of the positive effects of the technological revolution that was at the origin of the long expansion. Webber and Rigby, for example, conclude about the downturn in economic activity of the mid-1970s:

> (T)o the extent there has occurred a slowdown, it was inherent in the dynamics of the golden age. That is, the forms of technical change that sustained the real-wage rises of the 1950s and 1960s also diminished the profitability of production; our present disarray is caused by the continuing lack of profits in production. (...) The end of the period of relatively rapid growth was the product not of mistakes of policy, nor of slower productivity growth, much less of intensified competition from imports, but of the fact that it was a period of rapid growth.
>
> (Webber and Rigby, 1996: 11)

The development of these waves is expressed (or summarized) in the rate of profit. After staying at high and rising levels during the phase of prosperity, it begins to fall during the recession as a consequence of, for example, social conflicts, wage increases, overaccumulation of capital, or a decline in productivity growth.[14]

There are different theories about which concrete mechanism ushers in a new expansive phase, but

> a central assumption of the long-wave idea (is) that eventually the trough of the wave will be reached and economic activity will turn up again. A new

sequence will be initiated on the basis of key technologies – some of which may be based on innovations which emerged during recession itself – and new investment opportunities.

(Dicken, 1998: 148)

Over the years researchers from various schools of thought have been studying long wave theory and testing its empirical validity. It is hardly surprising that in times of volatility and change like the turn of the twenty-first century, many economists and research institutions turn to Kondratiev for explanations. Discussing the so-called 'New Economy,' Kleinknecht (2000), for example, argues that Kondratiev's theory enables us to understand how the cluster of new, fast-growing technologies introduced in the 1980s is now pulling the whole economy towards a higher growth path.[15] Economists at the ING Bank and Rabobank, two of the biggest Dutch banks, as well as the president of Robeco, one of the world's biggest mutual funds, all also invoke Kondratiev to explain the economic impact of new Information and Communication Technologies (ICT).[16]

But up to this day the existence of long cycles or waves has remained a subject of considerable controversy among economists. Paul Samuelson once called them 'science fiction,' and in a 1978 issue of the *Citibank Monthly Economic Letter* they were described as a myth spread by people who believe in a mystical unfolding of history (quoted in Goldstein, 1988: 21–22). Doubts about the empirical evidence for the existence of such cycles are partially responsible for this controversy.[17] But more importantly, many scientists and observers have theoretical reasons not to accept the presence of endogenous long cycles of boom and bust. Shutt summarizes this skepticism in a polemical way:

> Confronted with the obstinate refusal of growth to revive, a significant number of economists and others have been inclined to flirt with quasi-metaphysical theories which supposedly give grounds for expecting a spontaneous recovery in the global economy irrespective of the revealed current tendency of market forces. According to such theories economic growth is governed by very long cycles (of fifty years or more), which their advocates claim can explain the ups and downs of the world economy at least since the Industrial Revolution, and that these unfold more or less independently of any 'man-made' events or influences such as world wars, political changes or innovations in technology. To anyone who recognizes economics to be a social science – and hence inherently subject to the unpredictable actions and reactions of ever-changing human society – such attempts to subject it to a series of rigid laws of motion can scarcely seem worthy a moment's consideration.

(Shutt, 1998: 194)

This criticism is not new.[18] The presumed regularity of long cycles was challenged as early as the 1920s. Mandel notes, for example, that Trotsky argued along the same lines against Kondratiev:

first that the *analogy* between 'long waves' and classical 'cycles' is false, i.e., that long waves are not possessed of the same 'natural necessity' as classical cycles. Second, that while classical cycles can be explained exclusively in terms of the internal dynamics of the capitalist mode of production, the explanation of long waves demands 'a more concrete study of the capitalist curve and the interrelationship between the latter and all the aspects of social life'.

(Mandel, 1972: 129)

Since these first debates, different factors have been emphasized as the main cause for Kondratiev cycles, such as technological developments affecting durable capital goods, cluster-like bursts of entrepreneurial innovation, excessive wealth concentration, and a low rate of profit in a depression, which induces capitalists to innovate to avoid going under.

But there has also been a further development of theories and empirical work building on the *critique* of Kondratiev cycles.[19] Such approaches begin from the idea that 'long-wave dynamics are shaped by a complex variety of cyclical, structural, and institutional forces' (Guttmann, 1994: 49), in which technological developments play an important but not decisive role. Consequently, these theories do not support the idea that a new long wave will come into existence endogenously after a long period of depression. It follows that in these approaches there is also no reason to assume that all long waves will have the same duration.[20]

So the question has to be posed as to which of these two approaches is the most suitable for an analysis of contemporary globalization? In many interpretations of the developments that have made contemporary globalization possible, technological change is cited as the fundamental cause. However, while the scope and effects of technological change have to be taken into account in analyses the causes and dynamics of increasing globalization since the early 1980s, it is intuitively easy to understand, first of all, why this kind of technological determinism does not hold. If technology were the driving force behind globalization, how could we account for the fact that there was less international trade for decades after the First World War than there was before 1914? Furthermore, it would be even more difficult to understand how the whole period from 1914 to about 1970 could have been one of 'illiberality in capital markets, with significant restrictions imposed by governments on international capital flows' (Adam, 1998: 559).[21]

New technological possibilities clearly do play a major role in internationalization and globalization. They make revolutionary changes possible. As soon as barriers (legal, social, fiscal or regulatory) to their application are removed or reduced, new applications and possibilities arise through a sort of self-reinforcing process, as more money and knowledge are invested in them. But this is not an autonomous process that takes place in a vacuum; institutional factors and relationships of forces delimit the playing field.[22] As Castells (1996: 5) argues in the Prologue to his monumental trilogy on the information society: 'Technology does not determine society: it embodies it. But neither does society determine technological innovation: it uses it.' For similar reasons, Dicken (1998: 145) proposes to consider technology as an '*enabling* or *facilitating* agent: it makes possible new structures, new organizational and geographical arrangements of economic activities, new products and new processes, while not making particular outcomes necessary.'[23]

Enabling or facilitating technologies allow companies, for example, to expand into new geographical areas. Low-cost sites can only be used if distances can be bridged without excessive costs and if such operations can be effectively coordinated and tracked. Development of these technologies is a precondition for development of international production and financial flows and transnational firms. Technologies in the fields of transport, communication, and organization of complex, spread-out activities are particularly important. But however important these technologies may be, they cannot be considered the causes of international production or transnational firms; they only make these phenomena possible. As if repeating a schoolbook caricature of Marxist theory, many accounts present globalization as the direct result of revolutionary technological change. But the application of these technological innovations is only possible thanks to social, that is economic, political, legal and institutional changes, nationally as well as internationally. The deterministic role that is assigned to technological developments in Kondratiev cycles is therefore very problematic, because technology cannot in itself explain contemporary globalization. For theories to be helpful in periodizing capitalism and understanding and characterizing globalization, they will have to be non-deterministic. In the next section three theories satisfying this condition will be introduced.

5.3   LONG SWINGS: THREE NON-DETERMINISTIC APPROACHES

In this section, three theoretical frameworks are introduced that were developed in the 1970s to analyze distinctive periods or stages in the history of capitalism. In my view, the essence of these three approaches is reflected well in the following description of long swings, stages of capitalism, or stages of accumulation:

> The long run evolution of our economy can (...) be conceptualized in terms of historically specific *accumulation regimes*, each with its own distinct institutional forms and modes of regulation. During the expansion phase of a long wave, these are capable of establishing and maintaining a relatively stable growth pattern. The shift toward the stagnation phase typically occurs when prevailing regulatory mechanisms are no longer able to cope with changing conditions in the structure of our economy. Economic imbalances and social tensions are allowed to build up to the point of structural crisis, at which point they destroy the cohesion of the existing accumulation regime in a series of ruptures. But this disintegration is simultaneously an impetus for massive reorganization efforts. Eventually these may go far enough to create

a new accumulation regime, with different social characteristics, regulatory mechanisms, and policy institutions. The precise outcome of this process is by no means predetermined.

(Guttmann, 1994: 56)

While some criticisms of and doubts about these various approaches will be mentioned, this section's aim is not to evaluate their application to concrete historical periods. Its goal is to prepare for the further elaboration in the final section of what may loosely be called 'long swing theories,' or alternatively 'theories of stages of accumulation,' based on these three approaches' main features.

5.3.1 Long wave theories

Long wave theories, which have gained some influence since the 1970s, go back directly to the debates at the beginning of the twentieth century over Kondratiev cycles introduced in the previous section.[24] Mandel is the most distinguished representative of all attempts to analyze long waves in a non-deterministic way, taking extra-economic factors and contingencies explicitly into account. Trotsky, as we have seen, rejected Kondratiev's use of the term 'long cycle' as an incorrect analogy with the normal business cycle, 'essentially because the sudden upward turning points of the long waves cannot be explained primarily by internal economic causes.' Following in Trotsky's footsteps, Mandel rejects

a Kondratieff type of theory of *long cycles* in economic development, in which there is, in the economy itself, a built-in mechanism through which an expansive long cycle of perhaps twenty-five years leads to a stagnating cycle of the same length, which then leads automatically to another expansive long cycle, and so on.

(Mandel, 1995: 16, 22)

Working in the same framework Barsoc argues:

There is no endogenous mechanism that makes the transition to a expansive long wave automatic after a recessive wave, or that guarantees the emergence of a new 'regulation'. Understanding the transition to a new upward phase requires taking 'extra-economic' factors into account.

(Barsoc, 1994: 57)

Although expressing skepticism about the existence of regular or systematic long waves, Maddison (1982: 85, 28) also comes close to this position when he argues that 'there have nevertheless been significant changes in the momentum of capitalist development.' His own analysis shows that 'the process of capitalist development has not been smooth. Within the capitalist period there have been distinct and important phases of development which are worthy of study, definition and causal interpretation.'

Integrating elements and categories from the Regulation approach, Barsoc (1994: 54–55) proposes that each long wave is characterized by a dominant mode of functioning of capitalism.[25] Four institutional forms support such a 'productive order': a mode of capital accumulation, a type of material forces of production, a mode of social control, and a type of international division of labor. Husson (1996) adds a particular 'reproduction scheme' as a fifth dimension, referring to classical Marxism as well as to a 'consumption norm,' which is important in the Regulationists' theories.

Critics of long wave theory concentrate mainly on its alleged mechanistic, economistic or deterministic character.[26] Another criticism often raised is the central place assigned in this approach to the tendency for the rate of profit to fall.[27] In addition – this is to a certain extent linked to the previous point – there have been criticisms of long wave theory's account of institutional aspects, which critics say is weaker than in the other approaches.

5.3.2   Regulation approach

The *Regulation approach* was developed in France during the 1970s and is best known through its representatives Aglietta, Boyer and Lipietz.[28] Over the years, members of this 'school' have gone in various directions, so that it is somewhat difficult to talk about *the* Regulation approach.[29] This was different at the beginning, when Regulationists, combining Marxian, Kaleckian and Keynesian insights, were characterized by the fact that they

> adopt a heterodox account of capital accumulation and emphasize the latter's socially embedded, socially regularized nature. They focus on the historically contingent ensembles of complementary economic *and extra-economic* mechanisms and practices which enable relatively stable accumulation to occur over relatively long periods, despite the fundamental contradictions, crisis-tendencies and conflicts generated by capitalism.
>
> (Jessop, 1997: 503)

The originality of this approach is, as Guttmann (1994: 55) argues, 'its focus on the real-life forces that have shaped the historic evolution of the capitalist system.' To facilitate such analyses and be able to integrate a broad range of factors and developments, Regulation theorists have developed a series of concepts and categories on different levels of abstraction. Their first level of analysis is a structural mode of production, such as feudalism or capitalism. Based on this foundation, for the capitalist mode of production sequential 'accumulation regimes' take shape between two structural crises, which is the second level of analysis. The third level of analysis concerns the specific configurations of social relations that can be identified during a period in a given geographic ensemble. Among these are a monetary regime, the prevailing forms of competition, the capital–labor relation, the form and policies of the state, and the international division of labor (Boyer and Saillard, 1995a).

Each of these configurations (or organizing forces) is subject to change, reflecting necessary adjustments in response to underlying tensions, Guttmann argues. Combined, they

> regulate our economy by coordinating its decentralized decisions and integrating its separate activities into a unified structure capable of forward motion. Replacing the static analysis of market equilibrium, the concept of regulation is used to show how various economic agents manage to achieve a certain degree of compatibility between their activities and of balance in their social relations. Different *modes of regulation* can be distinguished, depending on the prevailing set of monetary rules, corporate organization and competition, wage labor nexus, public policies, and international arrangements
>
> (Guttmann, 1994: 55–56)

Although some Regulationists have argued that discontent with structuralist variants of Marxist theory helped motivate them to develop a new theory, they have nonetheless sometimes been criticized for being too 'structuralistic' or 'functionalistic.' They have also been criticized for neglecting existing periodizations of capitalist development in other approaches. In addition, Brenner and Glick (1991) have argued that by concentrating on institutions of wage labor and mass consumption they have neglected inter-capitalist competition.

5.3.3 Social structures of accumulation

The Social Structure of Accumulation (SSA) approach, which is probably the least known, was introduced in the US in 1978 by Gordon and took its more definitive form in the beginning of the 1980s. Apart from Gordon, its best-known representatives are Bowles, McDonough and Weisskopf.[30]

The term 'SSA' refers to the whole set of institutions that support the process of capital accumulation. The approach's central idea is that each long period of relatively stable economic expansion requires an effective SSA. As in long wave theories and the Regulation approach, such an institutional set-up (SSA) promotes growth and stability for a certain period of time, but eventually declines. What then follows is a period of stagnation and instability, until a new SSA is built.[31]

Theorists who consider themselves part of the SSA approach recognize the influence of several intellectual traditions, most importantly Marxist theories, Keynesian thought, institutionalist tradition in American economics (Veblen, Commons), and long wave theories. One of their motivations for developing the SSA approach was the need they felt to make sense of historical patterns, bearing in mind that individual capitalist economic systems and the world system as a whole go through periodic booms and contractions. SSA researchers noted that such alternating long swings were associated with clustered institutional changes, which do not take place gradually but in a discontinuous manner. They have set themselves the task of explaining such patterns.

SSA researchers view long swings as in large part the product of the success or failure of successive social structures of accumulation in facilitating capital accumulation, and refer to the periods featuring those respective social structures of accumulation as stages of capitalism.[32] Their analysis

> does not suggest that the expansion and contraction phases of a long swing will last any specific number of years and certainly does not indicate that each long swing will have the same duration. On the contrary, we expect that the duration of each phase of a long swing is best understood within the specific context of each stage of capitalism.
>
> (Gordon *et al.*, 1994: 25)

The SSA school is often seen as the US counterpart of the (French) Regulation school, with a more individualistic (as opposed to structuralist) approach – for some critics too individualistic. Critics see its focus on a single country and its generalization from the US national situation, as well as the relatively sketchy character of some of its concepts and categories, as important weaknesses.

Notwithstanding differences among – and incidentally also within – these approaches, they have a remarkable number of features in common.[33] This is shown by the fact that over the years there has been considerable cross-fertilization, in which concepts and approaches have been productively borrowed and reciprocally integrated.[34] Finally, a review of interpretations of the origins and end of the expansionist decades after the Second World War also shows that there is much common ground. Rather than concentrating on deepening the distinctions and focusing on inconsistencies, elaborating the insights that these approaches share, therefore appears to be the most fruitful means of clarifying issues around globalization. This makes all the more sense since – as we have seen – none of the three approaches is uncontested, let alone dominant.

In the Regulation approach, research focuses on 'the historically contingent ensembles of complementary economic and *extra-economic* mechanisms and practices which enable relatively stable accumulation to occur over relatively long periods, despite the fundamental contradictions, crisis-tendencies and conflicts generated by capitalism' (Jessop, 1997: 503). These concrete historical realities can be characterized as *stages of accumulation*: 'segments of the overall history of the capitalist mode of production' with an 'integrated "total" character.'[35] From a long wave perspective these distinctive periods consist of a 'peculiar interweaving of internal economic factors, exogenous "environmental" changes, and their mediation through sociopolitical developments' (Mandel, 1995: 76). And in the SSA framework, a 'stage of capitalism can be conceived as the ensemble of economic, political, and ideological institutions which serve to reproduce capitalist relations of production and accumulation.' In this perspective, capitalism 'proceeds from one stage to the next when the SSA undergoes disintegration, producing crisis. The crisis can only be resolved through the construction of a new SSA, inaugurating a new stage of capitalism' (McDonough, 1994: 80).

While the Regulation approach calls successive stages of capitalism accumulation regimes, these are called long waves and social structures of accumulation, respectively, in the other two frameworks. Questions of terminology are important, but what really matters is content. I submit that semantic discussions can be avoided.

To sum up, the three theories presented in this section – the Regulation approach, the SSA approach and a variant of long wave theories – all developed in the 1970s, allow for a non-deterministic understanding of distinctive periods or stages in the history of capitalism. Notwithstanding differences among these approaches, they have a remarkable number of features in common. Given the cross-fertilization that has already taken place among them, further elaboration of a theory of stages based on their shared properties therefore seems not only possible but also promising.

5.4 A THEORY OF STAGES OF ACCUMULATION

In this section a theory will be set out to conceptualize different stages of accumulation, building on major elements of the three approaches introduced in the previous section. Especially since we are trying to come to grips with a 'moving target' as challenging as economic globalization, a certain dose of eclecticism, allowing for open exchanges and borrowing of categories, concepts, and premises, is called for.

Our point of departure is that elaboration of a theory of stages is necessary if we want to be able to analyze contemporary globalization's central features and dynamics. Why? Because such a theory allows for the integration of historical changes in a theorization of contingent regimes, which have their own specific institutional interrelations against the backdrop of the general requirements for accumulation that are necessary for reproduction of the capitalist economy.[36] Stages of capitalism defined in the above-mentioned way allow us to understand tidal economic changes while incorporating social, political and institutional dimensions. This makes possible a qualitative comparison of economic realities that – at least on the surface – seem to be similar. So a different light may, for example, be shed on some of the contributions that have been made by globalization skeptics who have argued that today's globalization is nothing new, since trade and financial flows were also heavily internationalized in an earlier historical period.[37]

The combination of the following eight elements is proposed as a tool to differentiate periods in the development of capitalism.

The first element of our theory of stages is that there are *general* requirements that are necessary for the reproduction of the capitalist system, of which capital accumulation is the motor. These necessities follow from the fact that capitalism is a generalized wage–labor system of commodity production for profit. The owners of the means of production (capitalists) employ producers (workers) and pay them wages, keeping the fruits of the labor process to sell at a profit. Necessities are conditions that have to be satisfied to guarantee the reproduction of capitalism, such as a legal system protecting property rights, the availability of workers, mechanisms of labor management, and the existence of an exchange system.

But – our second element – capital accumulation is not simply an economic process. Economic relations are *socially embedded* and must therefore be placed in their social context. A wide range of economic, political and social institutions as well as social forces have to be taken into account in order to understand how real economies operate. Among the important – changing – institutional arrangements are the provision of money and credit, state involvement in the economy, and how conflicting class interests are dealt with.

Third, the *concrete* forms capitalism takes are therefore not immediately or exclusively defined by the requirements for accumulation. The structure and actual content of institutions that are required for the reproduction of capitalist relations are not predetermined by the general requirements for capitalist production and accumulation, but mediated by the (changing) relationships of forces between (opposite fractions of) capital, (different groups within) labor, and (different) social movements. As a result, concrete studies are always necessary to grasp the relationship between the general requirements of capital and the specific form capitalism takes.

These three elements, which have a certain relative autonomy, together form a dynamic structure of the system.[38] While the actual functioning of capital accumulation is co-determined by the relationship of forces and by the ensemble of economic, political and social institutions, the actual functioning of capital accumulation in its turn co-determines relations among and within classes and social movements and the form and operation of institutions. To give an example: when accumulation stagnates because profit rates have declined, unemployment rises. This weakens the position of workers and trade unions not only in direct negotiations and conflicts with employers, but also in tripartite institutions, where inversely employers' organizations will strengthen their position. The effect of this change can affect, for example, labor market regulation, unemployment benefits, etc.

What else can be said about the dynamic of this system? Our fourth element introduces the concept of periods, or stages of accumulation. A stage of accumulation is suitable for analysis at an intermediate level. As a category it is more general and abstract than concrete accounts of capitalist development at a certain moment in time, but more specific and concrete than – necessarily abstract – theories of capitalism in general. Different stages of accumulation are characterized by a dominant mode of functioning of capitalism.

However – this is our fifth element – the concrete form of these stages of accumulation is not predetermined. Because social actors have a certain relative autonomy – contrary to the mechanical approach to the development of capitalism in orthodox economics and some variants of Marxism, which, different as they are, both treat economic agents as passive bearers of relations of production and thus become theories of historical inevitability. The result of struggles – between, e.g. workers and employers – is not known in advance.[39] Because the outcome of such struggles is of essential importance for the forms and policies of institutions, for the development of different components of the profit rate, and for the specific evolution of production relations, the trajectory of capitalist development is *contingent*.

Finally, it is necessary to say more about the development and dynamics of stages, and about how they come to alternate. To begin with it is necessary to distinguish two meanings of economic stagnation – our sixth element. The accumulation process causes periodic crises (i.e. the business cycle). Under normal conditions imbalances in accumulation will be corrected endogenously within the existing set of institutions. But there are also long periods of structural stagnation overarching the business cycle, which are characterized by a reduction in rates of accumulation and economic growth over a longer period of time. The relative stagnation of capitalism since the mid-1970s is the most recent example of the latter. Note that, due to the business cycle, there are periods of upturn and recession within such a stage of relative stagnation.

A new stage of accumulation – our seventh element – has always begun up until now with a long period of expansion that is eventually followed by a long period of stagnation. The concrete circumstances under which such turns from expansion to stagnation take place differ and have to be analyzed case by case. But such a turnaround occurs essentially because at a certain moment the inner conflicts of the capitalist mode of production can no longer be bridged over. Concrete expressions of this state of affairs are a steady decrease in the rate of profit, a stagnation of economic growth, and a concomitant increase of unemployment. As a consequence, the existing equilibrium in and between capital and labor and social movements and the set of institutions in place are put under new strains and begin to change. Periods of structural stagnation can therefore be interpreted as harbingers of transitions between different stages of accumulation, and occur when previous constellations of processes of accumulation and institutions that once positively reinforced each other become incompatible.

Finally, once economic stagnation has set in, a process of reorganization of the whole system begins. Any possible resolution of stagnant (or depressive) phases has as its basic preconditions a sharp rise in the rate of profit and a corresponding overhaul of outworn institutional forms. However, since, as we have seen, contingent outcomes of struggles and conflicts of interest co-determine the conditions, supporting structures and institutions of capital accumulation, there is no guarantee that a successful new ensemble will emerge. Since there is no automatic mechanism that leads to the passage from a stagnant to an expansionist period, it cannot be taken for granted that – even substantial – reorganizations of the business sector and institutions will usher in a new expansive phase. Incidentally, this also implies that there is no reason to expect a stagnant phase of a stage of accumulation to last any particular number of years, or that different long swings will have the same duration.

These elements together form a theoretical framework for analyzing and comparing different periods or stages in the development of capitalism. This framework will be used in the final chapter to analyze contemporary globalization.

5.5   SUMMARY AND CONCLUSION

In this chapter, we have constructed a framework in which to conceptualize stages of accumulation. The rationale for analyses at such an intermediary level – more abstract than detailed accounts of capitalism and more concrete than its general laws of motion – is that economic development is neither random nor completely determined by general laws and tendencies: different historical periods can be distinguished in social formations. The best-known description of specific periods in the history of capitalism is the theory of Kondratiev cycles, which were discovered and discussed as early as the 1920s. The (possible) existence of such cycles is also known in mainstream economics, thanks to Schumpeter, who gave them their name. But the deterministic role assigned to technological developments by the Kondratiev cycles theory makes it unsuitable in explaining contemporary globalization, since technological developments in themselves cannot account for the acceleration of economic internationalization during the last decades of the twentieth century.

Subsequently, three theories developed in the 1970s – the Regulation approach, the SSA approach and a variant of long wave theories – have been presented that allow for a non-deterministic understanding of distinctive periods or stages in the history of capitalism. It is remarkable that, notwithstanding differences among them, these approaches have a number of features in common. This has already made some degree of cross-fertilization possible.

Building on these approaches' common properties, a theoretical framework has been formulated in the final section that can be used to conceptualize different stages of accumulation. Our point of departure is that a theory of stages is needed to analyze contemporary globalization, because such a theory allows for the integration of historical changes in contingent regimes with specific institutional interrelations, against the backdrop of the basic requirements for reproduction of the capitalist economy.

With that aim, eight elements were developed in a framework for analyzing and comparing different periods of capitalist development and making sense of their dynamics and inner conflicts. There are, to begin with, general requirements for the reproduction of the capitalist system. However, capital accumulation is not simply an economic process. A wide range of institutions and social forces have to be taken into account in an understanding of how real economies operate. The concrete forms capitalism takes are therefore not defined exclusively by the necessities of accumulation, but dependent on the changing relationship of forces in and among capital, labor and social movements. These three elements together form the dynamic structure of the system.

It follows that while the concrete forms capitalism assumes are characterized by a dominant mode of functioning of capitalism, the trajectory of capitalist development is not predetermined. Social actors have a certain relative autonomy and the outcome of their struggles is of essential importance for the development of the profit rate and the specific evolution of production relations.

For an understanding of the development and alternation of stages, it is necessary to differentiate between two kinds of economic stagnation. In addition to periodic crises – the business cycle – there are also long periods of structural stagnation, which are characterized by a significant reduction in rates of accumulation and economic growth over a longer period of time. The latter are harbingers of transitions between different stages of accumulation, and occur when processes of accumulation and institutions run into serious problems. Concretely, a new stage of accumulation has always begun up until now with a long period of expansion that is eventually followed by a long period of stagnation. Such a turn from expansion to stagnation occurs essentially because at a certain moment the inner conflicts of the capitalist mode of production can no longer be bridged over. This results in a fall in the rate of profit, leading to a decrease in accumulation, stagnation of economic growth and employment creation, and changes in and a reconsideration of the existing relationship of forces in and among classes as well as economic, social, and political institutions. The resolution of stagnant (or depressive) phases has, therefore, as its basic preconditions a sharp rise in the rate of profit and a corresponding overhaul of former institutional forms.

Once economic stagnation has set in a process of restructuring begins, which may give way to a new stage of accumulation and a new expansionist phase. However, since contingent developments of institutions and outcomes of struggles co-determine the conditions, supporting structures and institutions of capital accumulation, there is no guarantee that a successful new ensemble will emerge. There is therefore no reason to expect that the expansive and stagnant phases of a long swing will last any specific number of years, or that long swings will have the same duration.

NOTES

1 Husson (1994) and Reati and Roland (1988) express this same opinion of the Regulation approach and long wave theory, but do not take the SSA approach into account.
2 See, e.g. Dicken (1998), van Duijn (1979), Kleinknecht *et al.* (1992) and OECD (1999).
3 Burbach and Robinson argue that claims of continuity at higher levels of abstraction risk becoming empty:

> If we break capitalism down into its most fundamental characteristics — the exploitation of labor by capital, commodity production, and the continued expansion of capitalism — then yes, nothing has changed. However, to take this view one could argue that nothing has changed since Columbus, or perhaps since the industrial revolution, if one defines the earlier period as mercantile capitalism.
>
> (Burbach and Robinson, 1999: 12)

4 Mavroudeas does not take this seriously when he denounces middle-range theories,

> particularly popular in periods when general-theoretical paradigms are in crisis'. Because 'of their inherently eclectic nature and their ability to conform with a wide

variety of more general theories and trends,' he says, 'they facilitate an accommodation between the previous theses of their contributors (albeit in a transforming fashion) and the new intellectual fashions.

(Mavroudeas, 1999: 323)

5 This is not only the case for capitalism. Fine and Harris (1979: 104–119) show that Marx periodized the history of feudalism, based on his understanding that modes of production give rise to distinct stages rather than to continuous trends.

6 See also Freeman and Louçã (2001). Similar observations are also made in other social sciences. Political scientist Gilpin, for example, explicitly refers to the same idea:

> (A)lthough a regularized, systematic and cyclical pattern of expansion and contraction may not exist, the modern world economy has in fact undergone a traumatic experience approximately every fifty years and has experienced alternating periods of rapid and slow growth. These massive swings up and down have affected mainly the price level; in some cases, however, they have entailed significant changes in economic output and in the rate of employment. Moreover, these erratic economic shifts have been global phenomena. Originating in the core economies, their effects have been transmitted through the market mechanism and the nexus of economic interdependence to the extremities of the planet, shattering individual economies and setting one economy against another as each nation has tried to protect itself against destructive economic forces. The periods of expansion and contraction have also been associated with profound shifts in the structure of the economic and political system.
>
> (Gilpin, 1987: 105)

7 Held teaches politics and sociology, McGrew teaches government, Goldblatt teaches social sciences, and Perraton teaches economics. Streeten, to give another example, argues in the same vein that it is impossible to make sense of globalization if one limits oneself to narrow economic phenomena and approaches:

> (W)e hear and read everywhere that interdependence among states (sometimes wrongly equated with integration) has increased dramatically. This can be seen in the spectacular growth of the trade-to-GNP ratio, which, for some countries, has doubled since the mid-1980s. It can also be observed in the globalization of production through foreign investment by transnational corporations; in the integration of international capital markets and portfolio investments; in the growth of international migration; and in the spread of cultural impulses such as television, styles in clothing, music, sport, sexual mores, and even crimes. At the same time there is a rise of religious fundamentalism and of the assertion of national identity by potentially 5,000 different peoples in the already proliferating 182 states. The main lessons are (1) that trade cannot be considered in isolation, but must be accompanied by an analysis of the flow of information, capital, people, and education and cultural impulses, in addition to monetary and fiscal policies; and (2) that economics no longer can be isolated from political science, philosophy, law and other disciplines.
>
> (Streeten, 1996: 354–355)

8 As Beniès argues:

> The new, post-Cold War world that is now being born is witnessing the emergence of a new era for capitalism, 'globalization', in which the old reference points have

disappeared and capitalism is the only credible perspective. This new world requires building a new theoretical framework.

(Beniès, 1998: 256)

9 Maddison reminds us that economists

generally devise more or less self-contained systems (to) explain economic development and do not like to give 'exogenous' events a major role. Some historians, by contrast, describe economic development as a chain of *ad hoc* events happening more or less by accident.

(Maddison, 1992: 28)

10 DeMartino argues that

forms of abstraction that treat the economy as a self-contained sphere of society, amenable to examination in isolation from non-economic factors, fail in principle to convey the complexity of economic events and the scope of economic possibilities. Just as all economic activities entail social and political relations, so are seemingly non-economic activities and practices shaped by economic processes.

(DeMartino, 2000: 83)

11 See, e.g. Kotz *et al.* (1994b).
12 See Barnett (1998). Although the idea that economic growth proceeds in a series of long cycles of approximately 50 years' duration is generally attributed to the Russian economist Kondratiev, he did not originate the idea. The Russian Marxist Parvus and the Dutch Marxist Fedder (pseudonym of van Gelderen) were earlier (see, e.g. Mandel, 1972: 108–145). On van Gelderen/Fedder, see also Kalshoven (1993).
13 On List see also Chapter 2.
14 See, e.g. Reati (1992: 255–256).
15 Kleinknecht, a renowned long wave researcher, holds that a new Kondratiev cycle probably began in the early 1993 or 1994: 'The gurus of the "new economy" have not studied enough economics. They do not know Kondratiev and the new literature about that. They rediscover the wheel and call it "new economy"' (Dikstaal, 2001: 47).
16 See Boonstra (2000), van Duijn (1998) and ING-Bank (2000). See also The Economist (1999).
17 The main problem is that 'statistical analysis of economic growth with regard to regular patterns requires the concept of cycle analysis. The analysis of cycles requires, on the other hand, the elimination of the non-cyclical or the so-called irreversible component of time-series, that is, the trend' (Metz, 1992: 82), which is not neutral for the final results. Underlining these difficulties, Metz came to almost diametrically opposite conclusions about the existence of long waves in his papers in 1992 (there is evidence) and 1998 (they have no meaning).
18 Shutt, however, overstates his cases when he writes that economics is 'inherently subject to the unpredictable actions and reactions of ever-changing human society.' If this were true that would preclude *any* social science.
19 When Boyer (2000a: 293) calls the appearance of Kondratiev-style cycles 'deceptive, since capitalism develops more in a spiral, never passing through the same configuration twice,' he echoes to a certain extent Trotsky's (1923) remark that if capitalism were characterized by reccurring cycles, 'history would never be anything more than a complex repetition, not a dynamic development.' (cited in Bensaïd, 1995: 67).
20 Freeman argues this point as follows:

Many long wave theorists argue that phases of expansion are sparked, in some way, by a semi-automatic or automatic process in which technical revolution, following Schumpeter's 'creative destruction', rekindles the dynamism lost in a previous long period of stagnation. This implicitly re-instates the factor of technology, which others take as exogenous, as a endogenous market phenomenon. When one reflects on this line of argument, one realizes it does not really address the problem. With enough equations we can make everything in the world a product of the market. But all we would do is define the market to include everything, and we would no longer have a theory of the market but a theory of society as a whole. If the 'market' is a distinct social institution, demarcated for example from government or at least aspects of government, then it should exhibit universal laws which apply under all governments. I want to be quite precise about what this endeavor consists of. The idea is not at all that the market operates independent of say, technology or politics. It interacts with them. But an interaction is not the same thing as an internal property or law.

(Freeman, 1999: 4)

21 See also Chapters 2 and 3.
22 As Dicken argues:

Technology is (. . .) not independent or autonomous; it does not have a life of its own. *Technology is a social process* which is socially and institutionally embedded. It is created and adopted (or not) by human agency: individuals, organizations, societies. The ways in which technologies are used – even their very creation – are conditioned by their social and their economic context.

(Dicken, 1998: 146)

23 Similarly Marx, who has often been accused of determinism, portrays 'technology more as an enabling factor than as an original cause, autonomous force, or determining factor' (Bimber, 1995: 95).
24 See, e.g. Mandel (1972, 1995) and Goldstein (1988).
25 See also Bensaïd (1995), Husson (1994) and Reati and Roland (1988).
26 While there is often truth in such criticisms, this can definitely not be said of Mandel, who consistently argued against such explicit or implicit presumptions in long wave theory (see, e.g. Mandel, 1992, 1995).
27 Incidentally, much of this criticism relies on interpretations of Marx's (1894) theory of the tendency of the rate of profit to fall as a theory of trend. Reuten (2002) shows that such an interpretation can hardly be based on Marx's own writings, since he developed the classical theory in this respect into a theory of cycles.
28 See, e.g. Aglietta (1997), Boyer (1987), Boyer and Saillard (1995a) and Verhagen (1993).
29 Jessop (1990) identifies seven different schools, which he categorizes in four approaches.
30 See, e.g. Verhagen (1993).
31 See, e.g. Kotz *et al.* (1994b).
32 McDonough makes a convincing case that

the social structure of accumulation approach developed by David Gordon and his collaborators is one of the legitimate heirs to the Marxian tradition of stadial theory begun at the turn of the century by Hilferding, Bukharin, and Lenin. This tradition held that the recovery of capitalism at the beginning of the twentieth century was due to a comprehensive society-wide reorganization of the institutional conditions of capitalist profitability. This new institutional configuration, involving political and ideological as well as economic institutions, formed the basis for the inauguration of a new stage of capitalism.

(McDonough 1999: 29)

He credits Gordon, and 'to a certain extent' Mandel, for recognizing 'a similar historical process taking place after World War II, creating a new postwar stage of capitalism.' McDonough also holds that with the intervention of Gordon, the Hilferding–Bukharin–Lenin

> theory of the highest stage of capitalism is transformed into a general theory of stages. This theory could then be applied to understanding the broad historical sweep of capitalist accumulation and crisis. Not incidentally, this perspective brings politics, ideology, and culture into the heart of the Marxist theory of capital accumulation.
>
> (McDonough, 1999: 29)

33 See, e.g. Verla (1987), Kotz (1994b), McDonough (1994) and Verhagen (1993).
34 See, e.g. Barsoc (1994), Husson (1994, 1996), Kotz (1994a), Kotz *et al.,* (1994b) and Reati and Roland (1988).
35 As Boyer argued:

> Structural crisis is any episode during which the very functioning of regulation becomes contradictory with the existing institutional forms, which in fact are abandoned, destroyed or passed around. More precisely, three features:
>
> • within the given mode of regulation, there exist no self-correcting mechanisms for the profit decline;
> • most of the institutional forms are destroyed;
> • way out of the trouble is not obtained by letting the economic mechanisms to play their role, since they are precisely coming into contradiction one with the other. Thus some strategic choice, made by leading firms, unions, governments are necessary to promote a new mode of development.
>
> (Boyer, quoted in Verhagen, 1993: 156).

36 For a systematic derivation of necessities and contingencies in capitalist economies, see Reuten and Williams (1989). As they put it,

> totality is an interconnected whole, and what it is is determined by phenomena which are necessary rather than contingent with respect to it. (...) The contingency of phenomena does not imply that there is no way of grounding them; the point is rather that the ground of their being is not internal but *external* to them, or exogenous. (...) In this sense, the contingent as such is non-essential to the totality of the existent (the object); or, to put it the other way around, the totality of the existent is indifferent to the contingent (which could be otherwise without changing the essence of the existent, that is its interconnectedness). So mere possibility is further determined as *necessity* by the derivation of its interconnectedness within the object totality. Indeed, interconnectedness then amounts to a circle of conditions of existence.
>
> (Reuten and Williams, 1989: 16; 24–25)

37 See also Chapters 1 and 3.
38 From the perspective of historical sociology, Shaw argues similarly:

> Understanding the major historical change of our own times (...) involves us in understanding the links between economic, cultural and political transformations, and between markets, state institutions and social movements. If they can be considered tasks for international political economy, they obviously involve understanding the field in the broadest sense. They bring into question the relationship between international political economy and other disciplines. In particular this proposal directs our attention towards the field's intersections with history and sociology. If global change is considered not just a set of relatively discrete processes, but as a profound and all-embracing transformation, then it takes us back to the foundations of our understanding of the modern world as well as forward to new ways of thinking.
>
> (Shaw, 2000: 230)

39 De Angelis (2000) argues, for example, that although recession generally weakens working class power this cannot be generalized. He points to the struggles of US workers and unemployed in the 1930s, which took place in the mids of the depression and forced a paradigm shift in economics and economic policy towards the postwar Keynesian order.

6 Globalization: a new stage of capitalism

There seems to be a widespread perception that the global economy now stands on the brink, but the brink of what remains the question.
(Bank for International Settlements, 70th Annual Report, 2000)

The aim of this chapter is to conceptualize economic globalization as a new stage of capitalism, which came into existence after the post-Second World War boom came to an end. The ensuing, unprecedented internationalization of the three circuits of capital has been accompanied by a rather one-dimensional internationalization of institutions and regulation. By way of conclusion it will be argued that the way global capitalism has changed since the end of the post-Second World War expansion has raised the profit rate but is not conducive to the emergence of a new global long boom with growth levels as high as those in the 1960s and 1970s.

Section 6.1 surveys central features of the restructuring of world capitalism since capitalism's golden years ended in the mid-1970s. Section 6.2 focuses more specifically on the requirements for accumulation laid out in Chapter 5 and analyzes the accelerated internationalization of capital, which has become a dominant feature of the world economy. Section 6.3 analyzes the internationalization of institutions and regulation, and the fourth section discusses whether a transnational state is being formed. Section 6.4 looks at the future of the global economy and briefly returns to the questions raised in the first chapter.

6.1 TRANSITION: THE RESTRUCTURING OF GLOBAL CAPITALISM

The accumulation regime that brought high levels of accumulation and growth to most parts of the world economy for almost three decades after the Second World War ran into serious trouble in the early 1970s. Worldwide, corporate profitability declined substantially from the mid-1960s to the early 1970s, dampening investment and resulting in a corresponding stagnation in aggregate output.[1] The theory of stages laid out in Chapter 5 would lead us to expect a transitional period of systemic restructuring once the expansionist period had ended and economic stagnation had set in.

This is indeed what happened. With the aim of pumping their profit rates back up, companies and their governmental allies began an offensive, whose contours are summarized as follows by Castells in his widely acclaimed trilogy on 'the information age':

> When the oil price increases of 1974 and 1979 threatened to spiral inflation out of control, governments and firms engaged in a process of restructuring in a pragmatic process of trial and error that is still underway in the mid-1990s with a more decisive effort at deregulation, privatization and the dismantling of the social contract between capital and labor that underlay the stability of the previous growth model. In a nutshell, a series of reforms, both at the level of institutions and in the management of firms, aimed at four main goals: deepening the capitalist logic of profit-seeking in capital-labor relationships; enhancing the productivity of labor and capital; globalizing production, circulation, and markets, seizing the opportunity of the most advantageous conditions for profit-making everywhere; and marshaling the state's support for productivity gains and competitiveness of national economies, often to the detriment of social protection and public interest regulations.
>
> (Castells, 1996: 10)

Firms reacted worldwide to falling profitability with new strategies, increasingly reliant on new information technologies, to reduce production costs (beginning with wage costs), increase productivity, expand markets and accelerate capital turnover. Governments turned from Keynesian to monetarist policies.[2] As a result, the institutional set-up of the postwar accumulation regime came under pressure, and institutional pillars that were functional in the postwar boom were put in question.

Rapidly increasing unemployment and increasing international competition played a crucial role. The huge rise in unemployment had an impact above all on the mode of accumulation and the mode of organization of social relations. In times of almost full employment, wage earners are in a position of strength; improvements can be won more easily and the threat of worsening conditions is easier to ward off. A rise in unemployment leads to a weaker union movement, which gives employers the nerve to take the offensive and begin undermining wage earners' rights and gains. So, rapidly rising unemployment was used, as in earlier periods of history, to impose lower wages and more work on those who had not (yet) lost their jobs. Employers also began to reorganize labor processes, imposing more flexibility in working hours and the wage system.[3] They launched a permanent process of restructuring, often including as an important element contracting out of work that was not – or no longer considered to be – part of their 'core business'.[4]

So, as soon as the expansive phase was over, national compromises with unions and governments, which in the previously existing institutional framework had generally been advantageous for capital, began to be perceived as an obstacle to the measures needed to raise the rate of profit. Less money was spent on concessions to wage earners, since there was less need for it as a result of the changed relationship of forces between capital and labor. The postwar agreement was as it were unilaterally abrogated. A prolonged period of struggle began among companies, unions and governments, with far-reaching liberalization, deregulation, privatization, and dismantling of social security and the public sector as major aims.[5]

This made the 1980s the decade of the so-called 'crisis of the welfare state'. A start was made with major reductions in social spending, as Keynesian policies were buried and replaced by a monetarist policy geared at maintaining price stability. 'Liberalization,' 'more competition' and 'more market' became core concepts in the new hegemonic paradigm among politicians and economists and in (international) policy institutions. As Castells (1996: 20) records, '(r)estructuring proceeded on the basis of the political defeat of organized labor in major capitalist countries, and the acceptance of a common economic discipline by countries of the OECD area.'

Not only in the OECD countries, we should add. On 6 October 1979 the new chairman of the US Federal Reserve, monetarist Paul Volcker, announced that it would drastically restrict the money supply in order to curb rapidly accelerating inflation. Other central banks followed and the result of these restrictive monetary policies was the generalized recession in 1980–1982. For many Third World countries this recession marked the real beginning of their troubles. As inflation declined, real interest rates skyrocketed on loans that they had easily obtained.[6] At the same time their possibilities for economic growth declined drastically as a result of the new recession. The result was the debt crisis. In 1982, Mexico was the first to announce that it could not meet the payments on its foreign debt; other countries followed.[7] This and subsequent debt crises have been used by creditor countries and international organizations to impose the end of protectionist measures and import substitution strategies and to open up markets in the South to trade, capital flows and investment in production facilities in exchange for new loans.[8] Palast (2002) has characterized the policies prescribed to these countries as the 'Four Horsemen of neoliberal policy: liberalized financial markets, reduced government, mass privatization and free trade.'[9]

The extension of potential markets thus obtained is one of the major changes that have taken place in the international division of labor. Another is the change in the position of the US, which until the early 1970s was the world's dominant economic, military and political power. Its position had begun to come under pressure as soon as Japan and Western Europe rebuilt their economies, but grew even shakier as international competition intensified because of economic stagnation. The collapse of the Bretton Woods framework in the early 1970s meant not only the end of a more or less stable international monetary system, in which exchange rates could only be changed in exceptional circumstances, but also the end of controls on cross-border capital flows. In reaction to the protectionism of the 1930s, the postwar international system was geared mainly towards expanding trade. In order to maintain the fixed exchange rates considered necessary for this purpose, national economies were sheltered to a certain extent from the rest of the world.[10] The existence of fixed exchange rates protected currencies from short-term fluctuations on the world market. At the same time countries kept a number of tools available to regulate international capital flows to a certain extent, through controls on cross-border capital transactions. Keeping these tools in reserve was a major element of the Keynesian conception of an active, interventionist state.[11] The end of the Bretton Woods system knocked these policy instruments out of governments' hands, as borders were opened to an immense increase in international capital flows with all their destabilizing consequences.

Finally, there was of course another fundamental change in the world that had major consequences for the evolution of capitalism. The fall of the Berlin Wall and the subsequent collapse of bureaucratic regimes in Eastern Europe and the Soviet Union in the early 1990s rapidly opened up an extensive area that had previously been closed off. This brought new prospects for investment, trade, production and sales.[12] The fall of the Wall did not only lead to the introduction of capitalist relations of production in Eastern Europe and the former Soviet Union; the tidal wave that swept across the world and successfully opened more and more Third World countries to capital and exports could also spread with fewer hindrances because there was no longer any 'real world' alternative to the International Monetary Fund (IMF), World Bank and financial markets.[13]

All in all, the restructuring of global capitalism that has taken place since the mid-1970s has not just led to a substantial increase of firms' profitability, but also to a new configuration of capitalism.[14] To get a feel of the scope of changes that have taken place, it is illuminating to briefly look at the modifications in what were considered pillars of the postwar productive order.

6.1.1   Taylorism

In general, the application of new communications technology and new management techniques in companies and institutions has changed the organization of labor or put it under increasing pressure, weakening employees' position and labor organizations.[15] Nevertheless, talk of 'the end of Taylorism' is only partially justified. New management techniques with a greater emphasis on teamwork (sometimes called 'Toyotist'), while widespread, are still far from universal. Also 'the triumphalist discourse in the creation of "high tech" jobs does not appear well founded' (Wilno, 2000: 30). In many expanding sectors, in fact, hierarchical management structures, rigid divisions of labor and repetitive work are overwhelmingly dominant.

6.1.2   Fordism

A fundamental break must be noted with 'Fordism' in the broad sense of the term, meaning the parallel, mutually reinforcing growth of production, labor productivity and working-class consumption. These postwar linkages have been pulled apart since the early 1980s. Increased productivity is no longer translated more or less automatically into increased working-class consumption.[16]

6.1.3 Keynesianism

As was outlined earlier, Keynesianism has become discredited among most economists and policymakers and only variants of neoclassical, pro-market policies are acceptable within the reigning economic consensus.[17] Key elements of the new orthodoxy are that monetary policy has to be used to control inflation, that governments have to balance their budgets and not use them to stimulate demand, and that unemployment is due to imperfections of the labor market and not to a lack of demand (Grieve Smith, 2002: 8).[18]

6.1.4 Hegemony of the USA

Absolute US economic hegemony, as it existed in the first decades after the Second World War, is a thing of the past. But predictions that Europe or Japan would take over the US' economic role, or that the world economy risked paralysis in the absence of a global hegemonic power, have turned out to be unwarranted, at least in the early years of the twenty-first century. Taking advantage of the dollar's central role, the growing openness of the world economy and the strength of the North American economy, the US has increasingly managed to reclaim its position as the world's most important economic and military power.[19] So, although the Bretton Woods system has collapsed, the world has not become leaderless.

Because of the changes in the world economy and the introduction of new information technologies, international organizations and policymakers have become quite upbeat about the world economy's future.[20] Their optimistic scenario is that a new global long boom – 'where world GDP growth could be in the 4 per cent per annum range and might lift world per capita GDP growth rates above the 3 per cent mark' (Michalski *et al.*, 1999: 8) – is around the corner. In a joint document, the IMF, OECD, UN and World Bank argue, for example, along these lines, setting out a set of policies they consider necessary for growth sufficient to reduce poverty drastically:

> Globalization offers enormous opportunities for the developing countries – better ways of tapping the world's knowledge, better technology for delivering products and services, better access to the world's markets. But taking advantage of the opportunities requires action. Countries have to lower their tariffs and other trade barriers and streamline their systems for the flow of imports, exports and finance. They also have to manage their inflation, interest and exchange rates – to be seen as good places for doing business. And they have to maintain consistent policies – to be credible to investors, both domestic and foreign. The high-income countries have their part to play too – reducing

tariff and other trade barriers to imports from developing countries and providing assistance to build the capacity to trade effectively.[21]

(IMF, OECD, UN and World Bank, 2000: 22)

But why proponents of the canonical policies of protecting internationalizing capital and capitalist relations expect such policies to lead to a new long global boom in the near future remains a mystery.[22] The long global boom does not seem to have begun so far, after all, despite two decades of neoliberal policies. True, the restructuring of world capitalism since the end of the post-Second World War long boom has had an impact on profitability. International organizations and financial analysts have reported that profit rates have increased to levels comparable to those of the late 1960s.[23] But it is remarkable that this upswing in the rate of profit has not given rise to a new global boom with increased worldwide economic growth.[24] The IMF's *World Economic Outlook* (1999b: 3) documents 'an average growth rate of world output in the 1990s of only 3 per cent, below the average growth rate of the 1980s (3.5 per cent) and the 1970s (4.5 per cent).'[25] Weisbrot *et al.* (2000) conclude from growth per capita data of 116 countries that the 'growth slowdown of the last two decades was a worldwide phenomenon.' They calculate that countries for which data were available had an (arithmetical) average rate of growth of output per person for the period 1980–2000 of 33 per cent, while for the period 1960–1980 this was 83 per cent. Growth has especially slowed in the less developed countries. Easterly (2001: 135) of the World Bank calculates that 'in 1980–1998, median per capita income growth in developing countries was 0.0 per cent as compared to 2.5 per cent in 1960–1979.'[26]

The connections among accumulation, rising productivity, economic growth and consumption that were characteristic of the postwar period have been broken. But at the turn of the century they had not been replaced by a new self-reinforcing positive dynamic. Lower growth on average, growing inequality, and financialization of the global economy (leading to short-termism and financial instability) make Boyer's expectation (1995) that 'bad capitalism' tends to drive out forms of 'good capitalism' seem more plausible than optimistic visions of an immanent global long boom that will be advantageous for all.[27]

In sum, our survey in this section shows the magnitude and depth of the changes that have taken place since the end of capitalism's so-called golden years. A period of systemic reorganization, which began with the onset of a period of lower average growth rates, has resulted in across-the-board liberalization, deregulation, privatization, dismantling of social security and the public sector, and a turn from Keynesian to monetarist policies. In addition, liberalization and deregulation of financial markets since the end of the Bretton Woods system have undermined the margins for independent policy choices on a national level. Profitability has subsequently increased and new markets have been opened, but contrary to expectations and previous experience, this recovery of profit levels has not given rise to a new global long boom with a high level of growth. The following sections will take a closer look at the internationalization of capital and institutions, and regulation.

6.2 AN UNPRECEDENTED INTERNATIONALIZATION OF CAPITAL

When the postwar productive order had lost its momentum and the long expansion ended, a period of reorganization began. One ensuing major change is the acceleration of international economic transactions. National states, which were previously rather autonomous, have faced what Boyer (2000a: 288–289) describes as 'a growing extroversion,' which is the consequence of the extension of world trade, variable exchange rates and the increasing number of financial innovations intended to create more 'globalized' markets. This means for Boyer that 'modes of regulation which were very largely autonomous have been increasingly subjected to the ups and downs of the international economy, over which national governments have little hold'.

Since the mid-1970s the world economy has rapidly become much more internationalized. Four developments stand out as especially important.

First, an increase in the number of really integrated global markets for goods and services, and especially for finance. This implies that the calculations behind economic decision making must take global conditions and prices into account. Since the 1980s, international trade in goods and services has on average increased twice as fast each year as world output; and as far as trade orientation is concerned, the world economy has never been as open as it is today.[28] But financial markets are doubtless the most globalized markets, and financial globalization and the corresponding increase in speculation have been spectacular. Deregulation and financial innovations – in 1980 financial futures, swaps and options still hardly existed – have significantly increased the economic weight of financial markets. Bond markets, stock markets and currency markets are connected – and mutually dependent – worldwide to an extent that has never been seen before in history. While it was still possible in the early 1970s to speak of national financial markets, this is no longer the case.

Second, the role and weight of multinationals in the world economy has increased immensely.[29] Companies prefer to plan and organize the conception, production, and distribution of their products and services not only regionally or bi-regionally but globally, with major consequences for their structures. Thanks to new information technology, production is increasingly being organized on an international scale. This implies for Standing that

> there is a *long-term* trend towards a single, borderless economy, which is being cemented by the trade liberalisation and the dismantling of tariff and non-tariff trade barriers under the aegis of the Uruguay Round and the World Trade Organization (WTO).[30]

> (Standing, 1999: 64)

The number of enterprises operating internationally is growing immensely. In 1999, according to UNCTAD (2000c: xv), there were 63,000 of such companies with at least 690,000 foreign affiliates. As an indication of their importance,

UNCTAD (2000c: xv–xvi) calculates that sales by foreign affiliates worldwide – $14 trillion in 1999, compared with $3 trillion in 1980 – are now nearly twice as high as global exports. The gross product that can be associated with international production was approximately 10 per cent of global GDP at the end of the twentieth century, compared with 5 per cent in 1982. Finally, Vernon (1998: 10) gives still another indication of multinationals' growing role in the world economy: 'the biggest couple of thousand of these companies account for about half the world's trade in goods, with about two-thirds of their trade taking place between related units of the same enterprise.' The significance of these data is magnified by the fact that the biggest internationally operating companies are operating mainly in world economy's most dynamic sectors, such as electronic products, chemicals, automobiles, drugs, machinery, and increasingly also in services such as banking and telecommunications. In sum, multinational companies have expanded considerably, both in number and in size, and gained in influence. The biggest companies' annual sales now dwarf the annual GDP of most countries in the world.[31]

Third, there has been a far-reaching globalization of a certain type of macroeconomic policies. This can be seen from the fact that variants of the same policy prescriptions are being followed – or pushed through, with the help of international organizations and the discipline imposed by 'the financial markets' – in all parts of the world. Creditor countries seized upon the 1980s debt crisis, for example, to end import-substitution strategies in the South and open Southern markets to trade and investment. Key elements of economic policies in the East, West, North and South are (a combination of) export-oriented growth, less governmental social policies, reduction of the public sector, deregulation, flexibilization, privatization, and priority to price stability.[32]

Finally, there is a trend towards more regional and global economic cooperation among countries.[33] One expression of this trend is the increased role and weight of supranational organizations, such as the G7, IMF, WTO, BIS and OECD. Another is the multiplication of regional agreements and blocs, such as the EU, NAFTA and MERCOSUR. Many analysts and observers expect such international bodies and forms of cooperation to steadily gain importance and coordinate and take over functions previously performed by national states. More international cooperation seems a logical step for governments increasingly losing control over their own territories as a result of the internationalization of markets for goods, services and finance, companies, and economic policies.

Each of these features of contemporary internationalization taken separately is significant. Combined, they represent a break with the world as we knew it during the post-Second World War golden years. But the question has to be posed whether these developments represent a qualitative change. It is here that the concept of the 'circuit of social capital' becomes of great significance. As we saw in Chapter 4, the analytical decomposition of this circuit into three separate – but indivisible – circuits of money capital, commodity capital and production capital allows for a differentiation of degrees of internationalization.

If we look at the current global economy from this perspective, there are three important observations to be made.

First and the most important, we can observe for the first time in history a combined internationalization of trade, finance and production.[34] As outlined in Chapter 4, internationalization of economic processes does not automatically involve the three circuits of capital in the same way. In the decades before the First World War, which are often compared with contemporary globalization, only trade and finance were strongly internationalized. While the combination of international trade and international capital flows is therefore not new, the accelerated internationalization of production capital since the early 1980s adds a new dimension to contemporary globalization, one that is without precedent.[35] So, although the world economy is still far from being as globalized as theoretically possible, there is now for the first time in history an increasing internationalization of all three circuits of capital.[36]

As we have seen, Ricardo held that international mobility of capital would undermine an essential assumption of his theory of comparative advantage from international trade.[37] Subsequently, Keynes and others argued that the combination of free trade and free movement of capital reduces the national states' ability to decide their own fate.[38] The addition of international production capital signifies that a qualitative new stage of internationalization has been reached.[39] All the more after the transformations in Eastern Europe and China, capitalism has become truly global for the first time. Capital now has more leverage than ever over national states, being able – if considered necessary for profitability – to (threaten to) move goods and services, finance, and/or production facilities to pressure national and/or regional constituencies into more capital-friendly policies.[40]

Second, in contrast with capitalism's golden years, 'the dynamism of direct investment has supplanted that of trade, and in its turn financial capital is piloting the redeployment of productive capital' (Boyer, 2000b: 289).[41] In the words of Bello *et al.* (2000: 4–5), the globalization of finance means 'that increasingly its dynamics serve as the engine of the global capitalist system'. This implies among others that it is now under certain circumstances more profitable to accumulate financial assets than to invest in real projects (Altvater, 2001: 74–75).

A central feature of the dominance of finance is the coming into existence of global norms for yields and profitability. This happens because

> (b)anks draw and place funds within an essentially globalized payments system, and the terms on which they do so are externally determined. Central banks certainly have some influence on the day-to-day price of these funds, but this influence is tightly constrained and has to be exercised in a way that does not threaten the stability of bond yields. Bonds are not only globally traded but also globally priced, and bond yields establish a reference point, for an marketed credit instrument.
>
> (Grahl, 2001: 35–36)

The fact that external finance still provides only a relatively small fraction of corporate investment resources, Grahl argues, does not mean that the effects of these developments are small, because (o)nce industrial borrowers begin to take the external costs of capital as the key hurdle for investment projects, and their customary creditors start to regard yields on organized asset markets as a base-line rate of return, then market terms and costs will inevitably start to be internalized – even if insider finance continues to prevail in a quantitative sense. Increasingly, to the extent that external finance is determined on the market, these terms and costs will be a matter of global forces.

(Grahl, 2001: 36)

Finance capital has become dominant and financial norms, promoting shareholder value, affect companies' mode of functioning and the distribution of income and wealth.[42] Shareholder value, Grahl explains,

is not – or not only – an ideology, but a real consequence of financial globalization. It represents a new balance of forces between proprietors and managers, very much in favour of the former. And it is driven not only by the as yet very limited cross-border market in equities, but also by the global transformation of currency and debt markets in ways which universalize these pressures, even in economies where equity itself is traded predominantly among domestic agents.

(Grahl, 2001: 40–41)

The ascendancy of finance has major consequences for nation-states' maneuvering room. As a result of financial deregulation after the break-up of the Bretton Woods agreement, most transactions in exchange markets are now speculative, and exchange rates depend on capital flows rather than trade flows.[43] Chesnais (1997a: 297) speaks about a 'globalized regime of accumulation with financial predominance,' which is definitely more constraining for states and more homogenizing than the post-Second World War 'Fordist accumulation regime'. Consequently, the space for different modalities of countries' participation in the international system has been gradually reduced. The opening up of national financial markets since the mid-1970s, which meant a radical break with the postwar regime, was of course a precondition for these changes.[44]

Finally, and also as a caveat in the face of (too) schematic interpretations, it must be stressed that there are no firewalls between the three circuits, and that the three types of capital are in reality often intermingled. As Bryan (1995b: 427) points out, 'mobility of capital occurs within as well as between individual capitals'. Since the mid-1970s the distinction between financial institutions and manufacturing companies has become hazier. Many companies now work with advanced financial management techniques, and multinationals like Ford, General Motors, Toyota and General Electric have major divisions or subsidiaries that compete with banks. A number of multinationals is earning more through financial transactions than by producing and selling the products that once made their fortunes.[45]

For a full understanding of how momentous the current internationalization of trade, finance and production is, still another dimension must be taken into account. Not only is capital extending capitalist social relations to more and more people and more and more aspects of people's lives, so as to be able to accumulate; this process also entails an expansion of the scale of production through the growth of individual capitals (*concentration of capital*) and the extension of command over capital via agglomeration of existing capitals, that is by way of mergers and acquisitions (*centralization of capital*).[46] The magnitude of this difference of scale is clearly visible in the following comparison by UNCTAD between the global mergers and acquisitions (M&A) boom at the turn of the millenium with a similar boom in the US a century earlier:

> Both M&A waves have been affected by major technological developments, new means of financing M&As and regulatory changes. But while the recent wave is an international one, the older one was confined to the United States. And just as the earlier boom in the United States contributed to the emergence of a national market for goods and services, and a national production system, complemented by a national market for firms, so is the current international boom reinforcing the emergence of a global market for goods and services and the emergence of an international production system, complemented by an increasingly global market for firms.
>
> (UNCTAD, 2000c: 19)

This development is clearly of great importance. Absolute and relative size make a big difference to the options available to companies that are involved in international trade, finance and/or production, and to their leverage over local, regional and national communities, authorities and interest groups.[47] To caricature a bit: 63,000 multinationals operating in two or three countries each, with a negligible size compared to these countries' GDP, have much less weight and influence than a couple of thousand multinational companies concentrated in the most dynamic sectors of the world economy, which together account for half the world's trade in goods. As we have seen, the latter is currently the case.

This state of affairs is the outcome of a long process of international concentration and centralization of capital. Before the end of capitalism's golden years, Mandel (1972: 310–342) distinguished three stages in this evolution:

- The early capitalist era of so-called free competition: relative international immobility of capital. Concentration remained predominantly national and centralization exclusively so.
- The era of imperialism: an increasing international concentration of capital, but hardly international centralization of capital. As competitive struggles among the big imperialist powers and fights for control over geographical zones intensified, national monopolies were pitted against each other.[48]
- The decades after the Second World War: the international concentration of capital started to develop into international centralization, as multinational companies became more and more the determinant form of big capital.

The trend towards increasing international concentration and centralization of capital accelerated after the end of the postwar productive order.[49] This is exemplified by the rapid growth in both number and size of the biggest multinationals – the companies involved in international trade, international finance and/or international production.[50]

In sum, the reorganization of the system that began after the end of the golden years has given rise to an unprecedented internationalization of the three circuits of commodity capital, money capital, and production capital, and to a concomitant accelerated internationalization of the concentration and centralization of capital.[51] In the process, finance capital has become dominant. The next section investigates to what extent institutions and state functions have also been internationalized.

6.3   ONE-DIMENSIONAL INTERNATIONALIZATION

The particular set of institutions that supported the expansionary phase after the Second World War ran out of steam in the mid-1970s. Worldwide, corporate profitability declined from the mid-1960s on, reducing accumulation and GDP growth. Since then sales, finance and production (all three circuits of capital), as well as the concentration and centralization of capital, have been internationalized to an extent that has never been seen before in history. As we saw in Chapter 5, there is no spontaneous symmetry between the general requirements for accumulation and institutional developments. The relationships of forces in and among capital, labor and social movements co-determine the concrete forms and contents of regulation and state functions. Section 6.1 showed that the restructuring of worldwide capitalism since the mid-1970s has proceeded on the basis of a reduction of the power and influence of organized labor in major capitalist countries and a narrowing of space for national development projects in the South. Fundamental changes in the conditions of accumulation have drastically shifted the relationships of forces to the benefit of capital, which has taken advantage of sharply increased unemployment and the debt crisis. The development of state functions and regulation reflects these shifts.

The unprecedented internationalization of capital since the mid-1970s has been accompanied by a rather one-dimensional globalization of regulation and governance. As Grant argues:

> The 1980s have seen an accelerating process of economic globalization, but a relatively limited development of political structures that can regulate this process. Indeed, the best developed mechanisms of governance that exist at the supranational level are intra- and interfirm: coordination within the new 'stateless firms' (. . .), and between firms through such devices as joint ventures and cartels. The chief executives of stateless firms claim with some justification that their enterprises 'change relations *between* companies. We function as a lubricant for worldwide economic integration' (. . .).

However, firms are not well placed to act as agents of international governance, particularly if the insertion of public policy objectives in the
decision-making process is thought to be desirable. International firms
create the need for improved international governance, but they do not and
cannot provide it.

(Grant, 1997: 319)

Concretely, the post-golden age world has seen a multiplication of attempts and
proposals to promote, establish or redefine the tasks and forms of (existing)
international organizations. But in light of the changed relationships of forces and
the predominance of market-oriented policies, it is no surprise that the most
serious initiatives have concentrated on encouraging and facilitating internationalization of the three circuits of capital: international trade, international finance
and international production.

To begin with, the World Trade Organization (WTO) was founded to guarantee the extension of international trade.[52] Policymakers, economists, international
organizations, and corporate lobbies use the comparative advantage theorem to
present the increasing globalization of trade as being in the interest of all
countries and peoples. International agreements therefore strongly discourage
tariff and non-tariff restrictions on cross-border trade, or outlaw them outright,
everywhere and in all situations, almost as a matter of principle.[53] As outlined in
Chapter 1, social movements and people's organizations increasingly challenged
the WTOs authority and jurisdiction at the end of the twentieth century, with
demands that included prioritizing social and ecological needs over expansion of
international trade.

Second, innumerable proposals have been made since the crisis broke out in
Asia for reorganization of what is called the 'international financial architecture'
and of the IMF in particular.[54] Policymakers, economists, international organizations such as the World Bank, and corporate lobbies present unrestricted international financial flows as conducive to global welfare, because they supposedly
give rise to an efficient allocation of financial means; they therefore promote
unrestricted financial flows all over the world. As was indicated in Chapter 1,
social movements from the North and South challenge this reasoning, pointing
among other things to the social effects of the Asian crisis and the structural
instability of globalized financial markets as a result of short-termism, herd
behavior, and contagion.[55] These problems are worrisome not only to critics of
globalized finance but also to its supporters, because as Aglietta (2000: 57)
argues, 'no central bank, not even among the most important, has today the clear
mandate to take responsibility for the stability of the whole of the global
financial system'. Therefore, 'in the absence of a lender of last resort, whose
actions result from a well-defined political cooperation, the risk is to be
confronted with situations in which the diagnosis of monetary authorities diverge
and contradictory interests lead to inactivity in front of a spreading crisis.'[56]

Finally, the last half of the twentieth century has seen a multiplication of
initiatives to stimulate and facilitate international production. As was outlined

above, the accelerated internationalization of the circuit of productive capital is a more recent phenomenon than the internationalization of trade and finance. This is reflected in what Estrella Tolentino (1999: 190–191) describes as the absence of international institutional structures to deal with multinationals and foreign direct investment (FDI): '(A) truly comprehensive set of rules at the global level has yet to emerge despite a long process of international rule building since 1948'. In the evolution of instruments dealing with transnational companies (TNCs) three phases can be identified since 1948, the last two decades of the twentieth century being the third:

> (T)he dominant approach regarding international rules relating to TNCs over the past two decades has been the promotion or facilitation of FDI expansion by defining the responsibilities of countries towards foreign investors. This shift was manifested in a marked tendency towards liberalization at the national level of host government policies towards TNCs since the early 1980s.[57]
>
> (Estrella Tolentino, 1999: 182–183)

Again, while policymakers, economists, international organizations and corporate lobbies argue that international production by multinationals is in everybody's interests, these companies have increasingly come under attack.[58] The best known example of this critical mood is the failure of attempts by the Organization for Economic Cooperation and Development (OECD) to codify and harmonize the rights of investing companies all over the world in a Multilateral Agreement on Investment (MAI). As Braunstein and Epstein (1999: 127) argue, the MAIs proponents failed to convince skeptical social movements – and in a country like France broader public opinion – of the treaty's benefits, 'often simply falling back on ideological or tautological claims.'

The powerful initiatives to encourage and facilitate the internationalization of trade, finance and production have not been accompanied by policies to globalize social rights, the provision of public goods, democracy, and environmental norms. International organizations promoting such policies are weak or hardly existent, and despite voluminous proof of the opposite the dominant claim is that 'free markets' will produce good social outcomes.[59] It is therefore no wonder that

> the mood of resistance to globalisation has visibly stiffened and sharply escalated. Among other factors, it has been spurred on by the highly visible social deficit caused by unfettered global market forces and civil society's growing scepticism that the existing global order can survive without major reform (...).
>
> The basic problem is that there is no provision at the global level for elementary social justice. The provision of social goods globally and other non-income objectives.
>
> (Drache, 2001: 2)

6.4 TOWARDS A TRANSNATIONAL STATE?

Few observers would disagree with the observation that today 'there does not exist – and will not exist for a long time – a supranational state that centralizes and comprises all the functions that were previously served by the various nation-states' (Boyer, 2000a: 296). But this diagnosis leads to two questions about the role and future of the state. First, will national states continue to be important structures within the international economic system, or is the increasing inter-nationalization of capital making nation-states redundant? Second, is the increasing international concentration and centralization of capital giving way to a reorganization of the relationship between dominant capitalist states, resulting in some form of *ultra-imperialism* or *super-imperialism*? Neither question is new; each has been discussed before in different contexts.

The rationale for the first question is what Murray (1971: 105–108) during a similar debate two decades ago called the 'growing territorial non-coincidence between extending capital and its domestic state.' Since then this contradiction has become much greater, and many politicians, journalists and researchers have in response declared the state (virtually) dead. Held, McGrew, Goldblatt and Perraton christen this position 'the hyperglobalist thesis,' which they summarize as follows:

> For the hyperglobalizers, globalization defines a new epoch of human history in which 'traditional nation-states have become unnatural, even impossible business units in a global economy' (...). Such a view of globalization generally privileges an economic logic and, in its neoliberal variant, celebrates the emergence of a single global market and the principle of global competition as the harbingers of human progress.
>
> (Held *et al.*, 1999: 3–5)

However, the idea that states can just fade away and leave the functioning of capitalism to 'the' market is totally untenable. The nation-state is definitely 'an historically specific form of world social organization' (Robinson, 2001: 1), but it nevertheless fulfills a number of economic functions that are indispensable for the reproduction of capitalism. These functions do not necessarily have to be – nor have they always been – executed by the 'mother states' of capital, but they have to be taken care of somehow.

At the time Murray (1971) listed the following six state functions: (1) guaranteeing property rights; (2) economic liberalization; (3) economic orchestration; (4) input provision (labor, land, capital, technology and economic infrastructure); (5) intervention for social consensus; (6) management of a capitalist system's external relations. We should now add at least a seventh to take account of the collapse of the then still functioning Bretton Woods system and the immensely increased weight of the financial sectot: (7) guarantor of the stability of the banking system (lender of last resort; supervision).

One can discuss whether all these functions still have the same weight today, but the main point to note is that capital requires a number of public functions to be performed. However, the capital's home government need not necessarily undertake this. The domestic state where capital originates from may do so, but there are alternatives, such as, foreign state structures, capital itself either singly or in conjunction with other capitals, or state bodies in cooperation with each other.

To make this point more concrete, let us look briefly at the present condition of the global economy from this perspective. With the collapse – and increasing integration into the capitalist world – of the former COMECON bloc and China's growing opening to foreign capital, point 6 is not a major concern at the moment. The same seems to be the case for point 4, although the structural decrease of public expenses, for example, education and transportation will have negative consequences in the longer term for the quality of labor, physical infrastructure and technological developments. On points 1 and 2, internationalizing capital has in general strengthened its position since the beginning of the 1980s, but increasing discontent with globalization, manifested in the impossibility of implementing the MAI and growing criticisms of the WTO, makes clear that these gains are neither unchallenged nor irreversible.

There are great difficulties with points 3 and 7, as reflected regularly in debates about the role and functioning of the IMF and in disagreements and conflicts of interest between the USA, the European Union and Japan over synchronization (or lack of it) of monetary and macroeconomic policies. Murray's (1971: 108) observation that there is 'a tendency for the process of internationalization to increase the potential economic instability of the world economy at the same time decreasing the power of national governments to control economic activity even within their own borders,' seems more true today than when he made it.

Finally, the lack of legitimacy (point 5) of the current mode of functioning of the global economy is a major weakness, because it is indissolubly linked to its results and effects. Thirty years ago, Mandel (1970: 22–23) invoked the *law of uneven and combined development* to make the point that imperialism, 'although it unites the world *economy* into a single world market, ... does not unify world *society* into a homogenous capitalist milieu. (...) (I)t maintains and strengthens to the utmost the *differences* between (these) societies.' Today this is even more the case. Almost no one denies any more that social differences have grown among countries and almost without exception within countries.[60] Since this increasing divergence is the opposite of the benign outcome that proponents of economic globalization hold out to countries and peoples that are willing to go along with the dominant economic prescriptions, the social consensus capitalism calls for is way out of reach.

So, while capital is increasingly internationalized, essential state functions are currently not being performed either by nation-states or by international institutions and collaborations of states. A prolonged period of trial and error so as to shift and reorganize responsibilities and tasks between national and international levels is the most likely perspective, with all sorts of conflicts because interests are divergent. This process has no predetermined outcome. Nation-states will definitely not disappear in the foreseeable future: 'at this point in history, the fading away of the nation-state is a fallacy' (Castells, 1997: 307). But neither will the current status quo last forever: 'we are not witnessing "the death of the nation-state", but its transformation' (Robinson, 1996a, b: 19). There are powerful pressures for mutations. And regional and global reorganizations ahead or already under way, such as the increasing economic integration of the European Union, will have significant implications for the organization of states.

This brings us to the second question: is the increasing international concentration and centralization of capital giving way to a reorganization of the relationship between dominant capitalist states, resulting, for example, in ultra-imperialism or super-imperialism? To begin with, this question is not new. As we have seen in Chapter 2, it has been discussed before, at the beginning of the twentieth century in debates about the character of imperialism, and also at the beginning of the 1970s in a controversy about the future relationship between the USA and Europe (Rowthorn, 1971; Mandel, 1972). This should make us beware of impressionistic conclusions. In addition, current developments are contradictory and have not yet matured, so that sweeping generalizations risk being outdated before they are printed.

For Burbach and Robinson (1999: 27), the 'open-ended and unfinished' process of globalization has by now evolved into a configuration where '(f)or the first time in history (...) we can speak of transnationalization of capital, a world in which markets are truly global and integrated. Capital ownership of the leading enterprises is also internationalized, with shareholders or financial institutions from various parts of the world being able to move their stockholdings in and out of any number of corporations and countries.' The extent to which this is today really the case is certainly open to debate,[61] but very few researchers would nowadays deny that there is a tendency – which is, incidentally, being challenged, and open to reversal – in that direction.

Burbach and Robinson go one step further when they argue that 'transnational class formation' is occurring and that a 'transnational capitalist class' (TCC) is emerging. Robinson and Harris (2000: 21) follow the logic of this argument to its conclusion with the thesis that economic forums such as the IMF, World Bank, WTO, G7 and OECD constitute 'an incipient TNS (transnational state) apparatus in formation.'[62] Since they also register the dominant role of finance capital,[63] their perspective is very reminiscent of ultra-imperialism – that is, a situation in which 'the international fusion of capital has advanced so far that all critical differences of economic interest between the capital owners of different nationalities disappear' (Mandel, 1972: 332).[64]

These different authors present their arguments for a TCC and TNS as no more than a tendency, and point to many contradictions and conflicts of interest that may block the future evolution of such a global-state-in-the-making.[65] But they do seem certain enough about the coming trajectory of the global economy to exclude other possible international structures explicitly (US dominance) or implicitly (continuing competition among blocs). But events so far hardly warrant such a choice. The two other models that were under consideration in past debates are not only still not excluded but also are in fact at least as likely.

First there is the case for super-imperialism – a situation in which 'a single imperialist power possesses such hegemony that the other imperialist powers lose any real independence of it and sink to the status of semi-colonial small powers' (Mandel, 1972: 331). Making the case for a form of super-imperialism today means of course arguing that the USA will become such a hegemonic power. Considering the relative strength of the US economy, the international role of the dollar, the extension of the dominance of shareholder value via globalized financial markets and US global military leadership,[66] it would be unwise to exclude this possibility.

The same is true for a third model, continuing competition among blocs. This would mean that, 'although the international fusion of capital has proceeded far enough to replace a larger number of independent big imperialist powers with a smaller number of imperialist super-powers, the counteracting force of the uneven development of capital prevents the formation of an actual global community of interest of capital' (Mandel, 1972: 332–333). Such an outcome can also not at all be excluded, given the dynamics of European integration and uncertainties about future developments in Asia (a bloc around Japan? what future role for China?).

To conclude, the acceleration of the internationalization of capital that has taken place since the end of the postwar expansion has not been paralleled by a similar internationalization of state functions. The idea that nation-states will disappear in the foreseeable future is therefore mistaken: states are not dying but changing. But neither will the present situation last. The disconnection between the increasing globalization of capital and the lukewarm internationalization of states and state functions is a major flaw of today's global economy, and attempts at reorganization are therefore inevitable. But since there are many conflicts of interest, the outcome is not predetermined: three models – a transnational state, US dominance, and continuing competition among blocs – are for the moment equally (un)likely.

6.5   WHITHER THE GLOBAL ECONOMY?

It is of course quite possible that the one-dimensional internationalization of regulation described in this chapter will proceed further, because it is after all instigated by and advantageous for capital. But as increasing support for movements against (the consequences of) contemporary globalization shows, the dilemma faced by the IMF, WTO and MAI – or similar treaties and organizations in the future – is that international organizations and regulations have to be effective as well as legitimate.[67] And as long as international regulation and governance is mainly directed towards facilitating expansion of international trade, international finance and international production, their effectiveness – no matter how well developed in itself – continually risks being undermined by their lack of legitimacy. It is therefore a serious deficiency that the increased internationalization of capital is not matched by a similar internationalization of provision of (global) public goods, guarantees of (global) democratic rights, establishment of a (global) civil society, transnational democracy, and protection of the (global) environment by international state-type organizations and institutions.[68]

To repair this shortcoming, a number of economists and international organizations have put forward programs for what we can call a 'global social contract' or 'new global compromise'. Their approach begins from the notion that the sustainability and credibility of globalization is not guaranteed under present conditions, but conditional on the fulfillment of a number of proposals to amend or improve the organization and functioning of the globalizing economy.[69] The social-democratic International, for example, calls for 'redefinition of the role of the Bretton Woods institutions' and 'a global recovery program promoting investment, trade, income, and employment'. It is of the opinion that '(t)o regulate globalization and to globalize regulation is not only a matter of concern to international financial institutions. It should be the means for a new international order, which can reinforce democracy and promote solidarity' (Socialist International Council, 1998).[70]

The International Labor Organization (ILO) is even more ambitious: 'If trade unions and other groups concerned with social and economic progress are to mitigate the serious problems and maximize the potential benefits provided by the new economic framework, it will require concerted action and support from international organizations with a mandate to promote socially sustainable economic growth' (Kyloh, 1996: 15). Consequently, the ILO promotes five sets of policies at different levels, for what it calls the 'governance of globalization': (i) Rebuilding strong trade unions and promoting collective bargaining. (ii) Multinational agreements, codes of conduct and social labeling. (iii) Influencing macroeconomic policy and promoting full employment. (iv) Influencing coordination of economic and social policies. (v) International labor standards.

Taken individually these proposals are not very radical. And excepting the last point, one cannot fail to notice their resemblance to what was more or less general practice during the golden years. However, in the present relationship of forces the combination is rather ambitious, because their implementation would imply a confrontation with the vested interests behind the internationalization of the three circuits of capital and their facilitating international institutions. As trade unions and other social movements have already discovered, these and similar proposals, such as the four global contracts that have been suggested by the Group of Lisbon (1996), are thus very difficult to enact.[71] The cumulative outcome of decades of deregulation and internationalization of trade, finance and production is a global configuration in which countries, peoples, communities, movements and organizations are permanently put in competition with each other – or threatened with competition from each other – for investments, jobs and welfare provisions – or inversely but with similar consequences, to pick up the bill for the provision of global public goods. Rodrik, therefore, argues that commentators are 'on to something' when they note that

> (g)overnments today actively compete with each other by pursuing policies that they believe will earn them market confidence and attract trade and capital inflows; tight money, small governments, low taxes, flexible labor

legislation, deregulation, privatization, and openness all around. These are the policies that comprise what Thomas Friedman (...) has aptly termed the Golden Straightjacket.

(Rodrik, 2000: 182–183)

Contemporary globalization has in this way created a global prisoner's dilemma that will be hard to break out of, even if the political will to do so becomes much greater than it has been so far.[72]

It is becoming more and more clear that the economic and institutional changes that have taken place in global capitalism since the mid-1970s have not only been insufficient for a new global growth regime, but are even countterproductive for such a perspective. The rise in inequality of income and wealth in and among countries since the end of the post-Second World War boom has become functional for the world economy, which is increasingly oriented towards the provision of luxury goods for the well-off and the short-termism of the financial sector. Widening social differences and uneven growth have thus become characteristic of the new accumulation regime.[73] As Durand (2000: 21) puts it, the current mode of accumulation of capital is 'geographically and socially exclusionary'. The implementation of new technologies 'comes up against a commodity logic that impoverishes their social effects.' The mode of social regulation 'functions on a mode of denial,' because public services and social protection are being cut back everywhere. And the international division of labor, which is to the benefit of vested interests, 'is founded on a profoundly unequal development and restores the most classic imperialist processes.'

This balance sheet of the restructuring of global capitalism since the mid-1970s raises the problem of a further delay of the dawn of a new global golden age. Wilno (2000: 34) suggests three reasons for this. First, the limitation of markets because of wage restraints in the advanced countries and structural adjustment policies in many countries of the South and East. Or as Greider (2001: 23) argues: 'Too many producers, too few consumers in a global system where too many workers cannot afford to buy the things they make – that's the central contradic- tion.' Second, there is a lack of congruence between social demand and the supply of commodities oriented by profit, and third the fragility of a macro-economic set-up that is largely dependent on the financial markets.

There is no inherent reason why capitalism cannot continue to function in this way for a prolonged period. But in the longer term the biggest weakness of a productive order that is not giving rise to a new global long boom with a high level of growth, and that is structurally incapable of distributing the fruits of its success in an egalitarian manner, is its increasing lack of legitimacy.[74]

In sum, the unprecedented internationalization of capital since the end of the golden age has been accompanied by important institutional changes that have facilitated the international expansion of trade, finance and production. Although the weight and role of international organizations such as the IMF and WTO have been strengthened, growing support for movements against (the consequences of) contemporary globalization points to the fact that international organizations and regulations have to be legitimate as well as effective. As long as international regulation and governance are one-sidedly directed towards facilitating expansion of international trade, international finance and international production, their effectiveness continually risks being undermined by their lack of legitimacy. Several international organizations and economists have, therefore, advanced programs for a 'global social contract' or 'new global compromise'. However, trade unions and other social movements have discovered that such proposals are very difficult to enact; contemporary globalization has created a global prisoner's dilemma that will be hard to break out of.

For the moment, prospects for a new worldwide long boom are dim. The rise in inequality of income and wealth in and among countries since the end of the post-Second World War boom has become functional for the world economy, which is increasingly oriented towards the provision of luxury goods for the well-off and the short-termism of the financial sector. The biggest weakness of this new productive order is its increasing lack of legitimacy.

6.6 CONCLUSION

By way of conclusion, we return briefly to the three puzzles that were posed in the first chapter as starting points for a new round of analyses and debates. Given that technology is not driving globalization, what is? Will globalization continue and spread, and if so under what conditions? And will globalization lift all boats in the long run, or are policy interventions and institutional changes necessary in order to bring about such a favorable outcome?

To begin with, our analysis showed that globalization is being driven by increasing internationalization of the three circuits of capital – international trade (*the global marketplace*), international finance (*the global casino*) and international production (*the global assembly-line*) – and the concomitant, increasing international concentration and centralization of capital. This characteristic of contemporary globalization, which distinguishes it from previous periods of international economic integration, has been a major contributor to the break-up of the institutional pillars of the postwar productive order, and is propelling further globalization.

The snowballing internationalization of capital has not been accompanied by a similar internationalization of state functions, however. In so far, as initiatives have been taken in that direction, they have focused on encouraging and facilitating international trade, international finance and international production, not on globalization of social and democratic rights, environmental norms, and provision of public goods for all. Under current conditions a favourable outcome that would 'lift all boats' is therefore extremely unlikely if not excluded.[75]

Finally, what does all this mean for the future of globalization? Even without globalization of social and participatory rights, contemporary globalization may well continue and spread. But this will only remain possible as long as, and in so far as countries and peoples can be bullied into accepting it. In Rodrik's words (2000: 185): 'One alternative possibility is that an ongoing series of financial crises will leave national electorates sufficiently shell-shocked that they willingly, if unhappily, don the Golden Straightjacket for the long run. This scenario amounts to the Argentinization of national politics on a global scale.' Obviously, this would not be a very healthy basis for further progress of globalization. Rodrik therefore considers it likely that 'governments will resort to protectionism to deal with the distributive and governance difficulties posed by economic integration.'

There is, however, a third, more promising possibility. The upshot of this analysis is that there are compelling reasons to doubt the compatibility of global equality, sustainability and democracy with increasing internationalization of trade, finance and production. The international movements that were mentioned in the first chapter were only the first contingent of the growing ranks of skeptics and dissenters from the dominant paradigm that theoretically and ideologically underpins contemporary globalization.[76] There is, therefore, hope that ideas, coalitions and broader public support for a different kind of globalization will gain strength and that the seeds of an alternative vision will sprout and mature.

NOTES

1 The rate of profit for the countries of the G7 went from 22.4 per cent in 1965 via 20.3 per cent in 1970 to 16.4 per cent in 1975 (OECD, 1994: Annex).
2 For Teeple (2000: 76), the abandonment of Keynesian policies, which were 'reflective of the interests of national capital in an age of late industrialization of Fordism,' was a result of the fact that they 'had lost their meaning as a philosophy of national economic management when the internationalization of capital began to undermine the economic policies of the nation-state.' As he sees it, 'the coming of monetarism did not represent a failure of Keynesianism, as some would argue, so much as a change of circumstances.' Monetarism 'represented the policies required by internationalized capital in a global economy, an arena in which political compromise with national working classes was a declining issue.' The turn to monetarism therefore 'represented the abandonment of national policies,' and 'the introduction of laissez-faire conducive to international capital, to competition at the international level, and to the levelling of conditions of national economies to standards of a common denominator.'
3 As Standing, senior economist at the International Labour Office, notes:

> The notion of 'labour market flexibility' has been a key euphemism of the last quarter of the twentieth century. It is not a neutral term: it is a euphemism for more than could be conveyed by any definition. Yet it prompts an image. Who could be against being 'flexible' or in favour of being 'inflexible'. Even more dubious uses of the term have been common. In many international reports and statements by public figures, calls for flexibility have been little more than ill-designed masks for proposals to lower wages or work protection. One claim or presumption of those who advocate more flexibility is that regulations, legislation, institutions and conventions apparently designed to protect workers and their families are often counter-productive, primarily because they raise unemployment. It is this that has given the topic of flexibility such a high profile.
>
> (Standing, 1999: 49)

4 See, e.g. Smith (1994, 2000).
5 The magnitude of the changes that took place is described a bit provocatively by George:

> In 1945 or 1950, if you had seriously proposed any of the ideas and policies of today's standard neoliberal toolkit, you would have been laughed of the stage or sent off to the insane asylum. At least in Western countries, at the time, everyone was a Keynesian, a social democrat or a social-Christian democrat or some shade of Marxist. The idea that the market should be allowed to make major social and political decisions; the idea that the State should voluntarily reduce its role in the economy, or that corporations should be given total freedom; that trade unions should be curbed and citizens given much less rather than more social protection – such ideas were utterly foreign to the spirit of the time. Even if someone actually agreed with these ideas, he or she would have hesitated to take such a position in public, and would have had a hard time finding an audience.
>
> (George, 2000: 27)

6 Western banks, who had had to find something to do with their 'petrodollars,' had among other things gladly lent to credit-hungry Third World governments.
7 See Solomon (1995: 193–273) for a description of the emergence of this debt crisis, the potential consequences for hundreds of Western banks, and the measures taken by the main industrialized countries' central banks and the IMF to prevent an international crisis of the financial system.
8 On the import substitution strategies, see also Chapter 2.
9 See Palast (2001) for the criticisms of these policy descriptions by Joseph Stiglitz, World Bank's former senior economist and winner of the 2001 Nobel Prize in economics.
10 See also section 3.1 of Chapter 3 on the macroeconomic policy 'trilemma'.
11 As Simmons argues:

> (G)overnments of the advanced industrialized nations have used capital controls as a key tool of economic policy. In the face of collapsing financial markets and downward spiraling trade, capital controls were employed primarily to try to stabilize currencies and prevent capital flight. (...) After World War II, however, a clear and distinctive justification for maintaining capital controls was articulated in both Britain and the United States: they could be used by governments to manage the domestic economy. (...) Thus, after World War II, a tight matrix of capital controls was continued in many countries of the OECD, and these were viewed not only as an instrument of exchange rate stabilization, but as a means to secure full employment and other national economic priorities. (...) Far from ensconcing principles of capital market liberalization parallel to those in the postwar institution for trade, the Bretton Woods agreement condoned capital controls not only for short-term management of balance-of-payments crises, but also for purposes of domestic economic management.
>
> (Simmons, 1997: 37–38)

12 But as Rigacci argues,

> We can say that up until now the Chinese market, the Russian market or that of the countries of Eastern Europe have not constituted a significant outlet for the products of the industrialized countries. It is true that Chinese imports have grown notably in the 1990s (from 50 to 150 billion dollars), but exports also increased (from 60 to 180 billions). Result: China enjoys a large trade surplus. As to Russia and other countries of Eastern Europe, they have rather registered a slowing up in

their trade. Conclusion: the countries of the former Soviet bloc and China remain, in the whole, marginal in relation to the world economy.

(Rigacci, 2000: 28)

13 Hutton (Giddens and Hutton, 2000: 11) argues that the former Soviet Union 'did have one good impact; it kept capitalism on its guard – in a sense it kept it aware that it had to have a human face'. Wilno holds that

> the collapse of the USSR which, although there were no tears to shed over what no longer constituted an alternative to capitalism, represented a considerable ideological victory for the latter, freeing it from any necessity of providing its legitimacy not only in the economic but also in the social arena.
>
> (Wilno, 2000: 34)

Another aspect was the support the Soviet Union sometimes used to give to Third World countries. This was of course not charity but a means of preserving its own sphere of influence, was (thus) not very reliable, and came with political strings attached. But sometimes it was better than nothing. Countries like Cuba lost an ally, major trading partner and economic patron almost overnight when the USSR collapsed.

14 As Castells argues:

> In capitalist economies, firms and governments proceeded with a number of measures and policies that, together, led to a new form of capitalism. It is characterized by globalization of core economic activities, organizational flexibility, and greater power for management in its relation to labor. Competitive pressures, flexibility of work, and weakening of organized labor led to the retrenchment of the welfare state, the cornerstone of the social contract in the industrial era. New information technologies played a decisive role in facilitating the emergence of this rejuvenated, flexible capitalism, by providing the tools for networking, distant communication, storing/processing of information, coordinated individualization of work, and simultaneous concentration and decentralization of decision-making. (...) In spite of a highly diversified social and cultural landscape, for the first time in history, the whole planet is organized around a largely common set of economic rules. It is, however, a different kind of capitalism than the one formed during the Industrial Revolution, or the one that emerged from the 1930s Depression and World War II, under the form of economic Keynesianism and social welfarism. It is a hardened form of capitalism, but it is incomparably more flexible than any of its predecessors in its means.
>
> (Castells, 1998: 357–358).

15 See, e.g. Coutrot (1998) and Gadrey (2000).

16 See, e.g. Hoang-Ngoc (1996), Husson (1996, 1999a, b) and Teeple (2000).

17 To give an example of how far this consensus went: Yergin and Stanislaw record that the German Christian Democrats

> adopted a program in 1947 which declared that 'the capitalist economic system' has failed 'the national and social interests of German people' and instead called for public ownership of the commanding heights and a 'considerable' degree of central planning 'for a long time to come.'
>
> (Yergin and Stanislaw, 1998: 33)

18 See, e.g. DeMartino (2000), Pollin and Zahrt (1997) and Sengenberger (1996).

19 See, e.g. Achcar (1998), Brenner (1998) and Gowan (1998).
20 According to a study by the Central Intelligence Agency (2000: 34), e.g. the 'global economy is well-positioned to achieve a sustained period of dynamism through 2015. Global economic growth will return to the high levels reached in the 1960s and early 1970s, the final years of the post-World War II "long boom".' Another example is IMF economist Mussa:

> (T)he prospect is that the process of global economic integration – which is being driven by essentially irresistible forces of technological advance – will take place through voluntary means. People around the world will decide to participate – through trade, through movements of people and capital, and through assessing information and taking advantage of new technologies – because they see the benefit to them of such participation. Unlike too many unfortunate episodes in the past, participation in the global economy will not occur at the point of a sword or facing the muzzle of a gun. This, perhaps more than anything else, provides the reasonable assurance that the fundamental forces that are driving global economic integration are, in fact, driving the world toward a better economic future.
>
> (Mussa, 2000: 19)

See also OECD (1999).
21 Similarly, the G7 heads of state committed themselves at their first meeting in 2001 to attain the United Nations target of halving global poverty by 2015. As the *Financial Times* (19 February 2001) notes: 'The target, which includes other goals such as universal primary education, was agreed in the early 1990s but has largely been seen as an aspiration rather than a policy guideline.'
22 Significantly, the International Fund for Agricultural Development (IFAD), a United Nations Agency, declared in its Rural Poverty Report 2001 (www.ifad.org) that the pledge to halve poverty by 2015 is doomed to failure: 'Progress in reducing rural poverty has stalled. In the 1990s, it fell to less than one-third of the rate needed to meet the United Nations' commitment to halve world poverty by 2015.' Similarly, OXFAM (2000: 10) calculated that the actual rate of poverty reduction on the world from 1990 to 1998 was less than one-third of what would be required to meet the 2015 target.
23 See, e.g. Duménil and Lévy (2000, 2001) and Husson (1999a).
24 See also Husson (2001). Economic developments in the US at the end of the twentieth century have sometimes been presented as the beginning of such a turnaround. But even the US economy in the 1990s

> did not remotely compare to that of the first *three* decades of the post-war era. Even during its supposedly epoch-making *four-year* economic expansion between 1995 and 1999, the business economy as a whole was unable to match its *twenty-three year* economic expansion between 1950 and 1973 in terms of the average annual growth of GDP (4.0 per cent versus 4.2 per cent), labour productivity (2.5 per cent versus 2.7 per cent) or real wages (2.1 per cent versus 2.7 per cent), or the rate of unemployment (4.7 per cent versus 4.2 per cent).
>
> (Brenner, 2001: 37)

25 In case the difference between these growth figures seem marginal, one way to illustrate that 1.5 per cent makes a big difference is to look at the implication of this extra annual growth for the number of years necessary to double total world output. With 3 per cent annual growth total world output doubles in a bit less than 24 years. With 4.5 per cent annual growth this takes roughly 16 years.

26 'In Latin America, GDP per capita grew by 75 per cent from 1960 to 1980, whereas from 1980 to 1998 it has risen only 6 per cent. For sub-Saharan Africa, GDP per capita grew by 36 per cent in the first period, while it has since *fallen* by 15 per cent' (Weisbrot *et al.*, 2000: 2).

27 Significantly, Crafts (2000: 52) also expresses such doubts in an IMF Working Paper: 'Finally, it should be recognized that the analysis in this section is quite skeptical of the projections of future growth performance that international organizations such as OECD seem to favor.'

28 See, e.g. Kitson and Michie (2000, Chapter 4).

29 This is not to say that big companies are now footloose. For a healthy dose of skepticism about such claims, see, e.g. Ruigrok and van Tulder (1995a), Doremus *et al.* (1998) and van Tulder *et al.* (2001).

30 These developments are outstandingly documented in the *World Investment Report* published yearly by UNCTAD.

31 See Went (2000: 18–20) for a list of the world's top 100 economies in 1998 (companies' sales and countries' GDP).

32 The same applies to the shock therapies in the East in the 1990s, see also George (2000).

33 See, e.g. Cohn (2000).

34 This development is sometimes epitomized in social movements by the trinity of the global market, the global workshop (or global assembly line), and the global casino.

35 The use of information technology allows for a reduction of intra-firm and inter-firm information costs and transaction costs, permitting

> multinational corporations to disperse their global production activities to a far greater extent than was hitherto possible and what emerges as a result is a correspondingly larger number of export platforms in an integrated system of production spread across a variety of different countries. 'Foreign affiliates', that is to say, 'no longer need to be freestanding and miniature versions of parent firms. Rather, they can fulfil specialized tasks in the framework of a global intra-firm division of labour, and trade the results via international communication networks' (UNCTAD, 1996: 106)
>
> (James, 2001: 157–158).

36 As DeMartino (2000: 160) argues, this was different during the post-Second World War 'golden age': 'By fixing capital (geographically, industrially), the state stripped the firm of the option of "exit" in pursuit of profits.'

37 See Chapter 2.

38 See Chapter 3.

39 Many 'still view global competition through the 200-year-old eyes of Adam Smith and David Ricardo, who saw trade as the chief form of economic exchange,' Quinlan and Chandler (2001) argue, but foreign direct investment 'has grown faster than either world output or global trade' since the 1970s, and companies from the US, Europe and Japan now sell many more goods and services abroad through their foreign affiliates than by exporting.

40 As Terry McDonough pointed out to me, there is now in a more meaningful sense an international capitalist class, an international working class and an international reserve army of labor.

41 See, e.g. also Bello *et al.* (2000), Boyer (2000a), Chesnais (1997a, b), Gowan (1998) and Robinson and Harris (2000). van der Pijl (2001: 12–13) argues that the 'regression from the emerging productive world economy to financial speculation' is one sign 'that a crisis of exhaustion is threatening a global society held together by capitalist discipline.'

42 See, e.g. Coutrot (1998, 1999), Cutler and Waine (2001) and Froud *et al.* (2001).

43 As Webber and Rigby (2001: 261) note, 'large capital inflows fuel rising asset prices, which tend to stimulate currency revaluations even as they tend to increase the trade deficit. Currency values and trade deficits are thus increasingly moving in non-orthodox directions, tending to increase disequilibrium.' See also Patomäki (2001).

44 The analysis of Bryan goes in the same direction:

> What makes the current period distinctive, is that the impact of "internationalisa-tion" is more pervasive than cross-border flows. There is a breaking down of the difference between cross-border and domestic flows, for they are all becoming subject to the same calculation. So in addition to cross-national resource flows, and more importantly, recent internationalisation is reflected in the impact of international forces on domestic resource uses. This impact is somewhat more nebulous than resource flows, for it involves an interpretation of the extent to which domestic resource uses are influenced by and subject to international movement of capital. Or, in sum: The mobility of money has served to subject all activities involving money to an international criterion of profitability.
>
> (Bryan, 1995a: 13, 61)

45 This raises a question, Nitzan and Bichler argue: how are we

> to classify conglomerates such as General Electric, DaimlerChrysler, or Philip Morris, which operate in hundreds of different sectors across the entire spectrum from finance, through raw materials, to trade, production, entertainment, advertising and distribution? Moreover, diversification has practically broken the functional connection between profit, which is reported in *business firms*, and industrial classification which is based on the *type of production* (. . .). The result is that the very meaning of "industrial", "commercial" and "financial" profit is no longer clear. For instance, in the national accounts, "manufacturing" profits denote the earnings of firms whose largest *single* line of business, measured in sales, is manufacturing. But if, as often is the case, manufacturing represents only a small part of such sales, the result is that the bulk of "manufacturing profit" in fact comes from lines of activity *other than manufacturing*! And the problem does not go away even if we limit ourselves to an individual firm. The difficulty here is due to non-arm's-length, intra-firm transactions and "transfer pricing". For example, if GE Capital subsidizes GE's jet-engine division by supplying it with cheap credit, the result is to lower profit in the former and raise in the latter, without any change in production and sales.
>
> (Nitzan and Bichler, 2000: 81–82)

46 See, e.g. Foley (1986) and Mandel (1972).

47 The following example shows why this issue is not only important for economically underdeveloped countries:

> The question, though, is whether Finland is becoming too dependent on Nokia. The company accounts for well over 20 per cent of Finland's exports, about a third of R&D expenditure, and is predicted to have generated about a quarter of the country's economic growth of nearly 6 per cent in 2000. Moreover, nearly all of Finland's biggest taxpayers work at Nokia and the company accounts for a staggering 70 per cent of the market value of the Helsinki Stock Exchange. (. . .) But many small and medium-sized companies depend on Nokia's continued suc-cess. And with slowing growth in demand for mobile phones and uncertainties surrounding the development of the mobile internet, Nokia is going to have to work hard to maintain its pre-eminence. "We have to hope that Nokia has made

the right decisions on technology," says Mr. Kotilainen' head of forecasting at the Research Institute of the Finnish Economy (Etla).

(*Financial Times* 3-1-2001)

48 See also Chapter 3.
49 As consecutive, World Investment Reports of the authoritative UNCTAD testify. In its 1993 report UNCTAD (1993: 98) analyzes, for example, the causes of the cross-border 'mergers-and-acquisitions boom' of the 1980s, while the 1999 report (UNCTAD, 1999: 94–101) discusses the specific characteristics of the 'present wave of M&As,' noting that '(t)he number and value of total cross-border M&As worldwide increased dramatically in 1998 over those in 1997'. See also the comparison earlier in this section between the contemporary global merger wave and an earlier US merger wave in the World Investment Report 2000.
50 As argued before, there are no firewalls among the three circuits, and two or all three types of capital are in reality often integrated in one company.
51 The notion that national markets and the so-called national 'Fordist compromises' became a straightjacket for firms and investors desperate for higher profits at the end of the postwar boom is generally accepted among long swing researchers. Nor is there disagreement about the results of the ensuing changes – which have been quite positive for capital in general: 'By extending its global reach, integrating markets, and maximizing comparative advantages of location, capital, capitalists, and capitalist firms have, as a whole, substantially increased their profitability' (Castells, 1996: 85).
52 See, e.g. also Nadkarni (1999).
53 See Chapter 2.
54 See, e.g. Eatwell and Taylor (2000), Eichengreen (1999), Harris (1999) and Michie and Grieve Smith (1999).
55 See, e.g. Bello *et al.* (2000). One of the two global scenarios to 2020 that are presented in a remarkable study by Shell (2002: 34) is the 'relatively unbridled capitalism of *Business Class*,' which 'leads to highly volatile markets. There are many short-term crises, and in weaker economies these have long-lasting effects.' On the economics of this scenario, which is basically a continuation of contemporary globalization, the study argues:

> In general, the global economy continues on its path of liberalisation and integration in spite of the increased inequality and volatility that results from economic integration. This is a world of economic peaks and valleys, prone to speculation and 'bubbles'. The logic of global capitalism leads to a relentless pursuit of efficiency, which, in turn, leads to high polarisation and volatility because capital and high quality labour move quickly to where the profits are made – the rich get richer because they're better placed to take advantage of opportunities. There are frequent, herd-like capital flows – one year, capital pours into local start-ups, the next everyone invests in China.
>
> (Shell, 2002: 36)

56 To cure these grave deficiencies Eatwell and Taylor (2000) propose the inauguration of a new organization, the World Financial Authority.
57 As DeMartino (2000: 14) also notes: 'Since the early 1980s in particular, nations across the globe have reduced or entirely rescinded all sorts of performance standards and other restrictions on foreign corporations in hopes of attracting investment, employment and income.'
58 One intriguing example is an opinion poll by *Business Week* (2000c), which showed that nearly three-quarters of North Americans believe that business has gained too much power over their lives.

59 Typical examples can be found in the supplement *The Economist* produced to counter criticisms of globalization:

> But the starting point for all liberals is a presumption that, under ordinary circumstances, the individual knows best what serves his interests and that the blending of these individual choices will produce socially good results. Two other things follow. The first is an initial scepticism, at least, about collective decision-making that overrides the individual kind. The other is a high regard for markets – not as a place where profits are made, it must be stressed, but as a place where society advances in the common good.
>
> (*The Economist*, 2001: 4)

60 One not so obvious example is Michalsky *et al.* (1999: 9) of the OECD Secretariat, who write: 'Inequality within and between nations has, from a number of perspectives, increased.'
61 See, e.g. Held *et al.* (1999), Hirst and Thompson (1996), Ruigrok and van Tulder (1995a, b) and Went (2000).
62 See also van der Pijl (1999).
63 Correctly, in my opinion, See also Chesnais (1997a, b, 1999).
64 A similar perspective is proposed by Castel (1998), who argues that ultra-imperialism is taking shape, and by Yaghmaian (1998), who proposes that '(a) supranational state (though tenuous and riddled with contradictions) is in the making, with a mandate to (de)regulate the conditions of accumulation on a worldwide basis by removing the national regulation of accumulation.'
65 Robinson and Harris (2000: 50) stress among others the essential point that '(n)o emergent ruling class can stabilize a new order without developing diverse mechanisms of legitimation and securing a social base.'
66 See Achcar (1998) and Gowan (1998).
67 See also Chapter 1.
68 On global public goods, see, e.g. Kaul *et al.* (1999). On transnational democracy, see, e.g. Giddens and Hutton (2000). On both issues see also DeMartino (2000).
69 Castells (1997: 253) argues, for example, that '(o)nly a global social contract (reducing the gap, without necessarily equalizing social and working conditions), linked to international tariff agreements, could avoid the demise of the most generous welfare states.'
70 The blatant discrepancy between fine statements of this kind and the actual deeds of many of the organizations that issue them should not go unmentioned.
71 Many will for that reason support Castells' gloomy conclusion (1997: 253) that 'a far-reaching social contract is unlikely.'
72 This is also the case with proposals to fundamentally alter the international monetary system, such as the one suggested by Guttmann:

> The emerging global accumulation regime requires an additional layer of management and regulation, based on new multilateral arrangements and international policy-making institutions. One of the most pressing issues in this transformation is the replacement of our current multicurrency system with a new kind of universal credit-money that provides the world economy with sufficient liquidity and balanced adjustments.
>
> (Guttmann, 1994: 427)

73 As Mishel, Bernstein and Schmitt show in their authoritative study on the US:

> Income inequality continued to grow in the 1990s, though at a slower rate than in the 1980s. Between 1989 and 1999, the share of total income received by the

> bottom 20% of households fell 0.3 percentage points, while the share received by the top 5% grew from 17.9% in 1989 to 20.3% in 1999. Income inequality continued to grow even during the boom in the second half of the 1990s. From 1995 to 1999, the real incomes of low-income families, or families in the 20th per centile, grew 2.6% each year, the same as for families in the middle (60th per centile) but far slower than the 3.5% rate for families at the top (95th per centile).
>
> (Mishel *et al.*, 2001: 3)

74 Many commentators and participants are aware of this. Yergin and Stanislaw (1998: 390) argue, for example,: 'Excessive concentration of wealth will undercut the legitimacy that a market-oriented system requires,' and they quote Peter Drucker, who warnes for a 'backlash of "bitterness and contempt" against the rich in the United States.' And Schrempp (2001: 6), chairman of the management board of DaimlerChrysler, one of the biggest multinationals in the world, argues that 'there are dangers in dismissing all critics of globalization as irrelevant or completely superficial'. Leaders in business and politics 'must not ignore the have-nots' and

> perhaps the developed world needs to ask itself today, can we afford another Marshall Plan? And maybe the question should be, can we afford not to have another Marshall Plan, to build political, economic and civil institutions that promote social equity and stability?
>
> (Schrempp, 2001: 8)

75 Similarly, Rodrik (2000: 185) argues that the likelihood of a new worldwide 'bargain,' guaranteeing global public goods and 'highly participatory political regimes,' is small.
76 See, e.g. Aguiton (2001) and Klein (2001).

Bibliography

Achcar, G. (1998) The strategic triad: the United States, Russia and China. *New Left Rev.*, **228**, 91–127.

Achcar, G. (ed.) (1999) *The Legacy of Ernest Mandel*. London: Verso.

Adam, C. (1998) In A. Levy-Livermore (ed.) *Internationalization and Integration of Financial and Capital Markets*.

Aglietta, M. (1982) World capitalism in the eighties. *New Left Rev.*, **136**, 5–41.

Aglietta, M. (1997) *Régulation et Crises du Capitalisme* (nouvelle édition revue et corrigée, augmentée d'une postface inédite). Paris: Éditions Odile Jacob.

Aglietta, M. (1998) Le capitalisme de demain. *Notes de la Fondation Saint-Simon* No. 101.

Aglietta, M. (2000) Comment stabiliser la finance globalisée? (interview). *Alternatives Economiques*, hors-serie No. 45.

Aglietta, M. and Moatti, S. (2000) *Le FMI de L'ordre Monétaire aux Désordres Financiers*. Paris: Economica.

Agosin, M. and Ffrench-Davis, R. (1996) In M. Ul Haq, I. Kaul and I. Grunberg (eds) *Managing Capital Inflows in Latin America*.

Aguiton, C. (2001) *Le Monde nous Appartient*. Paris: Plon.

Albelda, R. and Tilly, C. (1994) In D. Kotz, T. McDonough and M. Reich (eds) *Towards a broader vision: race, gender, and labor market segmentation in the social structure of accumulation framework*.

Albo, G. (1997) In L. Panitch (ed.) *A World Market of Opportunities? Capitalist Obstacles and Left Economic Policy*.

Albritton, R., Itoh, M. Westra, R. and Zuege, A. (eds) (2001) *Phases of Capitalist Development. Booms, Crises and Globalizations*. Houndmills, Basingstoke: Palgrave.

Altvater, E. (2001) In L. Panitch and C. Leys (eds) *The Growth Obsession*.

Altvater, E. and Mahnkopf, B. (1996) *Grenzen der Globalisierung*. Münster: Westfälisches Dampfboot.

Amable, B., Barré, R. and Boyer, R. (1997) *Les Systèmes d'innovation à l'ère de la globalisation*. Paris: Economica.

Andreff, W. (1996) *Les Multinationales Globales*. Paris: La D'écouverte.

Andriessen, J. and van Esch, R. (1993) *Globalisering: een zekere trend*. Discussienota 9301. Den Haag: Ministerie van Economische Zaken.

Archibugi, D. and Michie, J. (1997a) In D. Archibugi and J. Michie (eds) *Technological Globalisation and National Systems of Innovation: An Introduction*.

Archibugi, D. and Michie, J. (1997b) In D. Archibugi and J. Michie (eds) *The Globalisation of Technology: A New Taxonomy*.

Archibugi, D. and Michie, J. (eds) (1997c) *Technology, Globalisation and Economic Performance*. Cambridge: Cambridge University Press.

Archibugi, D. and Michie, J. (1998) Technical change, growth and trade: new departures in institutional economics. *J. Econ. Surv.*, **12**(3), 313–332.

Arthur, C. (1998) In C. Arthur and G. Reuten (eds) *The Fluidity of Capital and the Logic of the Concept*.

Arthur, C. and Reuten, G. (eds) (1998a) *The Circulation of Capital: Essays on Volume Two of Marx's Capital*. New York: St. Martin's Press.

Arthur, C. and Reuten, G. (eds) (1998b) *Marx's Capital II. The Circulation of Capital: General Introduction*.

Bairoch, P. (1993) *Mythes et Paradoxes de L'histoire Économique*. Paris: La Découverture, 1999.

Bairoch, P. and Kozul-Wrig0ht, R. (1996) Globalization myths: some historical reflections on integration, industrialization and growth in the world economy. *UNCTAD Discussion Papers* No. 113, March 1996.

Baker, D., Epstein, G. and Pollin, R. (eds) (1998a) *Globalization and Progressive Economic Policy*. Cambridge: Cambridge University Press.

Baker, D., Epstein, G. and Pollin, R. (1998b) In D. Baker, G. Epstein and R. Pollin (eds) *Introduction*.

Baldwin, R. and Martin, P. (1999) Two waves of globalization: superficial similarities, fundamental differences. *NBER Working Paper Series* No. 6904, January 1999.

Bank for International Settlements (BIS) (1999) *Central Bank Survey of Foreign Exchange and Derivatives Market Activity 1998*. Basle: BIS.

Bank for International Settlements (BIS) (2000) *70th Annual Report 1 April 1999–31 March 2000*. Basel: BIS.

Barkin, D. (1998) *Wealth, Poverty and Sustainable Development*. Mexico: Editorial Jus, S.A. de C.V.

Barnett, V. (1998) *Kondratiev and the Dynamics of Economic Development. Long Cycles and Industrial Growth in Historical Context*. Basingstoke: Macmillan.

Barsoc, C. (1984) *Les lendemains de la Crise*. Montreuil: La Brèche.

Barsoc, C. (1994) *Les rouages du capitalisme. Eléments d'analyse économique marxiste*. Montreuil: La Brèche.

Bellamy Foster, J. (1994) Waste away. *Dollars and Sense* No. 195, September–Oktober, 7.

Bello, W. (1998) The end of the Asian miracle. *The Nation*, **266**(2), 12/19 January, 16–21.

Bello, W. (2000) Why reform of the WTO is the wrong agenda. *Focus-on-Trade* No. 43.

Bello, W., Bullard, N. and Malhotra, K. (eds) (2000) *Global Finance. New Thinking on Regulating Speculative Capital Markets*. London and New York: Zed Books.

Beniès, N. (1998) In R. Poulin and P. Salama (eds) *Chômage, précarité et pauvreté dans les pays capitalistes développés*.

Bensaïd, D. (1995) *La Discordance des temps: Essais sur les crises, les classes, l'histore*. Paris: Les Éditions de la Passion.

Berger, S. and Dore R. (eds) (1996) *National Diversity and Global Capitalism*. Ithaca and London: Cornell University Press.

Bernstein, A. (2001) Low-skilled jobs: do they have to move? *Business Week* (5 March 2001), 68EU9–68EU10.

Bhagwati, J. (1997) The global age: from a sceptical south to a fearful north. *The World Econ.*, **20**(3) (May 1997), 259–283.

Bhagwati, J. (1998) The capital myth: the difference between trade in widgets and dollars. *Foreign Affairs*, **77**(3) (May/June 1998), 7–12.

Bhagwati, J. (1999) It's a small world after all. The *Wall Street Journal Europe*, **XVII** (5 May 1999).

Bhagwati, J. (2000) *The Wind of the Hundred Days. How Washington Mismanaged Globalization*. Cambridge and London: MIT Press.

Bimber, B. (1995) In M. Roe Smith and L. Marx (eds) *Three faces of technological determinism*.

Bischoff, J. (1999) *Der Kapitalismus des 21. Jahrhunderts. Systemkrise oder Rückkehr zur Prosperität*. Hamburg: VSA.

Blaug, M. (1968) *Economic Theory in Retrospect*. Homewood, IL: Richard D. Irwin.

Blaug, M. (1992) *The Methodology of Economics. Or how Economists Explain*. 2nd ed. Cambridge: Cambridge University Press.

Blaug, M. (2000) *Endogenous Growth Theory*. Research Memorandum in History and Methodology of Economics, Amsterdam, No. 00–7.

Blaut, J. (1997) Evaluating Imperialism. *Science & Society*, **61**(3), 382–391.

Bonefeld, W. and Holloway, J. (eds) (1991) *Post-Fordism & Social Form: A Marxist Debate on the Post-Fordist State*. Houndmills: Macmillan.

Boonstra, W. (2000) Niets nieuws onder de zon. Het debat over de Nieuwe Economie. www.rabobank.nl.

Bordo, M. and Eichengreen, B. (1993) *A Retrospective on the Bretton Woods System: Lessons for International Monetary Reform*. London: University of Chicago Press.

Bordo, M. and Schwartz, A. (1997) Monetary policy regimes and economic performance: the historical record. *NBER Working Paper Series* No. 6201.

Bordo, J., Eichengreen, B. and Irwin, D. (1999) Is globalization today really different than globalization a hundred years ago? *NBER Working Paper Series* No. 7195.

Boughton, J. (1997) From Suez to Tequila: the IMF as crisis manager. *IMF Working Paper*, WP/97/90.

Boyer, R. (1987) *La Théorie de la Régulation: Une Analyse Critique*. Paris: La Découverte.

Boyer, R. (1995) In R. Boyer and Y. Saillard (eds) *Du Fordisme Canonique a une Variété de Modes de Developpement*.

Boyer, R. (1996) In S. Berger and R. Dore (eds) *The Convergence Hypothesis Revisited: Globalization but Still the Century of Nations?*

Boyer, R. (2000a) The political in the era of globalization and finance: focus on some *régulation* school research. *International Journal of Urban and Regional Research*, **24**(2), 274–322.

Boyer, R. (2000b) Is a finance-led growth regime a viable alternative to fordism? a preliminary analysis. *Economy and Society*, **29**(1), 111–145.

Boyer, R. and Drache, D. (eds) (1996) *States Against Markets: the Limits of Globalization*. London and New York: Routledge.

Boyer, R. and Durand, J.P. (1998) *L'après Fordisme* (nouvelle édition augmentée). Paris: Syros.

Boyer, R. and Saillard, Y. (eds) (1995a) *Théorie de la Régulation: L'État des Savoirs*. Paris: La Découverte.

Boyer, R. and Saillard, Y. (1995b) In R. Boyer and Y. Saillard (eds) *Un précis de la Régulation*.

Braga de Macedo, J., Eichengreen, B. and Reis, J. (eds) (1996) *Currency Convertibility: The Gold Standard and Beyond*. New York: Routledge.

Brainard, S. and Riker, D. (1997) Are US multinationals exporting US jobs? *NBER Working Paper Series* No. 5958.

Braunstein, E. and Epstein, G. (1999) In J. Michie and J. Grieve Smith (eds) *Creating International Credit Rules and the Multilateral Agreement on Investment: What are the Alternatives?*

Brenner, R. (1998) The economics of global turbulence. A special report on the world economy, 1950–98. *New Left Rev.*, **229**, 1–265.

Brenner, R. (2000) The boom and the bubble. *New Left Rev.*, **6** (new series), 5–43.

Brenner, R. (2001) The world economy at the turn of the millenium toward boom or crisis? *Review of International Political Economy*, **8**(1), 6–44.

Brenner, R. and Glick, M. (1991) The regulation approach: theory and history, *New Left Rev.*, **188**, 45–119.

Bruton, H. (1998) A reconsideration of import substitution. *J. Econ. Lit.*, **36**(2), 903–936.

Bryan, D. (1995a) *The Chase Across the Globe: International Accumulation and the Contradictions of the Nation State*. Boulder, San Francisco and Oxford: Westview Press.

Bryan, D. (1995b) The internationalisation of capital and Marxian value theory. *Camb. J. Econ.*, **19**(3), 421–440.

Bullard, N. (1998) *Taming the Tigers: The IMF and the Asian Crisis*. London: CAFOD.

Burbach, R. and Robinson, W. (1999) The fin de siècle debate: globalization as epochal shift. *Science and Society*, **63**(1), 10–39.

Burtless, G. (1995) International trade and the rise in earnings inequality. *J. Econ. Lit.*, **33**(2), 800–816.

Business Week (2000a) *Editorials: What's Behind the Global Backlash*, 24 April, 76.

Business Week (2000b) *New Economy, New Social Contract*, 11 September, 80.

Business Week (2000c) *Special Report. Global Capitalism: Can it be made to Work Better?* 6 November, pp. 40–68.

Business Week (2000d) *Globalization: Lessons Learned*, 6 November, 136.

Caldwell, B. (1982) *Beyond Positivism: Economic Methodology in the Twentieth Century*. London: Unwin Hyman.

Calvo, G. and Mendoza, E. (1997) Rational herd behavior and the globalization of securities markets. *Discussion Paper* No. 120. Institute for Empirical Macroeconomics, Federal Reserve Bank of Minneapolis.

Campbell, M. and Reuten, G. (eds) (2002) *The culmination of capital: essays on volume three of Marx's capital*. New York: Palgrave.

Castel, O. (1998) *Le processus de mondialisation: la naissance de l'ultra-imperialisme*. Unpublished paper.

Castells, M. (1996) *The Information Age: Economy, Society and Culture, vol. I: The Rise of the Network Society*. Massachusetts and Oxford: Blackwell.

Castells, M. (1997) *The Information Age: Economy, Society and Culture, vol. II: The Power of Identity*. Massachusetts and Oxford: Blackwell.

Castells, M. (1998) *The Information Age: Economy, Society and Culture, vol. III: End of Millennium*. Massachusetts and Oxford: Blackwell.

Cervantes Martínez, R., Gil Chamizo, F., Regalado Alvarez, R. and Zardoya Loureda, R. (1999) *Transnacionalización y desnacionalización. Ensayos sobre el capitalismo contemporáneo*, Havana. Paper.

Chau, N. and Kanbur, R. (2000) *The Race to the Bottom, From the Bottom*. Paper, November 2000.

Chesnais, F. (1994) *La Mondialisation du capital*. Paris: Syros.

Chesnais, F. (coord) (1996a) *La mondialisation financière: Genèse, coût et enjeux*. Paris: Syros.

Chesnais, F. (1996b) Mondialisation du capital & régime d'accumulation à dominante financière. *Agone: Philosophie, Critique & Littérature* No. 16.

Chesnais, F. (1997a) *La Mondialisation du Capital* (nouvelle édition augmentée). Paris: Syros.

Chesnais, F. (1997b) L'émergence d'un régime d'accumulation mondial à dominate financière. *La Pensée*, **309**, 61–85.

Chesnais, F. (1999) *Tobin or not Tobin? Une taxe internationale sur le capital*. Paris: L'Esprit Frappeur.

CIA (Central Intelligence Agency) (2000) *Global Trends 2015: A Dialogue About the Future with Nongovernment Experts*. Washington, DC: CIA.

Clarke, S. (ed.) (1991) *The State Debate*. Houndmills: Macmillan.

Cody, H. (2000) Consolidation produces giants hoping for better performance. *Pulp & Paper*, **74**(11), 37–44.

Coggins, B. (1998) *Does Financial Deregulation Work? A Critique of Free Market Approaches*. Cheltenham: Edward Elgar.

Cohn, T. (2000) *Global Political Economy: Theory and Practice*. New York: Addison Wesley and Longman.

Corsetti, G., Pesenti, P. and Roubini, N. (1998) *Paper tigers? A preliminary assessment of the Asian crisis*. Paper for NBER-Bank of Portugal International Seminar on Macroecnomics, 14–15 June 1998.

Coutrot, T. (1998) *L'Entreprise néo-libérale, nouvelle utopie capitaliste? Enquête sur les modes d'organisation du travail*. Paris: Éditions la Découverte.

Coutrot, T. (1999) *Critique de l'organisation du travail*. Paris: Éditions La Découverte.

Coutrot, T. and Husson, M. (1993) *Les destins du tiers monde: analyse, bilan et perspectives*. Paris: Éditions Nathan.

Cox, K. (ed.) (1997) *Spaces of Globalization: Reasserting the Power of the Local*. New York: The Guilford Press.

Crafts, N. (2000) Globalization and growth in the twentieth century. *IMF Working Paper*, WP/00/44.

Crotty, J. (2000) Structural contradiction of the global neoliberal regime. *Rev. Radical Polit. Econ.*, **32**(3), 361–368.

Cumings, B. (1998) The Korean crisis and the end of 'Late' development. *New Left Rev.*, **231**, 43–72.

Cutler, T. and Waine, B. (2001) Social insecurity and the retreat from social democracy: occupational welfare in the long boom and financialization. *Review of International Political Economy*, **8**(1), 96–117.

Daly, H. (1995) Against free trade: neoclassical and steady-state perspectives. *J. Evol. Econ.*, **5**, 313–326.

Daly, H. (1996) In J. Mander and E. Goldsmith (eds) *Free Trade: The Perils of Deregulation*.

De Angelis, M. (2000) *Keynesianism, Social Conflict and Political Economy*. Houndmills: Macmillan.

DeFreitas, G. (1998) In D. Baker, G. Epstein and R. Pollin (eds) *Immigration, Inequality, and Policy Alternatives*.

DeMartino, G. (1999) Global neoliberalism, policy autonomy, and international competitive dynamics. *J. Econ. Issues*, **XXXIII**(2), 343–349.

DeMartino, G. (2000) *Global Economy, Global Justice: Theoretical Objections and Policy Alternatives to Neoliberalism*. London and New York: Routledge.

DeRosa, D. (2001) *In Defense of Free Capital Markets. The Case Against a New International Financial Architecture*. Princeton, NJ: Bloomberg Press.

de Vroey, M. (1983) De huidige krisis. Diagnose en strategische perspectieven. *Tijdschrift voor Politieke Ekonomie*, **7**(2), 102–130.

Desai, M. (1979) *Marxian Economics*. Oxford: Basil Blackwell.

Dicken, P. (1998) *Global Shift: Transforming the World Economy* 3rd ed. London: Paul Chapman Publishing.

Dikstaal, N. (2001) CAO: vangnet voor losers (interview with Alfred Kleinknecht). *Intermediair* (25 January), 45–47.

Dockès, P. and Rosier, B. (1992) In A. Kleinknecht, E. Mandel and I. Wallerstein (eds) *Long Waves and the Dialectic of Innovations and Conflicts.*

Dore, R. (1996) In S. Berger and R. Dore (eds) *Convergence in Whose Interest.*

Doremus, P., Keller, W., Pauly, L. and Reich, S. (1998) *The Myth of the Global Corporation.* Princeton, NJ: Princeton University Press.

Dorman, P. (2001) *The Free Trade Magic Act. In Dubious Study First You See the Benefits of Globalization, then You Don't.* Washington, DC: Briefing Paper Economic Policy Institute.

Dos Santos, T. (1970) The structure of dependence. *Am. Econ. Rev.*, **60**(2), 231–236.

Dos Santes, T. (1978) *Imperialismo y Dependencia.* Mexico: Ediciones Era.

Drache, D. (ed.) (2001) *The Market or the Public Domain? Global Governance and the Asymmetry of Power.* London and New York: Routledge.

Drucker, P. (1997) The global economy and the nation state. *Foreign Affairs*, **76**(5), 159–171.

Duménil, G. and Lévy, D. (2000) *Crise et sortie de crise. ordres et désordres néolibéraux.* Paris: PUF.

Duménil, G. and Lévy, D. (2001) In R. Albritton, M. Itoh, R. Westra and A. Zuege (eds) *Periodizing Capitalism: Technology, Institutions and Relations of Production.*

Dumez, H. and Jeunemaître, A. (2000) How far can globalization go? *World Cement*, **31**(8), 16–24.

Dunford, M. (2000) In R. Palan (ed.) *Globalisation and Theories of International Relations.*

Dupont, M. (1987) In M. Dupont, F. Ollivier, A. Taillandier and C. Verla (eds) *Les horizons de la crise.*

Dupont, M., Ollivier, F., Taillandier, A. and Verla, C. (1987) *La Crise, les crises, l'enjeu.* Montreuil: PEC.

Durand, M. (2000) Lessons of a mini-crash. *Int. Viewpoint*, **322**, 17–21.

Easterly, W. (2001) The lost decades: developing countries stagnation in spite of policy reform 1980–1998. *J. Econ. Growth*, **6**, 135–157.

Eatwell, J. and Taylor, L. (2000) *Global Finance at Risk: The Case for International Regulation.* New York: The New York Press.

Economist (1996) 'Schools brief: the miracle of trade', 27 January, 65–66.

Economist (1997a) 'Schools brief: trade winds', 8 November, 99–100.

Economist (1997b) '1897 and 1997: the century the earth stood still', 20 December, 71–73.

Economist (1999) 'Eureka! A survey of innovation in industry', 2 February.

Economist (2000a) 'The case for globalization', 23 September, 17–18.

Economist (2000b) 'Anti-capitalist protests: angry and effective', 23 September, 97–103.

Economist (2001) 'Globalisation and its critics. A survey of globalisation', 29 September.

Edwards, S. (1993) Openness, trade liberalization, and growth in developing countries. *J. Econ. Lit.*, **31**(3), 1358–1393.

Eichengreen, B. (1996) *Globalizing Capital: A History of the International Monetary System.* Princeton, NJ: Princeton University Press.

Eichengreen, B. (1999) *Towards a New International Financial Architecture.* Washington, DC: Institute for International Economics.

Eichengreen, B. and Flandreau, M. (1996) In J. Braga de Macedo, B. Eichengreen and J. Reis (eds) *The Geography of the Gold Standard.*

Elliot, L. and Denny, C. (2002) Top 1% earns as much as the poorest 57%. *The Guardian* (18 January 2002).

Ellman, M. (2001) *A.G. Frank's World System Theory*. Paper.

Emmanuel, A. (1972) *Unequal Exchange: A Study of the Imperialism of Trade*. New York: Monthly Review Press.

Estrella Tolentino, P. (1999) In J. Michie and J. Grieve Smith (eds) *Transnational Rules for Transnational Corporations: What Next?*

Faux, J. (1997) The 'American model' exposed. *The Nation,* **265**(13), (27 October 1997), 18–22.

Faux, J. and Mishel, L. (2000) In W. Hutton and A. Giddens (eds) *Inequality and the Global Economy*.

Feenstra, R. (1998) Integration of trade and disintegration of production in the global economy. *J. Econ. Perspect.*, **12**(4), 31–50.

Feldstein, M. (2000) Aspects of global economic integration: outlook for the future. *NBER Working Paper Series* No. 7899, September 2000.

Feldstein, M. and Horioka, C. (1980) Domestic saving and international capital flows. *Econ. J.*, **90**, 314–329.

Felix, D. (1995) Financial globalization versus free trade: the case for the tobin tax. *UNCTAD Discussion Papers* No. 108.

Felix, D. (1998) On drawing general policy lessons from recent Latin American currency crises. *J. Post Keynesian Econ.*, **20**(2), 191–221.

Fine, B. and Harris, N. (1979) *Rereading Capital*. London and Basingstoke: Macmillan.

Fine, B., Lapavistas, C. and Milonakis, D. (1999) Addressing the world economy: two steps back. *Capital & Class*, **67**, 47–90.

Flandreau, M., Le Cacheux, J. and Zumer, F. (1998) In D. Begg, J. von Hagen, C. Wyplosz and K. Zimmermann (eds) *Stability Without a Pact? Lessons from the European Gold Standard*, 1880–1914.

Foley, D. (1986) *Understanding Capital. Marx's Economic Theory*. Cambridge: Harvard University Press.

Foreman-Peck, J. (1995) *A History of the World Economy. International Economic Relations Since 1850*. New York: Harvester Wheatsheaf.

Frank, A. (1998) *ReORIENT: Global Economy in the Asian Age*. Berkeley, CA: University of California Press.

Frankel, J. (2000) Globalization of the economy. *NBER Working Paper Series* No. 7858.

Freeman, A. (1998) GATT and the World Tråde Organisation. *Labour Focus on Eastern Europe*, **59**, 74–93.

Freeman, A. (1999) *New Paradigm or New World Order? The Return of Classical Imperialism and the Dynamics of the US Boom*. Paper, 7 May 1999.

Freeman, A. (2000) *Crisis and the Poverty of Nations: Two Market Products Which Value Explains Better*. Paper, 4 June 2000.

Freeman, C. (1997) In D. Archibugi and J. Michie (eds) *The 'National System of Innovation' in Historical Perspective*.

Freeman, C. and Louça, F. (2001) *As Time Goes By. The Information Revolution and the Industrial Revolutions in Historical Perspective*. Oxford: Oxford University Press.

Freeman, R. (1995) Are your wages set in Beijing? *J. Econ. Perspect.*, **9**(3), 15–32.

Frémaux, P. (1998) *Sortir du Piège. La gauche face à la mondialisation*. Paris: Syros.

Frey, B. and Weck-Hannemann, H. (1996) In D. Greenaway (ed.) *The Political Economy of Protection*.

Friedman, M. (1953) *Essays in Positive Economics*. Chicago and London: University of Chicago Press.

Friedman, T. (1999) *The Lexus and the Olive Tree: Understanding Globalization*. New York: Farrar, Strauss and Giraux.

Froud, J., Johal, S., Haslam, C. and Williams, K. (2001) Accumulation and conditions of Inequality. *Rev. Int. Political Econ.*, **8**(1), 66–95.

Fulcher, J. (2000) Globalization, the nation-state and global society. *Sociol. Rev.*, **48**(4), 522–543.

Gadrey, J. (2000) *Nouvelle Économie, Nouveau Mythe?* Paris: Flammarion.

Galbraith, J. and Jiaqing, L. (1999) Inequality and financial crises: some early findings. *UTIP Working Paper* No. 9.

Galbraith, J., Darity, W. and Jiaqing, L. (1998) Measuring the evolution of inequality in the global economy. *Working Paper Center for Economic Policy Analysis*, **3**(4).

Galbraith, J., Jaiqing, L. and Darity, W. (1999) Measuring the evolution of inequality in the global economy. *UTIP Working Paper* No. 7.

Gardiner, P. (1968) In D. Sills (ed.) *The Philosophy of History*.

Garretsen, N. and Peeters, J. (1999) Globalisering en armoede. *ESB* No. 4222, pp. D10–D13.

Garrett, G. (2000) The causes of globalization. *Comp. Polit. Stud.*, **33**(6/7), 941–991.

Geary, D. (1987) *Karl Kautsky*. Manchester: Manchester University Press.

George, S. (2000) In W. Bello, N. Bullard and K. Malhotra (eds) *A Short History of Neoliberalism: Twenty Years of Élite Economics and Emerging Opportunities for Structural Change*.

Gertler, M. (1997) In K. Cox (ed.) *Between the Global and the Local: The Spatial Limits to Productive Capital*.

Giddens, A. and Hutton, W. (2000) In A. Giddens and W. Hutton (eds) *In Conversation*.

Gill, S. (1992) In R. Miliband and L. Panitch (eds) *The Emerging World Order and European Change: The Political Economy of European Union*.

Gilpin, R. (1987) *The Political Economy of International Relations*. Princeton, NJ: Princeton University Press.

Giussani, P. (1996) Empirical evidence for trends toward globalization. *Int. J. Polit. Econ.*, **26**(3), 15–38.

Glombowski, J. (1987) Lange golven, regulatiewijzen of sociale accumulatiestructuren? *Vlaams Marxistisch Tijdschrift*, **21**(2), 7–24.

Glyn, A. and Sutcliffe, B. (1992) In R. Miliband and L. Panitch (eds) *Global but Leaderless? The New Capitalist Order*.

Goldstein, J. (1988) *Long Cycles, Prosperity and War in the Modern Age*. New Haven, CT: Yale University Press.

Gordon, D. (1988) The global economy: new edifice or crumbling foundations. *New Left Rev.*, **168**, 24–64.

Gordon, D. (1994) In D. Kotz, T. McDonough and M. Reich (eds) *The Global Economy: New Edifice of Crumbling Foundations*.

Gordon, D., Edwards, R. and Reich, M. (1994) In D. Kotz, T. McDonough and M. Reich (eds) *Long swings and stages of capitalism*.

Görg, C. and Hirsch, J. (1998) Is international democracy possible? *Re. Int. Polit. Econ.*, **5**(4), 585–615.

Gowan, P. (1997) The dangers of facade cosmopolitanism. *Labour Focus on Eastern Europe* **58**, 4–14.

Gowan, P. (1998) *The Globalization Gamble: The Dollar/Wall Street Regime and Its Consequences*. London and New York: Verso.

Gowan, P. (2001) Neoliberal cosmopolitanism. *New Left Rev.*, **11**, 79–93.

Grahl, J. (2000) Money as sovereignty: the economics of Michel Aglietta. *New Polit. Econ.*, **5**(2), 291–316.

Grahl, J. (2001) Globalized finance. *New Left Rev.*, **8**, 23–47.

Grahl, J. and Teague, P. (2000) The *Régulation* School, the employment relation and financialization. *Economy and Society*, **29**(1), 160–178.

Grant, W. (1997) In J. Rogers Hollingsworth and R. Boyer (eds) *Perspectives on Globalization and Economic Coordination*.

Greenaway, D. (ed.) (1996) *Current Issues in International Trade*. Houndmills: Macmillan.

Greider, W. (1997) *One World, Ready or Not*. New York: Simon and Schuster.

Greider, W. (2001) A new giant sucking sound. *The Nation*, **273**(22), (31 December), 22–24.

Grieve Smith, J. (1997) In J. Michie and J. Grieve Smith (eds) *Devising A Strategy for Pay*.

Grieve Smith, J. (1999) In J. Michie and J. Grieve Smith (eds) *A New Bretton Woods: Reforming the Global Financial System*.

Grieve Smith, J. (2002) *Tackling the World Recession*. Working Paper. London: Catalyst.

Group of Lisbon (1996) *Limits to Competition*. Cambridge: MIT Press.

Guttmann, R. (1994) *How Credit-money Shapes the Economy. The United States in a Global System*. Armonk, New York, London: M.E. Sharpe.

Harris, L. (1999) In J. Michie and J. Grieve Smith (eds) Will the Real IMF Please Stand Up: What Does the Fund Do and What Should it Do?

Harvey, D. (1982) *The Limits to Capital*. London and New York: Verso, 1999.

Harvey, D. (1995) Globalization in question. *Rethinking Marxism*, **8**(4), 1–17.

Hausman, D. (ed.) (1984) *The Philosophy of Economics*. Cambridge: Cambridge University Press.

Hay, C. and Marsh, D. (1999) Introduction: towards a new (international) political economy? *New Polit. Econ.*, **4**(1), 5–23.

Held, D., McGrew, A., Goldblatt, D. and Perraton, J. (1999) *Global Transformations. Politics, Economics and Culture*. Stanford: Stanford University Press.

Helleiner, E. (1994) *States and the Reemergence of Global Finance: From Bretton Woods to the 1990s*. Ithaca and London: Cornell University Press.

Henderson, W. (1983) *Friedrich List: Economist and Visionary 1789–1846*. London: Frank Cass.

Higgott, R. (1999) Economics, politics and (international) political economy: the need for a balanced diet in an era of globalization. *New Polit. Econ.*, **4**(1), 23–36.

Hilferding, R. (1910) *Finance Capital: A Study of the Latest Phase of Capitalist Development*. London, Boston, Melbourne and Henley: Routledge & Kegan Paul, 1981.

Hirsch, J. (1991) In W. Bonefeld and J. Holloway (eds) *Fordism and Post-Fordism: The Present Social Crisis and its Consequences*.

Hirst, P. and Thompson, G. (1996) *Globalization in Question*. Cambridge: Polity Press.

Hirst, P. and Thompson, G. (1997) In J. Rogers Hollingsworth and R. Boyer (eds) *Globalization in Question: International Economic Relations and Forms of Public Governance*.

Hoang-Ngoc, L. (1996) *Salaires et emploi: Une critique de la pensée unique*. Paris: Syros.

Hobson, J. (1902) *Imperialism*. Ann Arbor: Ann Arbor Paperbacks, 1965.

Hodgart, A. (1977) *The Economics of European Imperialism*. London: Edward Arnold.

Hodgson, G. (1988) *Economics and Institutions*. Cambridge: Polity Press.

Hodgson, G. (1999) *Economics and Utopia. Why the Learning Economy is Not the End of History*. London and New York: Routledge.

Horman, D. (1996) *Les societés transnationales dans la mondialisation de l'économie.* Brussels: GRESEA.

Howard, M. and King, J. (1992) *A History of Marxian Economics vol. II, 1929–1990.* Houndmills: Macmillan.

Hossein-zadeh, I. and Gabb, A. (2000) Making sense of the current expansion of the US economy: a long wave approach and a critique. *Rev. Radical Polit. Econ.*, **32**(2), 388–397.

Huffschmid, J. (1999) *Politische Ökonomie der Finanzmärkte.* Hamburg: VSA.

Hummels, D., Rapoport, D. and Yi, K. (1998) Vertical specialization and the changing nature of world trade. *Econ. Policy Rev. Federal Reserve Bank NY*, **4**(2), 79–99.

Hurrell, A. and Woods, N. (1995) Globalisation and inequality. *Millennium: J. Int. Stud.*, **24**(3), 447–470.

Husson, M. (1994) In Sebaï and Vercellone (eds) *L'école de la régulation après la crise.*

Husson, M. (1996) *Misère du capital: Une critique du néoliberalisme.* Paris: Syros.

Husson, M. (1999a) Riding the long wave. *Hist. Mater.*, **5**, 77–102.

Husson, M. (1999b) In G. Achcar (ed.) *After the Golden Age: On Late Capitalism.*

Husson, M. (2001) *Le grand BLUFF capitaliste.* Paris: La dispute.

Hutton, W. and Giddens, A. (eds) (2000) *Global Capitalism.* New York: The New Press.

IMF, OECD, UN and World Bank (2000) *A Better World of All: Progress Towards the International Development Goals.* www.paris21.org/betterworld.

ING-Bank (2000) *MKB-Miljoenennota 2000.* Amsterdam: ING.

International Labour Office (ILO) (1996) *World Employment 1996–97: National Policies in a Global Context.* Geneva: ILO.

International Labour Office (ILO) (1998) *World Employment 1998–99: Employability in the Global Economy. How Training Matters.* Geneva: ILO.

International Monetary Fund (IMF) (1997a) *World Economic Outlook.* Washington, DC: IMF.

International Monetary Fund (IMF) (1997b) *International Capital Markets: Developments, Prospects, and Key Policy Issues.* Washington, DC: IMF.

International Monetary Fund (IMF) (1999a) *World Economic Outlook (May 1999).* Washington, DC: IMF.

International Monetary Fund (IMF) (1999b) *World Economic Outlook (October 1999).* Washington, DC: IMF.

Irwin, D. (1996a) The United States in a new global economy? A century's perspective. *Am. Econ. Rev.*, **86**(2), 41–46.

Irwin, D. (1996b) *Against the Tide: An Intellectual History of Free Trade.* Princeton, NJ: Princeton University Press.

Itoh, M. and Lapavitsas, C. (1999) *Political Economy of Money and Finance.* Houndmills: Macmillan Press.

James, H. (1996) *International Monetary Cooperation Since Bretton Woods.* Washington, New York and Oxford: IMF and Oxford University Press.

James, J. (2001) Information technology, cumulative causation and patterns of globalization in the third world. *Rev. Int. Polit. Econ.*, **8**(1), 147–162.

Jameson, F. (2000) Globalization and political strategy. *New Left Rev.*, **4**, 49–68.

Jessop, B. (1990) Regulation theories in retrospect and prospect. *Economy and Society*, **19**(2), 153–216.

Jessop, B. (1991) In W. Bonefeld and J. Holloway (eds) *Polar Bears and Class Struggle: Much Less than a Self-criticism.*

Jessop, B. (1997) Review essay. Twenty years of the (Parisian) regulation approach: the paradox of success and failure at home and abroad. *New Polit. Econ.*, **2**(3), 503–526.

Johnson, H. (ed.) (1968) *Economic Nationalism in Old and New States*. London: George Allen and Unwin.

Johnston, D. (1996) The imperative of free trade. *OECD Observer*, **201**, 4–5.

Jomo, K. (ed.) (1998) *Tigers in Trouble. Financial Governance, Liberalisation and Crises in East Asia*. London: Zed Books.

Julius, D. (1999) In OECD *Policy Drivers for a Long Boom*.

Kahan, A. (1968) In H. Johnson (ed.) *Nineteenth-century European Experience with Policies of Economic Nationalism*.

Kalshoven, F. (1993) *Over Marxistische Economie in Nederland, 1883–1939*. Amsterdam: Thesis Publishers.

Kanbur, R. (2001) *Economic Policy, Distribution and Poverty: The Nature of Disagreement*. Paper. Cornell University, Ithaca, NY.

Kaplinksy, R. (2001) Is globalization all it is cracked up to be? *Rev. Int. Polit. Econ.*, **8**(1), 45–65.

Katouzian, H. (1980) *Ideology and Method in Economics*. London and Basingstoke: Macmillan.

Kaul, I., Grunberg, I. and Stern, M. (eds) (1999) *Global Public Goods: International Cooperation in the 21st Century*. New York: UNDP.

Kautsky, K. (1914) Ultra-imperialism. *New Left Rev.*, **59**, (1970), 41–46.

Kautsky, K. (1915) The necessity of imperialism. In *Selected Political Writings* (P. Goode, Trans.). London and Basingstoke: Macmillan, 1983.

Kearny, A. (2001) Measuring globalization. *Foreign Policy*, **122**, (January–February), 56–65.

Kébabdjian, G. (1994) *L'Economie mondiale: enjeux nouveaux, nouvelles théories*. Paris: Editions du Seuil.

Kemp, T. (1967) *Theories of Imperialism*. London: Dobson Books.

Kenwood, A. and Lougheed, A. (1992) *The Growth of the International Economy 1820–1990*. London: Routledge.

Keynes, J. (1926) *The End of Laissez-Faire*. London: Hogarth Press.

Keynes, J. (1935) *The General Theory of Employment, Interest, and Money*. San Diego, CA: Harcourt Brace & Company, 1991.

Keynes, J. (1980) In D. Moggridge (ed.) *Activities 1940–1944: Shaping the Post-War World: The Clearing Union*. Collected Writings. vol XXV. London and Basingstoke: Macmillan.

Kitschelt, H., Lange, P., Marks, G. and Stephens, J. (eds) (1999) *Continuity and Change in Contemporary Capitalism*. Cambridge: Cambridge University Press.

Kitson, J. and Michie, J. (2000) *The Political Economy of Competitiveness. Essays on Employment, Public Policy and Corporate Performance*. London and New York: Routledge.

Klant, J. (1972) *Spelregels voor Economen*. Leiden: Stenfert Kroese.

Klein, N. (1999) *No Logo. Taking Aim at the Brand Bullies*. New York: Picador.

Klein, N. (2001) Reclaiming the commons. *New Left Rev.*, **9**, 81–89.

Kleinknecht, A. (2000) De vijfde van Kondratieff. *ESB*, **4245**, 171.

Kleinknecht, A. and ter Wengel, J. (1996a) Feiten over globalisering. *ESB*, **4076**, 831–833.

Kleinknecht, A. and ter Wengel, J. (1996b) Een overschat fenomeen. *ESB*, **4080**, 918–920.

Kleinknecht, A. and ter Wengel, J. (1998) The myth of economic globalization. *Camb. J. Econ.*, **22**(5), 637–648.

Kleinknecht, A., Mandel, E. and Wallerstein, I. (eds) (1992) *New Findings in Long-wave Research*. New York: St. Martin's Press.

Kotz, D. (1994a) In D. Kotz, T. McDonough and M. Reich (eds) *Interpreting the social structure of accumulation theory*.

Kotz, D. (1994b) In D. Kotz, T. McDonough and M. Reich (eds) *The regulation theory and the social structure of accumulation approach.*

Kotz, D. (2001) In R. Albritton, M. Itoh, R. Westra and A. Zuege (eds) *The State, Globalization and Phases of Capitalist Development.*

Kotz, D., McDonough, T. and Reich, M. (eds) (1994a) *Social Structure of Accumulation. The Political Economy of Growth and Crisis.* Cambridge: Cambridge University Press.

Kotz, D., McDonough, T. and Reich, M. (1994b) In D. Kotz, T. McDonough and M. Reich (eds) *Introduction.*

Kotz, D., McDonough, T. and Reich, M. (1994c) In D. Kotz, T. McDonough and M. Reich (eds) *Afterword: New International Institutions and Renewed World Economic Expansion.*

Kozul-Wright, R. (ed.) (1998) *Transnational Corporations and the Global Economy.* Houndmills: Macmillan.

Kozul-Wright, R. and Bairoch, P. (1998) In R. Kozul-Wright (ed.) *Globalization Myths: Some Historical Reflections on Integration, Industrialization and Growth in the World Economy.*

Krausz, T. (1997) *Selected Essays from Eszmélet – Consciousness.* Budapest: Eszmélet and Labour Focus on Eastern Europe.

Krueger, A. (1997) Trade policy and economic development: how we learn. *Am. Econ. Rev.*, **87**(1), 1–23.

Krugman, P. (ed.) (1986) *Strategic Trade Policy and the New International Economics.* Cambridge: MIT Press.

Krugman, P. (1987) Reprinted in J. Overbeek (ed.) (1999) *Is Free Trade Passé? Econ. Perspect.*, **1**(2), 131–144.

Krugman, P. (1995) Growing world trade: causes and consequences. *Brookings Pap. Econ. Activity*, **1995**(1), 327–362.

Krugman, P. (1998) Saving Asia: it's time to get radical. *Fortune*, **138** (7 September), 74–80.

Krugman, P. (1999) *The Return of Depression Economics.* New York and London: W.W. Norton.

Krugman, P. and Obstfeld, M. (2000) *International Economics. Theory and Policy*, 5th ed. Reading, MA: Addison–Wesley.

Kuttner, R. (1992) *The End of Laissez-Faire.* Philadelphia: University of Pennsylvania Press.

Kyloh, R. (1996) *Governance of Globalization: ILO's Contribution.* Draft Paper: International Labour Organization.

Lang, T. and Hines, C. (1993) *The New Protectionism: Protecting the Future Against Free Trade.* London: Earthscan Publications.

Lazarus, N. (1998) Charting globalization. *Race & Class*, **40**(2/3), 91–109.

Leamer, E. (1995) The Heckscher–Ohlin model in theory and practice. *Princeton Studies in International Finance*, **77**.

Leiderman, L. and Razin, A. (1994) *Capital Mobility: The Impact on Consumption, Investment and Growth.* Cambridge: Cambridge University Press.

Lenin, N. (1917) *Imperialism, the Highest Stage of Capitalism: A Popular Outline.* Moscow: Progress Publishers, 1975.

Levi-Faur, D. (1997) Friedrich List and the political economy of the nation-state. *Rev. Int. Polit. Econ.*, **4**(1), 154–178.

Levy-Livermore, A. (1998) *Handbook on the Globalization of the World Economy.* Cheltenham: Edward Elgar.

Lipietz, A. (1999) In OECD *Working for World Ecological Sustainability: Towards a 'New Great Transformation'.*

Lipsey, R. (1999) In OECD *Sources of Continued Long-run Economic Dynamism in the 21st Century*.

Lipsey, R., Blomström, M. and Ramstetter, E. (2000) Internationalized Production in World Output. *NBER Working Paper Series*. No. 5385.

List, F. (1837) *The Natural System of Political Economy*. London: Frank Cass, 1983.

List, F. (1841) *The National System of Political Economy*. London: Longman, Green and Co., 1904.

Livingstone, K. (1997) Democracy versus the market in the globalised economy. *Labour Focus East. Eur.*, **58**, 35–43.

Longworth, R. (1998) *Global Squeeze: The Coming Crisis for First-world Nations*. Lincolnwood: Contemporary Books.

Louça, F. (1997) *Turbulence in Economics: An Evolutionary Appraisal of Cycles and Complexity in Historical Processes*. Cheltenham: Edward Elgar.

Louça, F. (1999) In G. Achcar (ed.) *Ernest Mandel and the Pulsation of History*.

Luttwak, E. (1996) Buchanan has it right. *London Review of Books*, 9 May 1996, 6–8.

Lutz, M. (1999) *Economics for the Common Good. Two Centuries of Social Economic Thought in the Humanistic Tradition*. London and New York: Routledge.

Luxemburg, L. and Bukharin N. (1972) *Imperialism and the Accumulation of Capital*. London: Allen Lane The Penguin Press.

McDonough, T. (1994) In D. Kotz, T. McDonough and M. Reich (eds) *Social Structures of Accumulation, Contingent History, and Stages of Capitalism*.

McDonough, T. (1995) Lenin, imperialism, and the stages of capitalist development. *Science and Society*, **59**(3), 339–367.

McDonough, T. (1999) Gordon's accumulation theory: the highest stage of stadial theory. *Rev. Radical Polit. Econ.*, **31**(4), 6–31.

McLellan, D. (1975) *Marx' Leven en Werk*. Amsterdam: Van Gennep.

McMichael, P. (2000) In R. Palan (ed.) *Globalisation: Trend or Project?*

Maddison, A. (1982) *Phases of Capitalist Development*. Oxford: Oxford University Press.

Maddison, A. (1999) Poor Until 1820. *The Wall Street J.*, 11 January 1999.

Magdoff, H. (1969) *The Age of Imperialism*. New York and London: Monthly Review Press.

Mahnkopf, B. (1999) In Panitch and Leys (eds) *Between the Devil and the Deep Blue Sea: The German Model Under the Pressure of Globalization*.

Mandel, E. (1964) After imperialism? *New Left Rev.*, **25**, 17–25.

Mandel, E. (1970) The laws of uneven development. *New Left Rev.*, **59**, 19–38

Mandel, E. (1972) *Late Capitalism* (J. de Bres, Trans.). London and New York: Verso, 1999.

Mandel, E. (1978) In K. Marx *Introduction*, 1884.

Mandel, E. (1992) In A. Kleinknecht, E. Mandel and I. Wallerstein (eds) *The International Debate on Long Waves of Capitalist Development: An Intermediary Balance Sheet*.

Mandel, E. (1995) *Long Waves of Capitalist Development: A Marxist Interpretation*. London and New York: Verso (2nd revised ed).

Mandle, J. (2001) Reforming Globalization. *Challenge*, **44**(2), 24–38.

Mander, J. and Goldsmith, E. (eds) (1996) *The Case Against the Global Economy and for a Turn Toward the Local*. San Francisco, CA: Sierra Club Books.

Maneschi, A. (1998) *Comparative Advantage in International Trade. A Historical Perspective*. Cheltenham: Edward Elgar.

Mankiw, G. (1997) *Macroeconomics* (3rd edition). New York: Worth Publishers.

Mankiw, G. (2000) *Macroeconomics* (4th edition). New York: Worth Publishers.

Manoïlesco, M. (1931) *The Theory of Protection and International Trade*. Westminster: P.S. King & Son.

Marrison, A. (1998) *Free Trade and its Reception 1815–1960, vol I: Freedom and Trade*. London: Routledge.

Marx, K. (1848) 'On the question of free trade'. In K. Marx *The Poverty of Philosophy*. London: Lawrence and Wishart, 1956.

Marx, K. (ed.) (1884) *Capital*, vol II. Harmondsworth: Penguin, 1978.

Marx, K. (ed.) (1894) *Capital*, vol III. Harmondsworth: Penguin, 1981.

Mavroudeas, S. (1999) Regulation theory: the road from creative Marxism to postmodern disintegration. *Science and Society*, **63**(3), 310–337.

Meiksins Wood, E. (1997) "Globalization" or "Globaloney". *Monthly Rev.*, **48**(9), 21–32.

Mensink, N. and van Bergeijk, P. (1996) Globlablablah. *ESB*, **4080**, 914–916.

Metz, R. (1992) In A. Kleinknecht, E. Mandel and I. Wallerstein (eds) *A Re-examination of Long Waves in Aggregate Production Series*.

Metz, R. (1996) In H. Thomas and L. Nefiodow (eds) *Langfristige Wachstumsschwankungen – Trends, Zyklen, Strukturbrücke oder Zufall?*

Michalet, C.A. (1976) *Le Capitalisme Mondial*. Paris: Quadrige/PUF, 1998.

Michalski, W., Miller, R. and Stevens, B. (1999) In OECD *Anatomy of a Long Boom*.

Michie, J. (1999) In J. Michie and J. Grieve Smith (eds) *Introduction*.

Michie, J. and Grieve Smith, J. (eds) (1995) *Managing the Global Economy*. Oxford: Oxford University Press.

Michie, J. and Grieve Smith, J. (eds) (1997) *Employment and Economic Performance: Jobs, Inflation, and Growth*. Oxford: Oxford University Press.

Michie, J. and Grieve Smith, J. (eds) (1998) *Globalization, Growth, and Governance. Creating an Innovative Economy*. Oxford: Oxford University Press.

Michie, J. and Grieve Smith, J. (eds) (1999) *Global Instability: The Political Economy of World Economic Governance*. London and New York: Routledge.

Miliband, R. and Panitch, L. (eds) (1992) *Socialist Register 1992: New World Order?* London: The Merlin Press.

Mill, J.S. (1844) *Essays on Some Unsettled Questions of Political Economy*. Clifton: Augustus M. Kelly, 1974.

Mishel, L. and Schmitt, J. (1995) *Beware the US Model: Jobs and Wages in a Deregulated Economy*. Washington, DC: Economic Policy Institute.

Mishel, L., Bernstein, J. and Schmitt, J. (2001) *The State of Working America*. Ithaca and London: Cornell University Press.

Mocsári, J. (1997) In T. Krausz (ed.) *How to Steal a Factory*.

Moody, K. (1997) *Workers in a Lean World: Unions in the International Economy*. London and New York: Verso.

Morris, D. (1996) In J. Mander and E. Goldsmith (eds) *Free Trade: The Great Destroyer*.

Murray, R. (1971) The internationalization of capital and the nation-state. *New Left Rev.* **67**, 84–109.

Mussa, M. (2000) *Factors Driving Global Economic Integration*, speech in Jackson Hole, Wyoming, at a Symposium sponsored by the Federal Reserve Bank of Kansas City on 'Global Opportunities and Challenges', 25 August. http://www.imf.org/external/np/ speeches /2000/ 082500.html.

Myrdal, G. (1954) In D. Hausman (ed.) *The Political Element in the Development of Economic Thought*.

Nadkarni, A. (1999) In J. Michie and J. Grieve Smith (eds) *World Trade Liberalization: National Autonomy and Global Regulation*.

Nederveen Pieterse, J. (1996) The development of development theory: towards critical globalism. *Rev. Int. Polit. Econ.*, **3**(4), 541–564.

Nelson, R. (1999) The sources of industrial leadership: a perspective on industrial policy. *De Economist*, **147**(1), 1–18.

Nicolaus, M. (1970) The universal contradiction. *New Left Rev.* **59**, 3–18.

Nitzan, J. and Bichler, S. (2000) In R. Palan (ed.) *Capital Accumulation: Breaking the Dualism of 'Economics' and 'Politics'*.

North, D. (1968) In D. Sills (ed.) *Economic History*.

Norton, B. (1988) Epochs and essences: a review of Marxist long-wave and stagnation theories. *Camb. J. Econ.*, **12**, 203–224.

Notermans, T. (1997) In K. Cox (ed.) *Social Democracy and External Constraints*.

O'Brien, R. (2000) In R. Palan (ed.) *Labour and IPE: Rediscovering Human Agency*.

O'Hara, P. (1994) An institutionalist review of long wave theories: Schumpeterian innovation, modes of regulation, and social structures of accumulation. *J. Econ. Issues*, **XXVIII**(2), 489–500.

O'Rourke, K. and Williamson, J. (1999) *Globalization and History. The Evolution of a Nineteenth Century Atlantic Economy*. Cambridge, MA: MIT Press.

Obstfeld, M. (1998) The global capital market: benefactor or menace? *NBER Working Paper Series* No. 6559.

Organisation for Economic Co-operation and Development (OECD) (1994) *Economic Outlook*. Paris: OECD.

Organisation for Economic Co-operation and Development (OECD) (1999) *The Future of the Global Economy. Towards a Long Boom?* Paris: OECD.

Ohmae, K. (1995) *The End of the Nation State. The Rise of Regional Economies*. New York: Free Press.

Oman, C. (1997) Technological change, globalisation of production and the role of multinationals. *Innovations, Cahiers D'économie de L'innovation* No. 5.

Orléan, A. (1999) *Le pouvoir de la finance*. Paris: Éditions Odile Jacob.

Overbeek, J. (1999) *Free Trade Versus Protectionism. A Source Book of Essays and Readings*. Cheltenham: Edward Elgar.

Overbeek, H. (2000) In R. Palan (ed.) *Transnational Historical Materialism: Theories of Transnational Class Formation and World Order*.

OXFAM (2000) *Growth with equity is good for the poor*. Policy Paper available at www.oxfam.org.uk/policy/papers/equity/fullequity00.htm.

Palan, R. (ed.) (2000) *Global Political Economy. Contemporary Theories*. London and New York: Routledge.

Palast, G. (2001) *The Globalizer Who Came in from the Cold*. www.gregpalast.com.

Palast, G. (2002) *Argentina: World Bank President's Secret Plan for Bleeding Nation. An Uncharming Mix of Self-delusion and Cruelty*. www.gregpalast.com.

Palloix, C. (1975) In H. Radice (ed.) *The Internationalization of Capital and the Circuits of Social Capital*.

Palloix, C. (1977) The self-expansion of capital on a world scale. *Rev. Radical Polit. Econ.*, **9**(2), 1–17.

Panitch, L. (ed.) (1997) *Socialist Register 1997. Ruthless Criticism of All that Exists*. Suffolk: Merlin Press.

Panitch, L. and Leys, C. (eds) (1999) *Socialist Register 1999: Global Capitalism Versus Democracy*. Suffolk: Merlin Press.

Panitch, L. and Leys, C. (eds) (2002) *Socialist Register 2002: A World of Contradictions*. Suffolk: Merlin Press.

Parry, G. and Steiner, H. (1998) In A. Marrison (ed.) *General Editors' Preface*.

Parrini, C. and Sklar, M. (1983) New thinking about the market, 1896–1904: some American economists on investment and the theory of surplus capital. *J. Econ. Hist.*, **43**(3), 559–578.

Patel, P. (1997) In D. Archibugi and J. Michie (eds) *Localised Production of Technology for Global Markets.*

Patomäki, H. (2001) *Democratising Globalisation: The Leverage of the Tobin Tax.* London and New York: Zed Books.

Pauly, L. and Reich, S. (1997) National structures and multinational corporate behavior: enduring differences in the age of globalization. *Int. Organ.*, **51**(1), 1–30.

Pen, J. (1967) *A Primer on International Trade.* New York: Random House.

Perraton, J., Goldblatt, D., Held, D. and McGrew, A. (1997) The globalisation of economic activity. *New Polit. Econ.*, **2**(2), 257–277.

Picciotto, S. (1991) In Clarke (ed.) *The Internationalisation of Capital and the International State System.*

Plender, J. (1997) *A Stake in the Future: The Stakeholding Solution.* London: Nicholas Brealey Publishing.

Pollin, R. (1998) Theory and policy in response to 'Leaden Age' financial instability: comment on felix. *J. Post Keynesian Econ.*, **20**(2), 223–233.

Pollin, R. and Zahrt, E. (1997) In J. Michie and J. Grieve Smith (eds) *Expansionary Policy for Full Employment in the United States: Retrospective on the 1960s and Current Period Prospects.*

Poulin, R. and Salama, P. (eds) (1998) *L'insoutenable misère du monde: économie et sociologie de la pauvreté.* Hull (Québec): Éditions Vents d'Ouest.

Prakash, A. (2001) The East Asian crisis and the globalization discourse. *Review of International Political Economy*, **8**(1) 119–146.

Prebisch, R. (1959) International trade and payments in an era of coexistence: commercial policy in the underdeveloped countries. *Am. Econ. Rev.*, **69**(2), 251–273.

Pritchett, L. (1995) Forget convergence: divergence past, present and future. *Finance and Development* (June 1995), 40–43.

Pritchett, L. (1997) Divergence, big time. *J. Econ. Perspect.*, **11**(3), 3–17.

Quinlan, J. and Chandler, M. (2001) The US trade deficit: a dangerous obsession'. *Foreign Affairs*, **80**(3), 87–97.

Radelet, S. and Sachs, J. (1998) *The East Asian Financial Crisis: Diagnosis, Remedies, Prospects.* Paper. Harvard Institute for International Development.

Radice, H. (ed.) (1975) *International Firms and Modern Imperialism.* Harmondsworth: Penguin.

Radice, H. (ed.) (1999) In L. Panitch and C. Leys (eds) *Taking Globalization Seriously.*

Rae, J. (1834) In R. Warren James (ed.) *Statement of some Principles on the Subject of Political Economy*, 1965.

Reati, A. (1992) Are we on the eve of a new long-term expansion induced by technological change? *Int. Rev. Appl. Econ.*, **6**(3), 249–285.

Reati, A. and Roland, G. (1988) Ondes longues et régulation: le cas allemand. *Cahiers Écon. Bruxelles*, **117**, 107–150.

Reich, R. (1992) *The Work of Nations. Preparing Ourselves for 21st Century Capitalism.* New York: Vintage Books.

Reich, M. (1994) In D. Kotz, T. McDonough and M. Reich (eds) *How Social Structures of Accumulation Decline and are Built.*

Reuten, G. (2002) In M. Campbell and G. Reuten (eds) *The Rate of Profit and the Opposition Between Managerial and Finance Capital.*

Reuten, G. and Williams, M. (1989) *Value-form and the State: The Tendencies of Accumulation and the Determination of Economic Policy in Capitalist Society.* London: Routledge.

Reuten, G. and Williams, M. (1993) The necessity of welfare: the systemic conflicts of the capitalist mixed economy. *Science and Society*, **57**(4), 420–440.

Ricardo, D. (1817) In P. Sraffa (ed.) *On the Principles of Political Economy and Taxation*, 1970.

Richardson, J. (1995) Income inequality and trade: how to think, what to conclude. *J. Econ. Perspect.*, **9**(3), 33–55.

Richardson, P. (ed.) (1997) Globalization and linkages: macro-structural challenges and opportunities. *OECD Economic Department Working Papers* No. 181.

Rigacci, G. (2000) The capitalist system has not overcome its long wave of stagnation. *Int. Viewpoint*, **325**, 26–29.

Robinson, J. (1968) *Economic Philosophy*. Harmondsworth: Penguin.

Robinson, W. (1996a) *Promoting Polyarchy: Globalization, US Intervention and Hegemony*. Cambridge: Cambridge University Press.

Robinson, W. (1996b), Globalisation: nine theses on our epoch. *Race & Class*, **38**(2) 13–31.

Robinson, W. (1998) Beyond nation-state paradigms: globalization, sociology, and the challenge of transnational studies. *Sociol. Forum*, **13**(4), 561–594.

Robinson, W. (2001) Social theory and globalization: the rise of a transnational state. *Theory and Society*, **30**(2), 157–200.

Robinson, W. and Harris, J. (2000) Towards a global ruling class? Globalization and the transnational capitalist class. *Science and Society*, **64**(1), 11–54.

Rodgers, J. (1998) In A. Levy-Livermore (ed.) *From Bretton Woods to the World Trade Organization and the Formation of Regional Trading Blocs*.

Rodrik, D. (1997a) *Has Globalization Gone Too Far?* Washington, DC: Institute for International Economics.

Rodrik, D. (1997b) *Globalization, Social Conflict and Economic Growth*. Revised edition (11 December 1997) of the Prebisch Lecture delivered at UNCTAD, Geneva, on 24 October 1997.

Rodrik, D. (1998) Who needs capital-account convertibility. *Essays Int. Finance*, **207**, 55–65.

Rodrik, D. (1999) *The New Global Economy and Developing Countries: Making Openness Work*. ODC Policy Essay 24, Washington, DC: John Hopkins University Press.

Rodrik, D. (2000) How far will international economic integration go? *J. Econ. Perspect.*, **14**(1), 177–186.

Roe Smith, M. and Marx, L. (eds) (1995) *Does Technology Drive History? The Dilemma of Technological Determinism*. Cambridge, MA: MIT Press.

Rogers Hollingsworth, J. and Boyer, R. (eds) (1997a) *Contemporary Capitalism: The Embeddedness of Institutions*. Cambridge: Cambridge University Press, 1998.

Rogers Hollingsworth, J. and Boyer, R. (1997b) In J. Rogers Hollingsworth and R. Boyer (eds) *Coordination of Economic Actors and Social Systems of Production*.

Rostow, W. (1960) *The Stages of Economic Growth: A Non-communist Manifesto*. London: Cambridge University Press, 1961.

Rowthorn, B. (1971) Imperialism in the seventies – unity or rivalry? *New Left Rev.*, **69**, 31–54.

Rowthorn, B. (1980) *Capitalism, Conflict and Inflation. Essays in Political Economy*. London: Lawrence and Wishart.

Rowthorn, R. and Kozul-Wright, R. (1998) Globalization and economic convergence: an assessment. *UNCTAD Discussion Papers* No. 131.

Rude, C. (1998) *The 1997–98 East Asian Financial Crisis: A New York Market-informed View*. Paper for United Nations Expert Group Meeting, New York, 21–23 July 1998.

Ruigrok, W. and van Tulder R. (1995a) *The Logic of International Restructuring*. London: Routledge.

Ruigrok, W. and van Tulder, R. (1995b) Misverstand globalisering, *ESB*, **4038**, 1140–1143.

Sachs, J. (1997) Power unto itself. *The Financial Times* (11 December 1997), 11.

Sachs, J. and Warner, A. (1995) Economic reform and the process of global integration. *Brookings Papers on Economic Activity*, **1995**(1), 1–95.

Salvadori, M. (1976) *Karl Kautsky and the Socialist Revolution 1880–1938*. London: New Left Books.

Sassen, S. (1996) *Losing Control? Sovereignty in an Age of Globalization*. New York: Columbia University Press.

Saurin, J. (1996) Globalisation, poverty, and the promises of modernity. *Millennium: J. Int. Stud.*, **25**(3), 657–680.

Schiller, D. (1999) *Digital Capitalism. Networking the Global Market System*. Cambridge, MA: MIT Press.

Scholte, J. (1997) Global capitalism and the state. *Int. Affairs* **73**(3), 427–452.

Schor, J. (1998) *The Overspent American. Upscaling, Downshifting, and the New Consumer*. New York: Basic Books.

Schrempp, J. (2001) *The New Context for Globalization: A Transatlantic Company's Response*. CEO Leadership Series of the National Chamber Foundation available at www.us.cgey.com.

Schumpeter, J. (1919) In J. Schumpeter *The Sociology of Imperialisms*, 1951.

Schumpeter, J. (1951) *Imperialism and Social Classes* (edited and with an introduction by P. Sweezy). Oxford: Basil Blackwell.

Schumpeter, J. (1954) *History of Economic Analysis*. London: Routledge, 1994.

Schwartz, P., Kelly, E. and Boyer, N. (1999) In OECD *The Emerging Global Knowledge Economy*.

Scott, B. (2001) The great divide in the global village. *Foreign Affairs*, **80**(1), 160–177.

Sebaï, F. and Vercellone, C. (eds) (1994) *École de la régulation et critique de la raison economique*. Paris: Éditions L'Harmattan.

Semmel, B. (1970) *The Rise of Free Trade Imperialism: Classical Political Economy, the Empire of Free Trade and Imperialism 1750–1850*. Cambridge: Cambridge University Press.

Semmel, B. (1993) *The Liberal Ideal and the Demons of Empire: Theories of Imperialism from Adam Smith to Lenin*. Baltimore and London: Hopkins University Press.

Sengenberger, W. (1996) *Full Employment: Past, Present and Future – An ILO Perspective*. Paper Presented at the Conference of the European Association for Evolutionary Political Economy (EAEPE), Antwerp, 7–9 November 1996.

Sennett, R. (1998) *The Corrosion of Character. The Personal Consequences of Work in the New Capitalism*. New York and London: Norton.

Serfati, C. (1996) In F. Chesnais (ed.) *Le role actif des groupes à dominante industrielle dans la financiarisation de l'economie*.

Sharma, K. (1998) *Understanding the Dynamics Behind Excess Capital Inflows and Excess Capital Outflows in East Asia*. Paper for United Nations Expert Group Meeting, New York, 21–23 July 1998.

Shaw, M. (2000) In R. Palan (ed.) *Historical Sociology and Global Transformation*.

Shell (2002) *People and Connections. Global Scenarios to 2020 – Public Summary*. London: Shell.

Shutt, H. (1998) *The Trouble with Capitalism. An Enquiry into the Causes of Global Economic Failure*. London and New York: Zed Books.

Sideri, S. (1970) *Trade and Power: Informal Colonialism in Anglo-Portuguese Relations.* Rotterdam: Universitaire Pers Rotterdam.

Siebert, H. and Klodt, H. (1999) In OECD *Towards Global Competition: Catalysts and Constraints.*

Sills, D. (ed.) (1968) *International Encyclopedia of the Social Sciences, vols 5 and 6: Complete and Unabridged.* New York: Macmillan Company & Free Press.

Simmons, B. (1999) In H. Kitschelt, P. Lange, G. Marks and J. Stephens (eds) *The Internationalization of Capital.*

Singer, D. (1999) *Whose Millennium? Theirs or Ours?* New York: Monthly Review Press.

Slaughter, M. and Swagel, P. (1997) The effects of globalization on wages in the advanced countries. *IMF Working Papers,* WP/97/43.

Smith, A. (1776) *An Inquiry into the Nature and Causes of the Wealth of Nations.* Indianapolis: Liberty Fund, 1976.

Smith, T. (1994) *Lean Production: A Capitalist Utopia?* Amsterdam: IIRE.

Smith, T. (1998) In C. Arthur and G. Reuten (eds) *The Capital/Consumer Relation in Lean Production: The Continued Relevance of Volume Two of Capital.*

Smith, T. (2000) *Technology and Capital in the Age of Lean Production: A Marxian Critique of the 'New Economy'.* New York: State University of New York Press.

Socialist International Council (1998) *To Regulate Globalization and to Globalize Regulation.* Declaration, Geneva, 23–24 November 1998.

Soenderberg, S. (2001) The emperor's new suit: the new international financial architecture as a reinvention of the Washington consensus. *Global Governance,* **7,** 453–467.

Solomon, S. (1995) *The Confidence Game: How Unelected Central Bankers are Governing the Changed World Economy.* New York: Simon & Schuster.

Soros, G. (1998) *The Crisis of Global Capitalism. Open Society Endangered.* Boston: Little, Brown.

Sraffa, P. (ed.) (1970) *The Work and Correspondence of David Ricardo,* vol 1. Cambridge: Cambridge University Press.

Standing, G. (1999) *Global Labour Flexibility: Seeking Distributive Justice.* Basingstoke: Macmillan.

Steedman, I. and Metcalfe, J. (1996) In D. Greenaway (ed.) *Capital Goods and the Pure Theory of Trade.*

Streeten, P. (1996) In Berger and Dore (eds) *Free and Managed Trade.*

Stubbs, R. and Underhill, G. (eds) (1994) *Political Economy and the Changing Global Order.* Houndmills: Macmillan.

Sutcliffe, B. (1998) In D. Baker, G. Epstein and R. Pollin (eds) *Freedom to move in the age of globalization.*

Sutcliffe, B. (2001) *100 Ways of Seeing an Unequal World.* London and New York: Zed Books.

Tanski, J. and French, D. (2001) Capital concentration and market power in Mexico's manufacturing industry: has trade liberalization made a difference? *J. Econ. Issues,* **XXXV**(3), 675–711.

Teeple, G. (1999) *On Globalization: A Critique of the Critics.* Paper Presented at British Columbia Political Science Association, 14–15 May 1999.

Teeple, G. (2000) *Globalization and the Decline of Social Reform.* Aurora: Garamond Press.

Thomas, H. and Nefiodow, L. (eds) (1996) *Kondratieffs Zyklen des Wirtschaft. An der Schwelle neuer Vollbeschäftigung?* Köln: Lindenthal-Institut, BusseSeewald, Herford, 1998.

Toporowski, J. (2000) *The End of Finance: Capital Market Inflation, Financial Derivatives and Pension Fund Capitalism.* London and New York: Routledge.

Toussaint, E. and Drucker, P. (eds) (1995) IMF/World Bank/WTO: the free market fiasco. *Notebooks for Study and Research (NSR)* No. 24/25.

Van Tulder, R., van den Berghe, D. and Muller, A. (2001) *Erasmus (S)coreboard of Core Companies. The World's Largest Firms and Internationalization.* Rotterdam: Rotterdam School of Management/Erasmus University.

Tylecote, A. (1994) Long waves, long cylces, and long swings. *J. Econ. Issues,* **XXVIII**(2), 477–488.

Tyson, L. (2000) Though it's a new economy, it's got some old flaws. *Business Week,* (10 January 2000), 9.

Ul Haq, I.K. and Grunberg, I. (eds) (1996) *The Tobin Tax: Coping with Financial Volatility.* New York and Oxford: Oxford University Press.

United Nations Conference on Trade and Development (UNCTAD) (1993) *World Investment Report 1993. Transnational Corporations and Integrated International Production.* New York: UNCTAD.

United Nations Conference on Trade and Development (UNCTAD) (1994) *World Investment Report 1994. Transnational Corporations, Employment and the Workplace.* New York: UNCTAD.

United Nations Conference on Trade and Development (UNCTAD) (1997) *Trade and Development Report 1997.* New York: UNCTAD.

United Nations Conference on Trade and Development (UNCTAD) (1998) *World Investment Report 1998. Trends and Determinants.* New York: UNCTAD.

United Nations Conference on Trade and Development (UNCTAD) (1999) *World Investment Report 1999. Foreign Direct Investment and the Challenge of Development.* New York and Geneva: UNCTAD.

United Nations Conference on Trade and Development (UNCTAD) (2000a) *Trade and Development Report 2000.* New York and Geneva: United Nations.

United Nations Conference on Trade and Development (UNCTAD) (2000b) *The Least Developed Countries 2000 Report.* New York and Geneva: United Nations.

United Nations Conference on Trade and Development (UNCTAD) (2000c) *World Investment Report 2000: Cross-border Mergers and Acquisitions and Development.* New York and Geneva: United Nations.

United Nations Development Programme (UNDP) (1997) *Human Development Report 1997.* New York and Oxford: Oxford University Press.

United Nations Development Programme (UNDP) (1998) *Human Development Report 1998.* New York: Oxford University Press.

United Nations Development Programme (UNDP) (1999) *Human Development Report 1999.* New York: Oxford University Press.

van Duijn, J. (1979) *De Lange Golf in de Economie. Kan Innovatie ons Uit Het dal Helpen?* Assen: Van Gorcum.

van Duijn, J. (1998) *Economie en Beurs.* Amsterdam: Uitgeverij Nieuwezijds.

van Paridon, K. (1996) 'Een relevantere handelsmaatstaf'. *ESB,* **4080**, 916.

van der Pijl, K. (1998) *Transnational Classes and International Relations.* London and New York: Routledge.

van der Pijl, K. (2001) In R. Albritton, M. Itoh, R. Westra and A. Zuege (eds) *International Relations and Capitalist Discipline.*

Verhagen, M. (1993) *Institutionele Veranderingen en Economische Dynamiek. Radicale en 'Régulation' Benaderingen Over Gedaanteveranderingen van het Kapitalisme.* Tilburg: Tilburg University Press.

Verla, C. (1987) In M. Dupont, F. Ollivier, A. Taillandier and C. Verla (eds) *Régularités et crises du capitalisme.*

Vernon, R. (1998) *In the Hurricane's Eye. The Troubled Prospects of Multinational Enterprises*. Cambridge: Harvard University Press.

Viner, J. (1955) *Studies in the Theory of International Trade*. London: George Allen & Unwin.

Vromen, J. (1995) *Economic Evolution: An Enquiry into the Foundations of New Institutional Economics*. London: Routledge.

Wade, R. (1996) In S. Berger and R. Dore (eds) *Globalization and its Limits: Reports of the Death of the National Economy are Greatly Exaggerated*.

Wade, R. (1998) *From Miracle to Meltdown: Vulnerabilities, Moral Hazard, Panic and Debt Deflation in the Asian Crisis*. Paper. Russell Sage Foundation, available at http://epn.org/sagc/asiac3a.html.

Wade, R. (2001) Global inequality: winners and losers. *The Economist*, **359**, (28 April), 79–82.

Wade, R. and Veneroso, F. (1998a) 'The Asian crisis: the high debt model versus the wall street-treasury-IMF complex. *New Left Rev.*, **228**, 3–23.

Wade, R. and Veneroso, F. (1998b) The gathering world slump and the battle over capital controls. *New Left Rev.*, **231**, 13–42.

Warren James, R. (1965) *John Rae Political Economist: An Account of His Life and a Compilation of His Main Writings* (2 vols). Toronto: University of Toronto Press.

Webber, M. and Rigby, D. (1996) *The Golden Age Illusion: Rethinking Postwar Capitalism*. New York: Guilford Press.

Webber, M. and Rigby, D. (2001) In R. Albritton, M. Itoh, R. Westra and A. Zuege (eds) *Growth and Change in the World Economy Since 1950*.

Weeks, J. (2001) In R. Albritton, M. Itoh, R. Westra and A. Zuege (eds) Globa-lize, Global Lies: Myths of the World Economy in the 1990s.

Weijers, H. (2000) *Uiteindelijk zal alles New Economy Worden*. Published on www.rabobank.nl.

Weisbrot, M., Naiman, R. and Kim, J. (2000) *The Emperor has No Growth: Declining Economic Growth Rates in the Era of Globalization*. Washington, DC: Briefing Paper Center for Economic and Policy Research.

Weisbrot, M., Baker, D., Kraev, E. and Chen, J. (2001) *The Scoreboard on Globalization 1980–2000: Twenty Years of Diminished Progress*. Washington, DC: Briefing Paper Center for Economic and Policy Research.

Weiss, R. (1968) In H. Johnson (ed.) *Economic Nationalism in Britain in the Nineteenth Century*.

Weiss, L. (1998) *The Myth of the Powerless State*. Ithaca, NY: Cornell University Press.

Weisskopf, T. (1994) In D. Kotz, T. McDonough and M. Reich (eds) *Alternative social structure of accumulation approaches to the analysis of capitalist booms and crises*.

Weller, C., Scott, R. and Hersh, A. (2001) *The Unremarkable Record of Liberalized Trade. After 20 Years of Global Economic Deregulation Poverty and Inequality are as Pervasive as Ever*. Washington, DC: Briefing Paper Economic Policy Institute.

Went, R. (1996a) *Grenzen aan de Globalisering?* Amsterdam: Het Spinhuis.

Went, R. (1996b) Globalization: myths, reality and ideology. *Int. J. Polit. Econ.*, **26**(3), 39–59.

Went, R. (1997) De sociale gevolgen van globalisering. *ESB*, **4125**, 804.

Went, R. (1999) *Beyond the Globalization of Inequality*. Paper for the Annual Meeting of the European Association for Evolutionary Political Economy (EAEPE), Prague, Czech Republic.

Went, R. (2000) *Globalization: Neoliberal Challenge, Radical Responses*. London: Pluto Press.

Williams, J. (1929) The theory of international trade reconsidered. *Econ. J.*, **39**, (June 1929), 195–209.

Williams, K. (2000) From shareholder value to present-day capitalism. *Economy and Society*, **29**(1), 1–12.

Williams, K. (2001) Theme section: trajectories of inequality. *Rev. Int. Polit. Econ.*, **8**(1), 1–5.

Williams, M. and Reuten, G. (1994) The political economy of welfare and economic policy. *Eur. J. Polit. Econ.*, **10**(2), 253–278.

Williamson, J. (1996) Globalization, convergence, and history. *J. Econ. Hist.*, **56**(2), 277–306.

Williamson, J. (1997) Globalization and Inequality, Past and Present. *The World Bank Res. Observer*, **12**(1), 117–135.

Williamson, J. (1998) Globalization, Labor Markets and Policy Backlash in the Past. *J. Econ. Perspect.*, **12**(4), 51–72.

Willoughby, J. (1995) Evaluating the Leninist theory of imperialism. *Science and Society*, **59**(3), 320–338.

Wilno, H. (2000) A New Productive Order? *Int. Viewpoint*, **325**, 29–35.

Wolf, W. (1997) *CasinoCapital. Der Crash Beginnt auf dem Golfplatz.* Cologne: ISP.

Wolfson, M. (2000) Neoliberalism and international financial instability. *Rev. Radical Polit. Econ.*, **32**(3), 369–378.

Wood, A. (1994) *North–South Trade, Employment and Inequality: Changing Fortunes in a Skill-driven World.* Oxford: Clarendon Press.

Wood, A. (1995) How trade hurt unskilled workers. *J. Econ. Perspect.*, **9**(3), 57–80.

World Bank (1999a) *Global Economic Prospects and the Developing Countries.* Washington, DC: The World Bank.

World Bank (1999b) *Global Development Finance 1999. Analysis and Summary Tables.* Washington, DC: The World Bank.

Wyplosz, C. (1998) *Globalized Financial Markets and Financial Crises.* Paper Presented at a Conference Organized by the Forum on Debt and Development, Amsterdam, 16–17 March 1998.

Yaghmaian, B. (1998) Globalization and the state: the political economy of global accumulation and its emerging mode of accumulation. *Science and Society*, **62**(2), 241–265.

Yergin, D. and Stanislaw, J. (1998) *The Commanding Heights. The Battle Between Government and the Marketplace that is Remaking the World Economy.* New York: Touchstone.

Index